REBEL LAW

FRANK LEDWIDGE

Rebel Law

*Insurgents, Courts and Justice
in Modern Conflict*

HURST & COMPANY, LONDON

First published in the United Kingdom in 2017 by
C. Hurst & Co. (Publishers) Ltd.,
41 Great Russell Street, London, WC1B 3PL
© Frank Ledwidge, 2017
All rights reserved.

Printed in the United Kingdom by Bell & Bain Ltd, Glasgow.

Distributed in the United States, Canada and Latin America by
Oxford University Press, 198 Madison Avenue, New York, NY 10016,
United States of America.

The right of Frank Ledwidge to be identified as the author
of this publication is asserted by him in accordance with the
Copyright, Designs and Patents Act, 1988.

A Cataloguing-in-Publication data record for this book
is available from the British Library.

ISBN: 9781849047982

This book is printed using paper from registered sustainable
and managed sources.

www.hurstpublishers.com

CONTENTS

INTRODUCTION

'Kingdoms are won and lost in the realms of law and legitimacy.'[1]

The genesis of this project lies in my work. By profession, I am a barrister, trained in the practice of law. For seven years, I practised my profession in England. Since the mid-1990s, I have worked in many countries and regions as an advisor on the development of institutions of justice: the Balkans, Iraq, the former Soviet republics of Central Asia, Ukraine, Afghanistan, Libya and Ethiopia. Occasionally, I have been called up to be deployed as a reserve military officer, in the Balkans and Iraq, although my trade within the military was intelligence. In both my military and my civilian capacity, almost every country in which I have worked, apart from the United Kingdom itself, has been either in the middle of conflict or recovering from it.

As a lawyer working with the day-to-day problems of ordinary people, one develops a keen awareness of the centrality of the law and ways of resolving disputes to most people. Whether those disputes arise from what we call 'civil' matters, relating to property or redress of grievance, or whether they revolve around criminal matters, is of central importance to the people involved. Beyond the day-to-day affairs of ordinary people, the law holds government together; after all, what is government but the authority to issue and enforce laws? What are courts but mechanisms to ensure compliance to those laws?

Working in those conflict zones, it was clear that the importance of courts and laws did not diminish even in the midst of communal violence or indeed civil war. On the contrary, often courts and law

1

assumed an even greater importance as the struggles went on. In Kosovo, during the war itself I observed the workings of Serbian 'security courts' imprisoning dozens of evidently innocent men. After the war, there was huge controversy about which laws were applicable after the departure of much of the paraphernalia of the Serbian state. In Central Asia, post-9/11 state misuse of laws relating to terrorism—with attendant internment—had the effect of exacerbating what was otherwise a perfectly containable problem. I remember meeting a prosecutor in the town of Namangan in the grotesquely corrupt state of Uzbekistan where hundreds of dissidents, particularly moderate Muslim men, had been imprisoned. The reasoning was that they were practising Muslims and therefore dangerous terrorists. I outlined to the prosecutor what had happened in Northern Ireland in the 1970s, with internment resulting in increasing support for insurgent groups and antagonism towards the government. A year later, the Uzbek state went beyond imprisonment and settled on out and out murder. In May 2005, 600 people seeking some form of political change were massacred in Namangan's town square. All this was largely common fare for the human rights lawyer.

It was only when I served as a justice advisor for the UK military mission in Helmand in Afghanistan in the early days of the disastrous war there that the real potential of courts used not against insurgents—in this case the Taliban—but by them, became very clear indeed. While the foreign mission, including myself, was trying to shore up a totally dysfunctional and entirely corrupt judicial system, our opponents in the Taliban were busy demonstrating to the people of Helmand what their version of justice looked like. For very many of those people, it looked a whole lot better than the one we were working on.

When I came back from Helmand, I wrote two articles. The first was published in the *RUSI Journal*, the second in the *Journal of the Royal Society for Asian Affairs*.[2] In those pieces, I suggested that despite a plethora of reports streaming from Afghanistan on the justice sector, and the efforts being put in to reform it, little had been written on its role in both powering and countering insurgency. The focus of the work being done in the sector had been on assessing and critiquing (largely negatively) the international efforts so far—often only from the point of view of development and the so-called security sector, mainly the police and military. I suggested that, within the world of counterinsurgency, the justice sector was, at best, a poor cousin of the so-called security sector reform field. 'Security Sector Reform', known as 'SSR', is a development buzz-phrase usually meaning police, military and prisons, with a cadet function being assigned to courts.

The strong implication of these articles was that the justice sector, meaning courts, should take a far more prominent role in the effort to 'stabilise' Afghanistan. It was not simply another social good, such as hospitals or roads. Nor was it just another component of the much-referenced SSR, but was intimately bound up with concepts of legitimacy and justice. It was a vital element, in other words, of any insurgency with political ambitions—which is to say, all of them.

By the same reasoning, in the end any successful counterinsurgency operation, if it has any ambitions to political effect, must take steps—or, more importantly, be seen to take steps—to address the legitimate grievances that insurgents use to generate and sustain popular support. A corrupt, discredited justice system only serves to fuel an insurgency that bleeds legitimacy from the government in key strategic areas of the country; and in current counterinsurgency thinking, 'legitimacy' is a vital component of the overall effort.

The articles suggested that while the central importance of justice had to some extent eluded counterinsurgency (COIN) theorists at that time, successful insurgents had often historically placed it at or near the top of their objectives. One of the central ideas of this book is that counterinsurgents need to do exactly the same. What they suggested, and what this book explicitly suggests, is that just as the state can use 'lawfare' in its own courts and judicial systems, so can insurgents. The idea of 'lawfare', defined as 'law used as a means of achieving military objectives', is an important element in this book.[3] *Rebel Courts* looks at the use of courts as a weapon on both sides of insurgencies largely at the level below the strategic, which is to say where wars are actually fought—in military terms, at the operational and tactical levels.

Lawfare: synthesising law and insurgency

In his study of warfare in the eighteenth century, *The Verdict of Battle* (2012), James Q. Whitman describes the institution of pitched battle as 'a form of trial ... a contained and economical way of resolving a dispute between two warring parties or countries'.[4] He saw battle and war in that period as a form of legal process. The idea of warfare, or more widely armed combat, as a form of legal proceeding was also a feature of combat in the Middle Ages.[5]

This book will try to show that matters have progressed from battle being seen as a 'trial or legal proceeding' to legal processes themselves being a form of warfare.[6] That insight itself is not particularly new. As will be described below, the concept has been refined into the word 'lawfare'. However, one of the original ideas that this book seeks to encapsulate is the degree to which the use of law and legal procedures has long been a tool of insurgent and counterinsurgent warfare—a weapon, no less.

David Kennedy, in his *War and Law* (2006), states:

> In large measure, our modern politics is legal politics; the terms of engagement are legal, and the players are legal institutions, their powers expanded and limited by law ... To say that war is a legal institution is not only to say that war has also become an affair of rules or the military a legal bureaucracy. It is also to say something about the nature of the politics continued by military means.[7]

This is certainly true of warfare today. Law has become part of modern warfare. Like cyberspace, 'legal space' has become a battlefield, and combatants are still feeling their way around it. It is not new in nature: at the tactical level—the level at which soldiers operate—the law has long been an environment within which soldiers have had to work. In 1837, General James Napier put the officer's dilemma with black humour: 'Confronted by a mob, his thoughts dwell on the (to him) most interesting question; "shall I be shot for my forbearance by a court-martial, or hanged for over-zeal by a jury".'[8]

The idea of the confluence of law and war itself is not new. Jeremy Bentham, the eighteenth-century philosopher and exponent of utilitarianism, wrote that 'Legislation is a state of warfare; political mischief is the enemy; the legislator is the commander the moral and religious sanctions his allies, punishment and rewards the forces he has under his command, punishment his regular standing force.'[9]

The term 'lawfare' itself seems first to have appeared in 2001, in a working paper for a conference at Harvard University by an American

INTRODUCTION

Air Force judge advocate, Charles Dunlap.[10] In a later essay, written when the topic of lawfare had well and truly entered academic discourse, Dunlap took the view that law had become a 'decisive element of 21st century conflict'.[11] He went on to cite the way in which opponents of the US conduct of the war in Afghanistan had criticised the use, for example, of drones. Has law, asks Dunlap, become 'a tool for the enemy'?[12] In the UK, the issues often referred to in the United States as lawfare have become part of the national discourse[13] as a result of several cases decided in UK courts arising out of events in Iraq and Afghanistan.[14] This has been described as the 'juridification' of (in this instance) the British armed forces.[15]

In *War and Law*, Kennedy observes that war, like other forms of discourse, is governed by rules. Indeed, it is regulated by law:

> We know the corporate world can kill ... law addresses these wrongs, parsing them out—permissible injuries or violations of the duty of care. We insure, we contract out, we buy property elsewhere, we zone the city to reduce or concentrate the threat—we sue, we negotiate, we demand regulation or prosecution or the death penalty. Somehow we thought war was different. But it turns out not to be.[16]

The idea of law being used as a weapon is arguably as old as international law itself. Certainly, in the twentieth century, it was a common feature of the discourse of conflict; territorial claims were discussed in terms of legal right. Ideas of law and legitimacy were used during the Second World War to achieve political effect. For example, after the Warsaw Uprising of 1944, Winston Churchill levered the international law on the treatment of prisoners of war to ensure the safety of the captured Polish Home Army fighters.

At the grand strategic level, where debate on the legal aspects of war played a major role in the creation of narrative, no country could afford to be credibly accused, at least after the Second World War, of acting outside the law. However egregiously a country behaved, or indeed behaves, the language of law is used to justify that action. It hardly needs to be said, but it is a worthwhile observation, that no country will ever admit to acting outside international law.

As well as being used as a justification, law is also used instrumentally. Combined with a significant level of realpolitik, over the last few decades it has been used with considerable impact. For example, the removal of Taiwan from its seat as one of the five members of the Security Council representing China at the United Nations has been seen as a component of a long-term political effort to deny Taiwan legitimacy.[17] Law and war, particularly *through* the twentieth century, were intimately intertwined. Questions of law have always infused questions of *ius in bello* and *ius ad bellum*. Lawfare's current strategic role has been extremely well covered by Orde Kittrie in his *Lawfare: Law as a Weapon of War* (2015),[18] which examines how governments and indeed some other actors, notably Hamas and Hezbollah, have used legal instruments, courts, treaties and, importantly, legal narrative and language to affirm or perhaps justify their own cases and attack those of their enemies.

As Kennedy puts it and Kittrie confirms: 'Law and force flow into one another. We make war in the shadow of law and law in the shadow of force. Law has infiltrated the decisions to make war and crept into the conduct of warfare.'[19]

The creation of the various ad hoc war crimes tribunals in the 1990s added another rather more obvious lawfare component to the conduct of warfare. The strategic effect of the indictment of Slobodan Milosevic by the International Criminal Tribunal for the Former Yugoslavia (ICTY) certainly contributed to the overall NATO political strategy of marginalising Serbia.[20] Serbian nationalists have always regarded the ICTY as a political tool in a continuing campaign against their country.[21] In the current decade, 'Law's ascendance as a means of warfare is tied to the ascendance of counterinsurgency as a form of warfare.'[22]

There is no question that awareness of the potential of the use of law as a weapon is growing. For example, China is said to maintain an entire department of the People's Liberation Army specialising in the strategic use of law as a weapon,[23] within the framework of the idea of the 'three warfares' (legal, media and psychological operations).[24]

Among advocates of lawfare as something new, there is an awareness of the fact that war is a political tool and that law is a component of political discourse. The kind of lawfare they describe often gives direct and speedy political or even military results. China's 2013 declaration of an Air Defence Identification Zone over strategically important parts of the East China Sea (and China's subsequent narrative positioning) has been cited as a recent example of strategic-level lawfare; indeed, the use of lawfare as part of the political component of warfare is the central point.[25] Yet there is nothing new or especially threatening about the use of law as a rhetorical instrument of policy, so long as it is fully realised that this is what is happening and appropriate countermeasures are adopted.

Strategic lawfare and narrative

The conservative philosopher Joseph de Maistre, writing shortly after Waterloo, famously said that battles are won or lost in the imagination, not on the battlefield. This, as Whitman has said, was 'a *bon mot* not a scholarly argument', but, the importance of narrative to warfare is as central now as it ever was.[26] As may be clear from the foregoing, much of that narrative is conducted on the terrain of the law.

The controversies surrounding most international conflicts are often communicated through the language of law. Borders are set by legal means, even though those borders may bear little relationship to areas occupied by peoples or tribes. On occasion, the controversies surrounding these controversial borders turn on the construction of a few words or phrases. As Kennedy says, 'War takes place on a terrain that is intensely governed—not by unified global institutions but by a dense network of rules and shared assumptions among the world's elites.'[27]

The implications of such rules and assumptions can be vast, especially for the physical terrains—literal 'territories'. By way of illustration, the Durand Line, drawn in the late 1890s by a team of British surveyors, largely governs the border between what is now known as Pakistan and Afghanistan. It also applies to the virtual territory of discourse and argument—narrative.

The effect of a consistent 'narrative of justice' and indeed notions of 'fairness' and 'legitimacy' is amply displayed in many insurgencies, powered as so many are by notions of legitimacy and justice.

As the strategist David Betz says, 'No narrative can survive, even in part, if it is based on a lie.'[28] This is true. We will see below, as an example, that the Taliban narrative is not based upon a lie, whereas the Afghan government's offer largely is, in that its offer of a working, fair justice system is more or less illusory. The idea that a narrative backed by factual or perceptual truth is vital to the conduct of war is reinforced in Emile Simpson's *War from the Ground Up* he says that 'to base one's entire strategy upon perception rather than on the reality that lies beneath it is highly unstable. In the aftermath of the global financial crisis, it is clear that narratives which depend massively on perception without a base in physical reality are very dangerous.'[29]

Nonetheless, there is no doubt at all that what government officials often call 'optics', or, in other words, what appears to be happening as opposed to what might actually be happening, is important. This is the province of 'media operations' or 'psychological operations'—categories now subsumed under the rubric 'information operations'.

Military doctrine is not blind to the necessity of maintaining a link between what a counterinsurgent asserts and what goes on in fact. It makes the link between honesty in narrative and legitimacy. The US Army Field manual on counterinsurgency rightly states that 'Counterinsurgents seeking to preserve legitimacy must stick to the truth and ensure that words are backed up by deeds.'[30] From the perspective of justice and courts, any rhetoric of justice founded on a reality of corruption will fail to ground a legitimate state, as observed above.

In his book on contemporary strategy, Hew Strachan refers to General Rupert Smith in seeing 'contemporary warfare [as] a form of theatre played out by a small, separate group (i.e. a professional and not a conscript army) orchestrated by a team of unseen directors, stage managers and lighting engineers, but watched by many more. The people are the audience for war.'[31]

In insurgencies, that audience is rather closer to the stage than in other forms of warfare, or indeed lawfare. As we will see, ideas of justice, as well as the practice of justice, are at the centre of many insurgencies. In the words of Michael Walzer, arguably the leading ethicist of war of the last half-century, 'In a war for hearts and minds, rather than for land and resources, justice turns out to be the key to victory.'[32] That is all very well. But what is justice? This is a rather subjective matter. Almost by definition, in insurgencies one man's justice is another man's justification for terrorism. This book will not deal with definitions of justice, nor will it ask whether the various causes for which insurgents fight are right and just or wrong and unjust. It does not aspire to comprise some grand unified theory of insurgency or counterinsurgency; what it does aspire to do is to illuminate a small and somewhat neglected patch of insurgent and counterinsurgency studies. I would argue that this small patch is nonetheless very important. Throughout the book, reference will be made to many wars and conflicts. However, some are covered more than others. The case of the Irish War of Independence (1919–21), its causes and conduct, appears in several chapters. Ireland was considered by some of its British rulers at the time as a rural backwater, a general approach that might be argued to have caused the war in the first place. Ireland was and is an integral part of Western European history and culture. More importantly for present purposes, its legal system was intimately wound into the English judicial system itself. Indeed, by virtue of being a common law system, it was more connected to British metropolitan legal culture than Scotland.

Afghanistan, a very different place, also appears regularly. Different it may be, but similar patterns appear in the way successful Afghan insurgents use justice systems. I include these two places in this book for two reasons. First, because I know about them. As well as holding joint Irish/UK nationality, my grandfather fought in the Irish War of Independence on the nationalist (i.e. insurgent) side. Indeed, I discovered deep into the research for this book that he was heavily involved in the so-called republican courts that you will read about later in the book. Similarly with Afghanistan, I spent several months there and have tried to keep in touch with what was happening. The course and conduct of the war there was also the subject of two other books I have written.

The second reason goes beyond personal links or knowledge. It is simply that they provide effective case-studies on how insurgents actually work with respect to using courts as weapons.

Chapter summaries

This book deals with how ideas of justice power insurgency. It also deals with a slightly different notion of justice, specifically the mechanisms by which disputes are resolved in a fashion that is accepted as just. We will see in Chapter 1 that perceptions of fairness in arriving at decisions that resolve or aim to resolve disputes play closely into a notion that has not yet been mentioned—legitimacy. Chapter 1 will affirm the centrality of notions of law, justice and acceptable dispute resolution systems to any society. It will show that legitimacy, which is seen as central to ideas of countering insurgency, is closely linked to ideas of justice. Indeed, it will be argued that legitimacy depends to a high degree not so much on any abstract notion of justice but on the ordinary people believing that they are being dealt with fairly. In answering the question 'why do we obey the law?', the chapter draws on research done by the Yale psychologist and lawyer Tom Tyler, which demonstrates that legitimacy is closely linked to perceptions of procedural regularity. In other words, is my dispute being resolved in a way that I consider to be fair? Dispute resolution is often considered to be contingent on the deciding authority, the state and its manifestations such as courts, having a monopoly of force. The chapter concludes with a brief look at legal pluralism, which might be seen as challenging the notion that a monopoly of force implies a unitary, formal system of justice.

Chapter 2, 'Needing a Better Deal', looks at why providing a working and fair, or apparently fair, system is productive to all combatants. In a competitive environment, the side in an insurgency that offers a better deal is likely to prevail. What matters is not so much the retention of 'hearts and minds', but rather the appreciation that whether you agree with the insurgent's agenda or not, they can do something for you that the incumbent counterinsurgent cannot. Hearts and minds take second place to an understanding that any dispute you have may be settled fairly and sustainably. The range of possible sectors within which this competition takes place is very wide. However, as many insurgent leaders have pointed out, no area is more important than land, and it is land reform and the adjudication of land disputes that form the centrepiece of this chapter.

The next two chapters look at the insurgent courts set up to provide those dispute resolution services. Chapter 3, 'Offering a Better Deal', looks at some of the insurgent courts of the twentieth century, leading off with the highly successful republican courts of the Irish War of Independence and ranging further from Nepal to Western Sahara. The IRA's judicial strategy represents the most complete manifestation of an insurgent judicial strategy at work, and it played a major role in sustaining a difficult military campaign, and also measuring the reach of the legitimacy attached to the rebel cause. Chapter 4, 'Caliphates of Law', takes a close look at the courts of contemporary insurgent groups, from the Taliban to the Islamic State, and argues that these represent another full realisation of importance of law and courts to successful insurgency as well as state-building. Whether outsiders like it or not, the bare truth of many of these arrangements is that they offer something better than the alternatives. The Taliban courts of Afghanistan resemble the IRA's campaign in that they are a vital part of the insurgent 'offer'. As with the Taliban, so for the short-lived Union of Islamic Courts of Somalia and indeed Islamic State; many of those subject to their rule see them as allowing a basic level of security. Chapter 5 takes the fight home, so to speak, with a look at how insurgents, their supporters or other actors concerned with how counterinsurgents operate, use courts and law. In Algeria, dissident French lawyer Jacques Vergès used what he called rupture strategy to attack the legitimacy of the government's courts. He would refuse to accept their authority. This in itself is nothing new, but its articulation and use as a deliberate 'judicial strategy', as Vergès called it, is innovative. The concept of 'disruptive litigation' is introduced, whereby courts are engaged in an assault on how counterinsurgents operate; we have seen this happen from Colombia to the United States, from Northern Ireland to Iraq. It has had a demonstrable effect on how counterinsurgent forces operate.

Chapter 5 is the watershed of the book. From here on, it is the counterinsurgent response to insurgent judicial approaches that we will be examining. Chapter 6 adopts a historical and empirical perspective to examine the British, French and Ottoman responses to ruling what is now called 'ungoverned space' in the nineteenth and twentieth centuries. The dilemma facing these powers was that they realised that the state-centric system from which they came would simply not work. Yet to retain the current legal and dispute resolution regimes was impossible—these were after all imperial regimes. It is from this period that the idea of the 'dual mandate'—the idea that dispute resolution can be delegated to customary or tribal courts without compromising imperial authority. This is the source of current ideas of 'legal pluralism' that may be crucial in the development of judicial strategies in insurgency.

While lessons drawn from imperial experience are often simply labelled as imperialist and therefore toxic, recent events have amply demonstrated that ignorance of experience drawn from 150 years of hard-earned and by no means always irrelevant struggle may be, and indeed have been, fatal to contemporary efforts. Chapter 7 looks at some of the traditional ideas relating to courts and justice in insurgencies and rebellions within the military–intellectual world of counterinsurgency doctrine and theory relating to courts and what is now termed lawfare. It goes on to examine how those theories were brought into practice in the 'classic' period of counterinsurgency in the 1950s in Malaya, Kenya and Cyprus. The Northern Ireland experience is examined largely through the perspective of the so-called 'Diplock Courts'. These cases are instructive as they demonstrate some of the dilemmas facing counterinsurgents. These dilemmas open space for the likes of Vergès to fill with various insurgent judicial strategies. Chapter 8 concludes the main body of the book. It begins with a look at how counterinsurgent lawfare is expressed in the military context in current US doctrine. It goes on to explore how both military theory and its civilian sister 'rule of law development' ideology have been assaulted in grand fashion in Afghanistan, specifically in the south of that country, and essentially defeated.

The book concludes with a series of recommendations as to how policy-makers and practitioners may take forward both more recent experiences and those of our imperial ancestors.

Several ideas are drawn together. First and foremost, assuming that lawfare is accepted to be a central part of contemporary warfare, is the need for a judicial strategy that is workable. Such a strategy must be developed alongside the other aspects of interventions or indeed domestic insurgency. It must be workable and based on good knowledge. If necessary, it should draw strength from ideas of legal pluralism and avoid being wedded too closely to paradigms that are simply inappropriate to most societies. Whether this is done in the context of a future UN mission in Syria or elsewhere, success in doing so will contribute a little to adding strength to any fragile settlement. Failure to do so opens up a key flank for insurgents to exploit.

What this book is not

Law and war is a vast topic; so is insurgency. This book does not aspire to be a full survey of either topic. It is necessarily selective in the cases it examines. It certainly does not claim to have discovered some form of silver bullet or panacea for insurgencies. I see law as a weapon that is available to insurgents and counterinsurgents alike to varying degrees, like air power, artillery or a cyber capability. This book is not intended as a contribution to the huge literature advising on counterinsurgency as a whole. Anyone interested in the intellectual pedigree of such thinking might wish to consult one of the many recent works on that topic.

Over the last two decades, writing on insurgencies and counterinsurgency has assumed something of the nature of theology, complete with orthodoxies, heresies and revered texts. Counterinsurgency lies at the confluence of the military and academic worlds and debates are often actively and sometimes amusingly vitriolic.[33] Given that both the military and academic worlds are notoriously prone to feuding and opaque rivalries, this is perhaps not surprising.

Among advocates for for population-centred counterinsurgency, a view abounds that this form of war is something entirely distinct from other forms of conflict. The US military guide to the topic calls it 'graduate-level warfare'.[34] If counterinsurgency is graduate-level warfare, one is inclined to wonder where that situates the astonishing organisation of the assault on Germany in 1944–5 or, on a smaller scale, the multi-dimensional, high-stakes retaking of the Falklands Islands in 1982. Both of these are so-called conventional operations. Is this 'undergraduate' warfare? One observes that the last fifteen years might indicate that no 'graduate' degrees have been earned. The search continues for silver bullets that might enable the defeat of rebellions. As mentioned earlier, no such solution will be found within these pages.

Rather than outlining a grand unifying theme or solution, this book aspires only to point up the importance of law and courts to the form of war we call insurgency. As such, its aim is to promote and perhaps provoke debate among those who make a living from writing about insurgencies and rebellions. More importantly, its objective is to prepare those who have to go and live among or indeed fight against insurgents. To repeat, there are no nostrums on offer here. There is no suggestion that the establishment of working and legitimate courts will win your insurgency or counterinsurgency campaign. Nor, indeed, do I argue that the absence of them will doom your rebellion to failure. As I observe in Chapter 3, the insurgent Tamil Tiger group that fought in Sri Lanka for over twenty years had a remarkable judicial system, complete with law schools and the full panoply of courts. Raw military force defeated them. The Kosovo Liberation Army, as far as I can tell, had few if any courts litigating civilian disputes; similarly, Libyan rebel courts did not rely on judicial strategy in any way in 2011; in both cases, NATO was decisive in winning their wars. No doubt many other such examples could be quoted. Lawfare is only one dimension of warfare. This book aims only to provide some thoughts that might result in one aspect of this form of warfare not being ignored or side-lined.

The central point to be taken away is that the judicial flank has been left open in many counterinsurgencies. At the very least, I hope that if, in future, the UK or the United States is involved in such conflicts, and they will be, that judicial flank is not ignored.

1

LAW, LEGITIMACY AND INSURGENCY

Legitimacy: the 'main objective'

'Law has become a mark of legitimacy and legitimacy has become the currency of power.'[1]

As kinetic combat takes place in a physical environment, in which all participants fight, so law may be a common language in the virtual fight for legitimacy. Not all counterinsurgents understand that justice is where the rubber of governance meets the road of the people. Counterinsurgents should be sure to treat it with the same regard with which some successful insurgents treat it.

From a military perspective, treating the justice sector in a post-conflict or 'state-building' context as an often unwelcome ancillary is a serious error. While the form that dispute resolution mechanisms take may change, the nature of justice as a social good is similar across all cultures. Similarly, the relationship between justice and legitimacy is often taken for granted.

To illustrate the point, I will, for a moment, come home. There may be some readers who have, at one time or another, found themselves in a British court. The fact of being in such a place has profound implications that extend beyond the fate of one's personal liberty or driving licence. For a start, there is an implicit acceptance of the court's authority. The presumption of legitimacy is so deep that it is almost never articulated. One could sit in British courts for many years without hearing the phrase 'I deny the right of this court to decide my case.' There may be those who find court rulings misconceived or just plain wrong. Arguments are often made about jurisdiction, but few outside the small 'insurgent' community of this country deny the right of the court to make those rulings. Facing everyone in a UK court (except the judge or magistrate) is a large royal crest over the judge's seat. For those who care to consider it, the implication is clear. Here resides authority based around common acceptance. There are no rivals to the courts here. Any proposed, or indeed existing, Sharia or Beth Din courts (dealing largely with family cases, with the consent of the litigants) will derive their authority, and more importantly, the enforceability of their decisions, from UK law. When something goes wrong, whether this is government misfeasance or private crime, we rely on courts to sort it out.

The ability and acceptance of the right to adjudicate in disputes is the ultimate expression of the right to rule—indeed of legitimacy. Once that sense is lost, as it was in early 1920s Ireland or early twenty-first-century Afghanistan, it is an uphill struggle to get it back. Complex insurgencies are powered by injustice, corruption and a sense of illegitimacy. Contrary to received governmental wisdom, they are not generally driven by a desire to see free and fair elections. Most ordinary right-thinking people have the provenance of their government well down their list of priorities. What is important is the knowledge that if you have a dispute with your neighbour over land, or with an individual over whether he stole your television set, it will be resolved fairly. Your livelihood may depend on that. In the absence of such a service, insurgents will happily and gratefully provide it themselves. Justice is a doubly dangerous weapon in the hands of an information-literate indigenous insurgent operation like the Taliban. 'Sometimes the best weapons are those which do not shoot', as the US Counterinsurgency Manual puts it.[2] Not only does the insurgent's ability to adjudicate in disputes in an accepted and purportedly fair fashion reinforce his claims to legitimacy, but it bleeds that legitimacy away from the government. As one commentator puts it, the setting up of separate courts is the ultimate 'non serviam', the ultimate denial of the right of the state to determine the outcome of disputes and consequently the ultimate denial of that state's legitimacy.[3]

What is legitimacy?

Legitimacy is the bottom line of accepted counterinsurgency theory. The US *Insurgencies and Countering Insurgencies Field Manual* (2014 edition of FM 3–24) declares legitimacy to be 'the main objective' of counterinsurgents.[4] No fewer than sixty-one paragraphs of that document mention legitimacy. It declares irregular warfare to be a 'violent struggle among state and non-state actors for legitimacy'.[5] The question of legitimacy is one aspect of what Kilcullen calls 'the theory of competitive control'.[6] Unlike conventionally understood forms of war, insurgency/counterinsurgency is not a contest to control territory or to destroy an enemy's ability and will to fight, but rather a competition between two opposing groups to be recognised by a particular population as its legitimate government. As Kilcullen says elsewhere: 'We can beat the Taliban in any military engagement, but we're losing in Afghanistan not because we're being outfought but because the Afghan government is being outgoverned.'[7]

Thus, law has a dual use in counterinsurgency: both as a tool for defeating criminal insurgents themselves (by imprisoning them) and as a means for governments to build legitimacy.[8] So what is legitimacy? And from where does it derive?

The generic term for the plethora of military documents dealing with definitions and approaches to a given problem is 'doctrine'. Doctrine on insurgency prescribes nostrums for inculcating this elusive quality of legitimacy. The 2006 edition of FM 3–24 sets out six 'possible indicators of legitimacy', which include the ability to provide security, the selection of leaders in a manner perceived to be just and fair, a high-level of political participation, a culturally acceptable level of corruption, a culturally acceptable level of social and economic development, and a high level of regime acceptance by major social institutions.[9]

Nowhere in this list is the ability to solve disputes. None of those indicators are of much use if the 'host population' turns to the insurgent to solve its problems. British and US counterinsurgency doctrine adopts the solution of 'building courts and training lawyers'.[10] The

British handbook, like its American counterpart, mandates military lawyers to undertake 'rule of law activities'.[11] These prescriptions are nothing more than afterthoughts, representing the notion that justice is an easy fix, brought into effect by the construction of courts and the training of lawyers and judges. As we will see in later chapters, this approach has borne very little fruit.

Legitimacy and 'social capital'

Social theorists have looked at legitimacy as the product of the accumulation of social capital. That capital can take the form of roads, schools, and water and electricity production and distribution. There is also the accumulation of rather less tangible 'symbolic capital'. This 'refers to those intangible accumulations that are rich with widely socially shared meanings that are often rooted in accumulations of physical capital but nevertheless distinct.'[12] There is no better example of symbolic capital than a functioning court.

For a state to be legitimate, the reservoir of symbolic capital must remain above a certain threshold. In practical terms, that reservoir will contain such elements as working courts, systems by which judgements can be enforced, and a certain minimum foundation in the relevant societies' mores and customs. It is the job of the insurgent to drain that reservoir and refill it with his own capital.

Hobbes' classic formulation posited the necessity of what amounted to a contract between the subject and the sovereign. It is this formulation that lies at the root of the stream of political philosophy known as 'social contract theory'. The idea of the state existing to restrict uncontrolled violence through the exercise of the monopoly use of its own violence is commonly accepted. That is indeed correct. If no social institutions existed that were prepared to accept the use of violence, then the concept of 'state' would be eliminated, and a condition would emerge that could be designated as 'anarchy', in the specific sense of this word. Of course, force is certainly not the normal or the only means of the state—nobody says that—but force is a means specific to the state and in theory the state should have a monopoly over its use.[13] Mao Tse-tung phrased much the same thought differently: 'Every communist must grasp the truth "political power grows out of the barrel of a gun" ... all things grow out of the barrel of a gun.'[14] Such power may indeed grow from cold steel, but power itself and legitimacy are made of very different substances.

A critique from legal anthropology

The idea that societies must in some fashion be based on the threat of force structured and authorised by a system of dispute resolution is by no means accepted by all legal anthropologists. Fernanda Pirie states that 'behind this [Hobbes'] model is the idea that human beings are by nature asocial and inclined to a state of conflict unless controlled and socialised by government'.[15] She is supported in this by, among others, Simon Roberts, another leading anthropologist of law. He says that many studies have undermined the:

> long-standing assumption that order is only conceivable if there are strong men in positions of authority ready to tell others what to do ... It is not the fault of anthropologists if the lessons of these studies, clear as they are, have yet to be absorbed by some legal and political theorists.[16]

Similarly, Bronislaw Malinowski was an early advocate of the idea that centralised government and laws are not necessary to the functioning of society.[17]

Indeed, it can be argued that, even in the West, most disputes are not in fact settled through state structures, but are resolved through negotiation. It is only when such negotiation fails that the state becomes involved. It can also be argued that some laws and codes have little impact on how disputes are actually resolved. There are examples of societies where the law is separate from any normative function, serving rather as, at best, guidance or even ritual decoration.[18] An example of this has been cited in the 'law' of the Old Testament of the Bible, which is accepted as 'law' by, for example, Christians, but not implemented, albeit for theological reasons.

However, for many of those who advocate counterinsurgency techniques, there is a presumption that if structures are mandated, funded and legislated for, they must exist and function. This is very, very far from the case.

The paradigm of Western state-centralist 'rule of law' has dominated counterinsurgency discourse. The technical word for this approach is 'centralism', defined by John Griffiths as the belief 'that law is and should be the law of the state, uniform for all persons, exclusive of all other law and administered by a single set of state institutions'.[19]

It is, says Griffiths, 'a myth, an ideal, a claim, an illusion'.[20] Centralism treats customary systems, which are often encountered in insurgency situations, as separate from the essential centrality of the state. Legal development expert Deborah Isser is right when she says that customary systems must be seen 'not as an isolated phenomenon but as an undeniable component of the justice landscape'.[21] That notwithstanding, in every member state of the United Nations there is a structure that approximates to a 'justice system' backed by, and at least ostensibly supportive of, the state itself.

Perceptions of fairness and legitimacy

Such a system will function better as a guarantor of a minimum of physical and economic security if it is, one 'of which the population approves'.[22] Such a structure might promote legitimacy in two ways: first, by restraining and defining the parameters of the state, thereby ensuring that a sense of justice is at least possible; and second, by providing a service. That service in turn affects and promotes the idea of a state, by reinforcing the state's power.

In his book *Why People Obey the Law* Tom Tyler claims that the impression of procedural fairness is the key factor in legitimacy.[23] What, though, is fairness? Is what is fair to Afghans different from what is perceived as procedurally fair in colonial Ireland of the eighteenth and nineteenth centuries, for example? It is no good just relying on common sense; perhaps we must look into social contract? If foreign (sometimes called 'exogenous') counterinsurgents can provide procedural fairness, can they develop legitimacy? Surely, according to Tyler, the answer is yes.

Colonial Ireland provides an example of a society where the structures largely existed and appeared to work. They looked and functioned procedurally in a similar fashion to those that existed at the time across the Irish Sea in England. In her study of the courts of the period, Heather Laird has found that the dynamics that allowed the courts in England to gain an acceptable level of legitimacy in the late eighteenth century did not function in Ireland.[24] She counterpoints the conclusions of E.P. Thompson, who took the view that in England there was at least the perception of the possibility of justice.[25] Laird says that: 'British law' was popularly interpreted as a foreign imposition that had displaced an earlier legal system.[26]

It is clear that the writ of the 'crown' courts—those run by the British administration—in the sense of their accepted authority certainly did not run throughout the land. One 'resident magistrate', a representative of the lowest level of judicial authority, was often incapable of recalling that 'Ireland was a part of the United Kingdom with representatives in parliament and not a far flung colony.'[27] Thus, the law acted as a driver of conflict rather than a system of resolution. There was little in the way of a perception of fairness. In other words, justice was not seen to be done.

What makes people obey the law?

In answer to the question 'why do we obey the law?', social theory generally offers two general positions, not necessarily mutually exclusive. Running through both is the idea that perception is, if not all, then certainly very significant. The first has been characterised as the 'instrumental' perspective, also referred to as 'social control'. This is concerned primarily with offering access to resources for compliance, or sanctions for failure to comply. Complementary to the 'social control' perspective has been the 'public choice' approach, which 'suggests that people are intrinsically motivated to maximize their personal gain in their behavior towards the law'.[28] Consequent to this approach, the view is taken that sanctions, as the necessary counterpoint to gain, provide the key impetus for compliance. Put simply, the 'social control' approach posits that the main driver is a system of rewards and punishments. This might also be termed a 'transactional' approach. However, democratic societies cannot function in a purely instrumental fashion. While it is a mischaracterisation that the 'social control' model is Pavlovian, there is surely more to compliance than a simple and constant weighing up of rewards and costs: 'it may not be effective enough to allow a complex democratic society to survive'.[29]

The second approach is known in general terms as the 'normative approach', which takes what might be regarded as a more nuanced view of the problem. Tyler posits that the strongest motivation for obedience to the law is not externally imposed, but is, in fact, what he calls 'internalised obligation', a major component of this being 'legitimacy', which, he says, 'rests on a conception of obligation to obey any commands an authority issues so long as that authority is acting within appropriate limits'.[30] The case Tyler makes is not that legitimacy displaces the social control approach, but rather that legitimacy is an important element in the exercise of authority.

In 1984, alongside Kenneth Rasinski, he conducted an extensive and comprehensive empirical study, known now as the Chicago study, to determine what it is that motivates that 'internal' obedience.[31] Its conclusions were complex. However, one particular aspect was clear: 'The way people assess procedural fairness is strongly linked to their judgements of whether the authority they are dealing with is motivated to be fair.'[32] Tyler concludes that 'people obey the law because they believe that it is proper to do so.'[33]

This conclusion may seem to be in accordance with intuition, that justice must be perceived as 'proper'. What Tyler offers is empirical evidence that this is the case. This is important; Tyler demonstrates that it is no good simply having courts that hand down decisions, even if those decisions are enforced. What he is saying is that it is vital that they are seen to be fair.

The importance of procedural fairness and its perception may be clear in societies with structured legal regimes.[34] The same seems to be the case with respect to some 'stateless' systems of governance and dispute resolution. For example, the *Xeer* system in Somalia is based around submitting disputes to nominated representatives of tribal or clan groups—individuals who are chosen for their impartiality and knowledge of tradition. A hearing is held, at which both sides present their 'cases', as it were. The nominated elders arrive at a decision and the parties are encouraged to accept it. Simon Roberts highlights the vital role played by the feeling that a decision has been arrived at in a manner acceptable to those involved in the dispute: 'Whether such a decision sticks depends upon whether both parties feel the judgement to be fair.'[35] This may seem entirely intuitive, and it is. As much of the rest of this book will seek to show, he is exactly right.

LAW, LEGITIMACY AND INSURGENCY

Implications for insurgents and counterinsurgents

The key point to be drawn from Tom Tyler's conclusions is that obedience is conditional upon legitimacy, the 'stakeholders' believe that, regardless of the result, it has been arrived at properly. This applies equally to Western societies: relatively secure, governed by largely well-understood norms and a common acceptance that courts, as arbiters of last resort, will act properly. Few will question the legitimacy of such courts, even if they may believe that its verdicts or judgements are wrong. This is by no means the case in countries racked by rebellion or indeed in very many countries of the world where the legitimacy of a given authority is contested or indeed simply not an issue at all, in that no one in their right mind would ever consider a highly corrupt court to be legitimate. They may see it as formally 'legal' but not legitimate. This is a vital issue for insurgents because courts are the most obvious expression of a government's power in a civilian (or indeed in the case of 'courts martial', military) context.

Tyler confirms that legitimacy is itself conditional on fair dealing by the authorities with the 'customers' of the service provided. An actor aspiring to 'intervene' in conflicts such as those in Afghanistan or Syria will require a deep awareness of the systems of dispute resolution. Successful insurgents and rebels understand the importance of perceptions, as we will see below, particularly in Chapter 4, which deals with 'caliphates of law'. In the Somali example, as indeed in many other tribal systems, the concept of legitimacy may well be rather more individually than institutionally based, or indeed might be based upon notions of honour. Societies such as this are not rare outside the Western context, as will be seen throughout this book.

The implications of this are extensive, if they can be applied to insurgencies. It casts doubt on the 'armed alms-giving' and 'institution-building' aspects of counterinsurgency as supports for legitimacy.[36] The implication here is that, without what might be called 'fair dealing' (with the cultural caveat mentioned above), no amount of granting of physical or social goods will work in what amounts to a system that either is or is perceived to be corrupt or for that matter outside applicable social mores.

Justice may be a central actor in insurgencies, because if a state is not able to dictate how disputes are resolved—a contemporary expression of 'monopoly of force'—it surely can have no claim to legitimacy. This does not necessarily imply that the state does the dispute resolution in the form of courts; it may mean the state devolving that responsibility to a non-state actor, or indeed the state having little, if any, practical role in basic dispute resolution at all.

The fact that non-state actors (a vital distinction from anti-state actors) may be 'doing' justice need not in itself imply a reduction in legitimacy for the state systems. Ideas of legal pluralism do not necessarily challenge state authority provided they are countenanced by the state in, for example, a constitution. On the contrary, it is simply an acceptance of reality and a state endorsement of that reality. In Ethiopia, for example, the reality of a multi-ethnic and deeply multicultural state is reflected in a constitution that allows extensive latitude to the various approaches to governance, including informal justice such as the *Xeer* system or many other tribal systems. In other words, Ethiopia practises a deep and explicit legal pluralism.[37] It does so without compromising the integrity or legitimacy of the state. It might be argued that this fundamentally challenges the Hobbesian form of the 'state monopoly on the use of force' model. Maybe it does, but it also achieves the essential objective of the state countenancing a working system of dispute resolution that is seen to be fair and procedurally appropriate.

As we shall see when we look at the Afghan case, when the state, in Afghanistan encouraged by foreign interveners, tries—however ineptly—to impose a system that is foreign to, and distrusted by, the great majority of citizens, the state sets itself against those citizens.

It is into situations like this that the insurgent, the subversive, will insinuate himself. He will seek to offer an alternative to the state-provided version. He will place great emphasis on making the insurgent version work. The more such an insurgent version works, the more it is embedded; set against a state version that clearly, or apparently, does not work.

Parallel systems in the West?

Even in highly developed societies such as the United Kingdom, the idea of legal pluralism is not entirely alien, and there have been occasions outside the forum of the Civil War (where competing systems of governance existed) when the concept of pluralism has been and continues to be practised.

Proponents of legal pluralism, usually arguing from a religious perspective, would not contend that acceptance of the legitimacy of one system, even within one state, implies the illegitimacy of all others within that state. It is not, as it were, a zero-sum idea. Rather, they posit that legitimacy is not necessarily rooted in one stream of authority. Such ideas are controversial in Western societies, it must be said. One such controversy arose when there were moves in the United Kingdom to allow some degree of jurisdiction, particularly in family matters, to religious courts—specifically the Sharia courts of the Islamic community and the Beth Din courts of the Jewish community. Particular comment was occasioned by a statement from the former lord chief justice of England and Wales, Nicholas Phillips:

> There is no reason why Shari'a principles, or any other religious code should not be the basis for mediation or other forms of alternative dispute resolution [with the understanding] … that any sanctions for a failure to comply with the agreed terms for mediation would be drawn from the laws of England and Wales.[38]

It is fair to say that this statement and others by similarly prominent public figures, such as Rowan Williams, the former archbishop of Canterbury, have stressed arguments directed at promoting 'custom and community'.[39] Opponents have been clear that providing some limited legal authority for Sharia courts was the first step towards supplanting English law.[40]

Further equally fundamental objections to allowing any jurisdiction at all to Sharia courts reference human rights, particularly the treatment of women in probate and divorce matters.[41] Concerns such as these led to the introduction by Baroness Caroline Cox of the Arbitration and Mediation Services (Equality) Bill (2012), the intention of which, among other provisions, was to ensure that Islamic courts in the UK complied fully with national law on equality,[42] and that no claim of 'the powers and duties of a court' would be lawful. Concerns about parallel systems of justice are not confined, therefore, to the world of insurgencies and rebellions.

Conclusion

Current counterinsurgency theory is based to a great degree on ideas of legitimacy within the state-construct. As far as it goes, that is all very well. However, the judicial system is where the mettle of claims to legitimacy and the right to govern is proved. The setting up of the paraphernalia of justice is only the first of many difficult steps to the fuzzily understood concept, perhaps the chimera, that is legitimacy.

However, help is available from the academy. It seems clear that one factor in whether a system of dispute resolution is acceptable—is legitimate—is whether it is perceived as procedurally fair. In other words, as Tyler says, so long as that authority is acting within appropriate limits, then it is likely to be obeyed. Clearly, the term 'appropriate limits' comprises a somewhat wide area of discretion.[43] The exercise of such authority may be through so-called formal means, such as courts, or more informal mechanisms such as what is sometimes called customary justice. From the counterinsurgent perspective, the important element is that, however a system is set up, if the aspiration is legitimacy it should be seen to be acting fairly.

This opens a new set of possibilities to the counterinsurgent; it opens the way to the potential of pluralism as may be seen in evolved rather than imposed multinational and multicultural societies such as Ethiopia. Indeed, even in developed countries such as the UK, legal pluralism is not as foreign as we may at first be inclined to believe.

Where systems are not perceived to be acting fairly or appropriately, the way is open for insurgents to fill the gap and offer, as we saw above, a 'better deal'. It is to them that we now turn.

2

NEEDING A BETTER DEAL

'The authority to resolve disputes can necessarily be exercised by only one body (pursuant to the state's "monopoly on the use of force" that is the first element of the "rule of law")—imagine the systemic breakdown that would result from two competing bodies claiming the power to resolve disputes.'[1]

For the first few years of this century I worked for the Organization for Security and Co-operation in Europe (OSCE). This is an international organisation similar to the United Nations. Like the UN, it operates missions throughout what it calls its 'space', namely Europe and the former Soviet Union. For three of those years, I was a senior human rights officer for the OSCE's mission in Albania. My job was to try to monitor and if possible help to improve the human rights situation in the country. A tall order, you might think, and you would be right. The mission had diplomatic status, so we were all technically members of a diplomatic mission led by an ambassador. Each of the senior members of the mission was able to 'call on' senior government officials or indeed ministers (who regularly changed in the carousel that is the Albanian government). As with any other similar job, when I arrived in Albania's capital Tirana in the summer of 2000, I was required to call on some of my future interlocutors to introduce myself.

I had almost no experience of dealing with relatively senior officials at that time in my career. I had been a barrister—a trial lawyer—for seven years in Liverpool, England. My work involved the day-to-day business of law in a major provincial city, particularly criminal and family work. Like most of the members of my profession at that time, I respected judges as successful and knowledgeable men and women with a difficult job that was almost always done well. Along with very high levels of competence, integrity was taken as a given. Taking bribes, for example, was unheard of. The worst behaviour I had seen was the obvious bias of some judges towards the police; and, in fairness, there were also some judges who were visibly biased against the authorities. Given that our juries almost as a rule reacted negatively to bias of any kind in a trial, justice was almost always done, and seen to be done. Aside from that, I had seen the odd older judge nod off on warm afternoons after a good lunch, and some members of the judiciary could occasionally be uncivil. That was the limit of improper behaviour. Overall, I believed, with some considerable justification, that I had worked in a well-funded system with a centuries' old tradition of self-regulated competence, integrity and professionalism of which I was very proud. Right or wrong, that was the culture in which I was professionally raised.

So when I was invited to go and call on a very senior member of Albania's judiciary, I was conditioned to consider this person as roughly equivalent to our lord chief justice. In other words, a supreme professional, someone who had largely achieved his success due to legal knowledge, application of critical skills, with a modicum perhaps of social capital backing him up. This was until I saw a large late model Mercedes car parked outside his office. This vehicle was not a limousine owned by the state, as I discovered when I asked the flunky who met us at the entrance to the senior judge's offices. It was owned, he said, by the judge. In fairness, in the UK it would not be unusual for a senior judge to have a large and expensive status symbol. However, such men and women generally have salaries greater than $600 a month. They may have earned their fortunes while practising as a lawyer. In civil law countries, however, you become a judge when you leave law school, not as in the UK and United States at the end of a successful legal career. In the case of this man, he would never have earned more than he did when I visited him.

When the meeting with this rather grand personage had finished, I asked my Albanian interpreter how the good judge could afford a

$70,000 car on his salary. 'Perhaps he saved up', she replied. Perhaps indeed. Rather more likely, as was quickly made clear, is that this man had been on the take for many years. Judicial advancement was not seen as a mark of professional skill so much as a surrogate cash machine. In other words, those who bring cases to court could be expected to pay bribes for a judgement in their favour. This was the ecology within which many Albanian lawyers worked. As one said to me, 'my job is not so much to argue the case as to determine the price that the judge will accept'.

As the years in Albania went on, I saw time and again the marks of a severely corrupt legal system. The world's leading anti-corruption NGO, Transparency International (TI), runs an annual table listing all the countries of the world in order not of how corrupt they are but according to perceptions of corruption.[2] On that list, Albania is at number eighty-eight out of 167 countries (Denmark is number one, Britain is at number ten, the United States is sixteen). TI says that 114 countries in the world can be said to have 'serious problems with corruption'.

I went on to work in the former Soviet Union, places such as Belarus, Ukraine and the Central Asian states. If anything, these countries are far more afflicted by corruption than Albania. In one major Central Asian state, I was told that a very senior judge had a practice of letting parties to cases know that he was 'open to offers'. Sealed bids were to be sent to the judge and the highest bidder would secure judgement in their favour. Clearly, in disputes over oil and gas fields, such bids were often very high indeed. Later in my time with the OSCE, a close colleague from Belarus expressed surprise that I had not heard of this way of conducting legal business before. It was very common indeed.

The misconception I had of the role and function of the senior Albanian judge was an example of what Jonathan Foreman in his superb dissection of the aid and development industry *Aiding and Abetting* calls the 'Nomenclatural Fallacy':

> The term refers to the way that aid officials and other foreigners often make the naïve mistake of assuming that officials in poorer/developing countries who possess titles such as 'policeman', 'judge' or 'minister' have the same functions as officials who bear those titles in their home countries ... in fact in many, many countries from Equatorial Guinea to India,

a 'policeman' is essentially a licensed and uniformed bandit; a judge may be a judicial entrepreneur rather than a dispenser of justice.[3]

In postmodern terms, this is an example of 'simulacrum'—the idea that in some societies there are elements of society that profess to be and on the face of it are one thing, but are in fact another. This may seem to be a court operating upon the principles of law and the constitution. However, it is in fact something rather different; it may be an arm of the security forces in some countries and have only a distant relationship to the law. It may be a pure cash generation device for judges and lawyers. It may be something of both; but it is not a court governed by the constitution and the law. In every developing country I have worked in, and indeed in some of those newer members of the European Union, I have found this to be common. It must be said that one does find exceptions. But they are precisely that, and are more often to be found at the bottom of the hierarchy than nearer the top. Sadly, this is the reality in which many people live. Official or judicial positions are bought and sold. They are considered to be investments. Consequently, the ideal of fair procedure is all too often simply little more than that, an ideal.

None of the places I have mentioned were at the time involved in insurgency or rebellion. However, after my seven years with the OSCE, it was very clear that grand corruption (which is to say the illegal appropriation of money by state officials—let's call it theft) was very common indeed among judges. It was even worse, far worse, later on in Helmand (see Chapter 8).

In her ground-breaking book, *Thieves of State*, Sarah Chayes describes the nature of the kind of gross corruption found in such places as Afghanistan.[4] Chayes had lived in Kandahar, the largest and most important city in southern Afghanistan, for nine years throughout the worst of the war. Initially as an NGO worker and then running a business (making scented soap), she learned the language and became intimately familiar with how difficult is the struggle of ordinary Afghans in such environments. She is conscious that ordinary people have to endure a great deal in insurgencies such as the one still tearing Afghanistan apart. One vital element driving the insurgency is corruption. However, she does not see this through the same eyes as many observers, such as myself, whose familiarity is often based upon very short acquaintance. Her perspective as an outsider, but one who saw the place as her home, is vital. While we might regard the Afghan 'government', such as it was, as ramshackle and incompetent, she saw it rather differently: 'It was not incapable. It was performing its core function with admirable efficiency—bringing power to bear where it counted. And it was assiduously protecting its own. Governing—the exercise that attracted so much international attention—was really just a front activity.'[5]

It was a simulacrum of government. And what was that 'core function'? She sees states such as Afghanistan as a 'vertically integrated organised criminal syndicate'. You or I might use the term, as she does, of a 'mafia', the core activity of which is 'not in fact exercising the functions of a state, but rather extracting resources for personal gain'.[6] That the state is simply a front for the extraction of resources from ordinary people to connected individuals is a truism fully recognised across huge swathes of the planet. The idea that state-forming is analogous to organised crime is well known to sociologists.[7]

In circumstances such as those in Helmand, where there was an intense insurgency, the state offered an even worse deal to the people than it otherwise might. Indeed, after nine years of international assistance, largely applied in the form of military power with the addition of vast amounts of civilian input, Afghanistan had sunk to being the most corrupt country in the world.[8]

In Afghanistan, there was and is little in the way of the kind of procedural fairness that is central to notions of anything approaching legitimacy. In such circumstances, people will start to look elsewhere for dispute resolution, if that 'elsewhere' offers a better package. In other words, if an insurgent group can solve your problem in a way that will be lasting and effective, you are likely to take advantage of that offer. In doing so, you may be according a measure of support, inadvertent or otherwise, to that insurgent group, but, you might think, so be it.

When I was based in Afghanistan, the military commander of the UK's Helmand mission wrote a 'campaign appreciation' (i.e. a plan) in which he, like many counterinsurgency operators, stated that 'the people are the prize', as if they were some inert object. This particular general is intelligent enough to understand that this was not the case. However, those words do describe a certain attitude of counterinsurgents who believe that this 'prize' might be won if the 'people' were somehow leveraged away from any kind of support for the insurgents; in the Afghan case, the insurgents were the Taliban. However, it can be strongly argued that ordinary people, apart from the militarily or the politically active, tend not to support one side or another. What they are interested in is being permitted to get on with their lives with the minimum of interference. People are not prizes. They are dynamic actors. There has been much study of how people really behave in rebellions and insurgencies. A good place to start is Stathis Kalyvas's *The Logic of Violence in Civil War* (2006).[9] One key factor lying at the heart of that and other such studies is that people will act according to their own interests and such interests are not always marked by the granting of social or economic goods. Similarly abstract notions of loyalty or allegiance to one or other political agenda is, in reality, a relatively rare motivation for people to fight or support one side or another.

Notions of legitimacy, whether or not driven by procedural fairness, will tend to attract support. But the interests of a given individual do not necessarily follow legitimacy. It is possible to accept that a government's cause is legitimate while simultaneously fighting for the government's opponents if those opponents are offering something better than the government. For example, no interest is more fundamental than property, and if rebels offer security of tenure, so be it. This book's central thesis is that when corruption, inefficiency or incompetence causes an incumbent government to fail to offer a good service, the opportunity exists for insurgents to enter the fray and provide a better one. The provision of such a service will anchor their role as a workable alternative.

Insurgents and justice

Insurgents recognise justice as a key centre of gravity in their effort. Successful insurgents have often been aware of this. If 'the population is the prize', it is won at least partly by providing justice—and being seen to do so—in an acceptable fashion. In so doing, the insurgent may establish and entrench his own legitimacy, while undermining that of the state he opposes. As dynamic and reactive actors, successful insurgents see courts and dispute resolution as an opportunity to take the initiative in a vital area of conflict. If, as Whitman has put it, 'Kingdoms are won and lost in the realms of law and legitimacy',[10] then successful insurgents, whether Afghan, Irish or African, instinctively understand this.

In any legitimate state, there is a requirement for executive (and to some extent legislative) functions. What is indispensable is the judicial branch—that element of government deputed to resolve disputes and grievances. When the insurgent can provide the means to settle grievances fairly, or to be perceived to do so, he is a long way down the road to replacing the most central of governmental functions.[11]

It is an axiom that, as the French counterinsurgency theorist David Galula put it, 'a revolutionary war is 20% military action to 80% political.'[12] Galula strongly implies that this proportion should also apply to counter-revolutionary war. In other words, the effort of the counterinsurgent should comprise at least 80 per cent political action. Going far further back into strategic history, Clausewitz articulated the surely obvious but hitherto unexpressed truth that war is a political act: 'We see, therefore, that war is not merely an act of policy but a true political instrument, a continuation of political intercourse carried on with other means. What remains peculiar to war is simply the peculiar nature of its means.'[13] If we accept that rebellions and insurgencies are 'war', as surely we must, the political element itself comprises a plethora of interwoven elements, one of which is justice and its various, manifestations.

Shadow states and competitive control

In such conflicts, insurgents often set up their own systems of government in direct competition with the incumbent (i.e. official) government. It has been suggested that shadow states, one term for the kind of government that is exercised by insurgents, require an element of territorial control to succeed.[14] But this is not necessarily so. Many insurgents can exercise control over the population without exercising total control over territory. For example, the Irish Republican Army of the Irish War of Independence just after the Great War held almost no territory in Ireland. It did, however, exercise effective control on behalf of its civilian authority, the Dáil Éireann (the parliament). Similarly, the Taliban of today's Afghanistan control a great deal of territory, and they are able to exercise real influence even in areas dominated by government forces. Territory can be useful, or it can simply act as a focus for incumbent state action. Legitimacy is not dependent on the possession of territory. While the possession and control of land may have a function, an absolute *sine qua non* is the ability to ensure that the insurgent government's strictures are obeyed and that its rule is enforced. This is not necessarily dependent on the exclusive possession of the land. So, to return to Helmand as an example, when NATO forces were there, the Taliban had exclusive control over only a few small pockets of the province. The vast bulk of the province was under the supposed control of the government, or such government as could be said to have existed, in that NATO and some Afghan army and police units seemed to provide what passed for security in many areas. Even so, the Taliban had a whole system of government, including a governor, administrators, judges and an entire hierarchy of courts, all of which functioned rather better than their official governmental opponents, as we will see in Chapter 4 below.

In Afghanistan, as conventional military forces cleared areas that were to be filled by 'governance', the kind of governance that filled the cleared space was all too often rather worse than the admittedly ramshackle Taliban equivalent. As David Kilcullen writes in *Out of the Mountains*, 'If your strategy is to extend the reach of a government that is corrupt, abusive, ineffective and alienates the people, then the better you execute that strategy, the worse things were going to get.'[15] Accordingly, people began to look to the Taliban for, among other things, dispute resolution; in other words, they were looking for justice.

The unpalatable truth is that 'Parallel structures undermine official statutes in the first place then displace them', where they can establish—by force or otherwise—sufficient legitimacy and capability, for example in enforcing decisions of governments and courts.[16] Once it is established, it is very difficult to displace, because 'the creation of a counterstate solidifies the insurgency's support among the population and it is the final step on its path to power.'[17]

Justice and injustice

Che Guevara, the well-known darling of 1960s revolutionaries and a face on a million T-shirts and posters, looked at the stages of a guerrilla war through the lens of the Cuban Revolution, in which he was a leader.[18] After its beginnings and initial contacts with the enemy, the next stage of development followed when a base area was selected and basic elements of settled life began. In the case of Cuba, they were a show factory, a cigar and cigarette factory, a printing press and other factories necessary for the maintenance of basic existence: crucially, he added, 'A court is established for the administration of justice.'[19]

Guevara attached great importance to the development and enforcement of revolutionary laws, particularly those pertaining to land reform.[20] The guerrillas 'issued a penal code, a civil code, rules for supplying the peasantry and rules of agrarian reform.'[21] The council was essentially the ruling authority for the guerrilla organisation. It is striking that the judicial element and attendant necessary expertise is so explicitly stated. Cuba, of course, is a clear example of that deficit discussed briefly above. The Cuban state prior to Castro's revolution, despite its protestations of democracy, was almost a pure plutocracy. No legitimacy of any real significance was to be derived from it in the minds of the Cuban people.

Justice is central to almost any insurgency. Journalist and author David Loyn claims that justice is the single most important issue for the people of Afghanistan.[22] 'Lack of justice is a key driver of the disillusionment felt by many Afghans across the country ... There is relatively little detailed research on individual motivations to join the insurgency, but grievances related to injustice are repeatedly mentioned in interviews and the literature.'[23] The question of injustice continues to appear in discourse concerning insurgency.[24] One problem facing counterinsurgents, or the civilians working alongside them, is that they are rarely aware of the deeper problems facing a given society. Nowhere was this clearer than when the soldiers of the British Army, largely drawn from a liberal and urban society, crashed into the intensely conservative, highly complex rural Afghan province of Helmand.

Helmand, 2010

In late 2010, a British Army unit pulls up to a bare concrete school building in Helmand, with a dozen or so men and boys as an audience. Inside the school, sitting around the sides of its only classroom, are forty farmers and local workers, all male. At the front of the room, also seated, are two heavily bearded men: the chief administrator of the district—the local town of a few thousand people and its surroundings—and his deputy. The soldiers set up a basic security cordon around the building, and their leader, a young captain in his mid-twenties, strides to the front and sits alongside the two men. He takes off his heavy body-armour and sets aside his rifle. He is accompanied by a younger, unarmed man, also in military fatigues. They are attending the village shura (meeting) to introduce themselves. The previous military unit, a US marine battalion, has just left the area and the British officer is commander of their far fewer replacements. The district chief nods impatiently to the captain to stand up and say his piece. The officer walks to the front of the classroom and begins: 'Gentlemen, you may have noticed that my soldiers and myself are dressed rather differently from the American marines that we have replaced. We may have different uniforms but we have the same mission.' The words are translated by the young man beside him into the local Pashto language. Some of the farmers wonder in what way exactly this fair foreigner in brownish green clothes with his group of similarly attired heavily armed friends differs from the last one who made a speech to the village shura a few months ago. 'All I want to say right now is that like my predecessor, me and my soldiers stand squarely behind your district chief, Mr Alizai, in his efforts to improve your government's service to you. Mr Alizai Sir, over to you.'

Sher Alizai, the representative of the government of the Islamic Republic of Afghanistan and a member of a tribe not well liked in that area, stands to address the shura:

> What kind of men are you? … that can sit in your homes and allow the men, these so-called Taliban who brought war to this district simply run your lives. You cower at home as they set up checkpoints outside your village. If you resist them, we will support you; and yet no, you let them rule your lives; I am here to tell you that this will not be tolerated. One other thing that you need to understand. The government owns all the land in these parts; land outside the limits of this town will be expropriated; it is not yours and it never was.

Very few if any such meetings containing frank exchanges rather than formulas of agreement were filmed, or in any event broadcast by embedded Western journalists. All such footage was subject to censorship;

something rarely acknowledged by journalists desperate to curry favour with their host units. This particular meeting was recorded in a remarkable film made by one of the shura's participants. He, along with a dozen others, had been given a camera by the Afghan Danish journalist Nagieb Khaja. The footage was turned into a film called *My Afghanistan*, released in 2012.[25] Unpeeling this encounter, which no doubt took place in one form or another many times over the last decade, would take a book in itself. Clearly little if any of the district chief's speech was translated to the blameless young officer. The truly vital element was the district governor's remark about the village land. But even if the speech had been fully and accurately translated, the importance of that statement to the soldiers' mission would in all likelihood not have been appreciated by the officer or his men. It was not lost on the farmers at the shura.

Judges have to adjudicate in many different types of cases. Disputes involving personal injury, marriage, children and divorce comprise the day-to-day work of any judge or court. However, no issue is more important than land. The central place that land occupies in any society is familiar to anyone with a mortgage or lease. The rules and laws governing its use and ownership are central to any family in almost any place. No area of litigation or judicial activity offers more of an opportunity for 'offering a better deal' than disputes over land. In rural economies, land is a matter of life and death.

The law of the land

Land and property, not always the same thing, are the most important economic assets in most, if not all, societies. Their use, possession and ownership (all contested concepts) are central to every person involved in business, agriculture and commerce the world over. As we will see, land is therefore very often equally central to rebellion and insurgency.

Each society has its own unique perspective on land and its use and ownership. Attitudes to land are often buried deep in ancient cultural and social conflict. This is the case even in the relatively stable United Kingdom. For example, in the UK there is a firmly held concept of trespass based firmly in the notion of private property—those who in the United Kingdom espouse the 'right to roam' derive their claims from ideas of communal ownership, or more accurately, communal rights over land. These are very deep waters, filled with complex philosophical and legal ecologies. Similarly, anyone in the UK who has had anything to do with the ownership of land or housing is closely familiar with the idea of a lease. Once again, this concept is derived from medieval ideas of landholding from feudal lords. Indeed, even today, no one in England truly owns their land; owners of land hold a tenancy from the crown as freeholders. The ultimate possessor of all land in England and Wales is the sovereign. This is why property that is land is often referred to as 'real' property. The 'real' meaning 'royal' in the old legal language of Norman French.

Familiarity with such concepts of tenancy or freehold is ultimately an unconscious function of residence in the common law worldwide These ideas, foreign as they are even to Europeans in the Roman law tradition, would be entirely alien to those Helmandi farmers for whom different rules apply to different kinds of land. For example, their legal culture, drawn as it is from a mixture of tribal tradition, often ignored national legal provisions, and local custom would recognise no such idea as freehold or ownership of pasture land at all. No one owns pasture land by definition. It belongs to no one.[26]

Land is always an intensely complex issue, even in developed and relatively peaceful states. It is the ultimate resource upon which all others depend, and consequently is bound up with the legal or quasi-legal regulation of resources, ranging from rights to minerals and water to rights of access and pasture. It is often the ultimate stake across the spectrum of conflict—from tribal or clan disputes over land or water ownership, to inter-state territorial war.

This is not a treatise on land law. However, aside from the central importance of land to everyone, there is one important point to be drawn from this: that the rules and laws relating to property and land are culturally specific and often highly complex, often almost impossibly so for outsiders without the time and patience to make sense of them. Getting them wrong can be catastrophic. This highlights the absolute necessity of understanding the legal system in which you are working.

The centrality of land to insurgencies

In the communist or peasant insurgencies that dominated Galula's thinking, the root cause co-opted deceitfully by communist insurgents such as Castro and Mao, says Galula, was land reform.[27] Whether deceitful or not, the question of land is central to the causes and resolution of rural insurgency in particular. The reason for this will be amply clear: land is at the heart of the interests of individuals, families, tribes, ethnic groups and nations. Its possession and denial have been at the root of conflicts from the earliest times until today. Indeed, some conflicts seem to persist for millennia or at the very least centuries—the 'native' Catholic Irish against the Protestant 'planters' of Ulster and the Arab–Israeli conflict being just two of the land wars that are better known. There are many others.

These conflicts often take the form of insurgencies against established orders—incumbent governments whose predations, often dressed up as land reforms, give rise to violent responses. Guevara explicitly states that land reform is a primary cause of insurgency: 'a few peasants, dispossessed of their land', he says, are ideal for forming the nucleus of a guerrilla band.[28] While the struggle is ongoing, a priority is to formulate agrarian policy. Furthermore, upon the success of the fight, he identifies land reform as one of the first elements to be resolved by the successful insurgents.[29]

In his 1961 book *People's War, People's Army*, Vo Nguyen Giap—the commander of the North Vietnamese forces during both the war against the French (ending in 1952) and the war against the United States and its client South Vietnam—is clear as to the importance of land as a driving issue in the strategy of the wars he fought.[30] 'The Vietnamese People's War of Liberation was a just war aiming to win back the independence and unity of the country, to bring land to our peasants and to guarantee them the right to it and to defend the achievements of the August revolution.'[31] As a statement of strategy and intention, that is clear and unambiguous. He goes on to be even clearer about the importance of land: 'The problem of land is of decisive importance.'[32] Giap's views are echoed by historian Eric Bergerud, who took the view that 'more than anything else it was the land issue that brought Diem [the South Vietnamese leader initially strongly supported by the United States] to ruin.'[33]

What has land and land reform to do with justice? For some, this may be an unnecessary question. The point here does not so much concern land policy itself, let alone the nature of the land or its ownership. The important issue is the ability for disputes, in this case, over the crucial question of land, to be resolved in an appropriate manner. This is usually done with the use of some form of court operating some form of law or custom. For insurgents, the question is whose courts make those decisions, and whether the decisions concerning the apportionment of land can be viewed as having been decided by the subjects of those decisions. In other words, are they conducted in a fair manner, the term rightly adopted by Tyler, as discussed in Chapter 1, and in a manner consistent with relevant and acceptable cultures and traditions? Failing to address these issues may cause structural problems that persist for decades or longer.

In his study of the British invasion and occupation of Iraq in the early twentieth century, Toby Dodge makes clear the importance of land to the Iraqi polity, even today: 'No policy debate was more important for the making of the Iraqi state than that over the system of land tenure and revenue.'[34] He sees the British failure in the 1920s to address this matter as a major cause of problems that arguably subsist as a root cause of conflict—and indeed insurgency—in Iraq to this day.[35]

Closer to home, the mid-nineteenth century 'Land Wars' in Ireland involved cattle rustling, low-level political activities and largely passive resistance. Such action included refusing to deal in any way with certain officials who had become involved in evictions from land. This gave us the term 'boycotting', after one of its early victims. Another method became known as the 'unwritten law', which developed, in due course, into something like a shadow legal system in the form of the Land League Courts. This grew out of the 'Irish National Land League', a formal movement founded in 1879 with the aim of returning land owned and controlled by largely absentee landlords to those who actually worked it. In this lay the seeds of Sinn Féin and the movement for Irish independence, as distinct from Home Rule. In turn, the nascent shadow state bore full fruit in 1919, during the Irish War of Independence; we will look at how effective that was in the next chapter.

Similarly, the British failure to deal properly with the serious issues of land tenure and ownership, to the extent that Western notions of ownership were appropriate, was a contributory cause of the Mau Mau rebellion in 1950s Kenya. The war was fought, more than for any other reason, against land appropriations. For a people whose identity and life was wrapped up around land, what was perceived as the theft of land struck deep. One Mau Mau fighter said this:

> [We were] told that we were fighting for our land, the land of the Kikuyu, which had been taken by the white people who had taken it for themselves. They could do whatever they wanted with the land.[36]

These were examples touching the British experience; there are many, many more.[37] Political scientist Samuel Huntington, who gave us the term 'clash of civilisations', summarised land's importance as a driver of rebellion: 'where the conditions of land ownership are equitable and provide a viable living for the peasant, revolution is unlikely. Where they are inequitable and where the peasant lives in poverty and suffering, revolution is likely if not inevitable.'[38]

Contemporary Afghanistan

Against that background, we return to Afghanistan in the early part of the twenty-first century, fought over by various armed groups, narco-gangs, bewildered but heavily armed foreign forces and those they supported in what NATO called the legitimate government.

In late 2012, I was sent an essay for private distribution by a former stabilisation officer in southern Helmand.[39] The paper attacks current ideas about 'stabilisation'. Stabilisation is an idea that assumes the ability of Western soldiers and bureaucrats to settle or resolve disputes in countries of which they have little knowledge or experience. The paper argues that such ideas are little more than self-delusion in the context of Helmand. He writes extensively about the endemic corruption in the Afghan government and security forces. He says this about the issue of land: 'The longer I have been here the more fundamental this issue has appeared. It is a crucial, enduring conflict driver and source of instability and yet it remains unresolved, untouched and parked as being too difficult.'[40]

The stabilisation officer goes on to outline the history of Helmand over the previous five decades. It is a history in which land and land use, as with every other rural community, is absolutely central. As in Kenya and rural Ireland, the way in which the land is used and held forms a deep, central cause of conflict. In my own period as a justice advisor for the British mission in the recent Helmand campaign, the land issue cropped up again and again, from the problem of refugees taking land that had been allocated to the government in the late 1980s, to constant, and often violent, disputes over the ownership of commercial or agricultural property. From the macro to the micro, land was central. This was important throughout Afghanistan, but in Helmand, with its important agricultural resources and potential, the land issue had become absolutely crucial.

Mike Martin, a Pashto-speaking writer, soldier and former cultural advisor in Helmand for several years, points out in his book *An Intimate War*. He that one particular Afghan law from the 1970s caused and continues to cause extensive conflict. Taraki decree number 8 of 1978 ('law number 8', as it is commonly known) was introduced by a communist government to regulate the holding of land and was intended to give land to families that had previously been landless sharecroppers.[41] The reform was arbitrary and poorly thought out. One militia leader told Martin that 'the mother of problems we have now is the land redistributions [at that time]'.[42] These land conflicts overlaid those from the 1950s, feeding the tribal and group rivalry. The details of these land conflicts are long and involved.[43] For present purposes, it may suffice to summarise them as involving extensive land theft by certain tribal and narcotics interests—some with stronger links to the government than others. Several cases of such land theft or extortion by government officials against landowners were outlined to me during my time in Helmand as justice advisor in that province.[44] All of them involved violence to a greater or lesser degree. Entire quarters of the capital Lashkar Gah were appropriated from owners who had fled the country and reallocated to others with connections.

Very frequently in the conflicts examined in this book and elsewhere, land and the controversies attached to the laws regulating its ownership have been key drivers of the insurgencies. In Helmand, it has been apparent to many observers that law number 8 has been a festering source of conflict for the three decades since it was promulgated in 1978.[45] There is evidence of a lack of awareness of the profound, fundamental importance of land to insurgencies in predominantly rural cultures.

Martin details how law number 8 has continued to drive conflict in Helmand right up to the present day, interfering as it has with deeply entrenched social systems. This was not an obscure issue on which a few scholars should have been free to discuss matters and pass judgement; it was directly relevant to a large number of landholders in Helmand. Indeed, it was a matter of common conversation. When I asked a Helmandi official in 2007 what particular legal problems might be a cause of conflict in Lashkar Gah, the official replied that the dispossession in the 1980s of an entire community of refugees who were now returning from Pakistan and living in an already inhabited area of the town was causing problems that the Taliban were exploiting.[46]

Yet there was never any move on the part of the Western powers to initiate reform on any scale of this crucial provision. It was 'parked as too difficult'. While at root there was a deeper problem at play in the Western, and particularly British, involvement in Helmand—a lack of understanding of all of the conflict dynamics—this was certainly an area where progress could have been made, or at least attempted. To have done so would have demonstrated an awareness of the necessity of seeing conflict through legal as well as military eyes. This awareness was largely absent. By way of anecdotal evidence, when I asked who owned the land on which the UK Provincial Reconstruction Team in Lashkar Gah had been billeted, no one in the camp seemed to know.[47] In another case, journalist Ann Jones reported that US forces had built a suspension bridge across a river in the east of Afghanistan at a cost of $1 million. They had not secured any land rights, and so no roads led to the bridge, which remained unused.[48]

The existing problems involving the issue of land in Afghanistan were exacerbated by recent government actions. The government of Afghanistan 'claims to own 86% of the land of Afghanistan and appears to be intent on asserting its claim to as much land as possible.'[49] This is contested by those who owned the land previously. Current formal governmental procedures for settling land disputes are regarded as complex, corrupt and lengthy.[50]

So, for those gathered to listen to the foreign soldier and the Afghan district chief on that hot Helmand day in 2010, the chief's words concerning the villagers' land belonging to the government were distinctly unwelcome. All of those present would have understood the deeply contentious context, to put it mildly, of those words; everyone except the foreign soldier who stated explicitly that he stood behind them and supported the speaker.

The need for 'a better deal'

Land is at heart a legal issue, and as a driver of insurgency—and therefore as a potential weapon against insurgents—it has been largely ignored. Insurgent courts can provide rebels with an opportunity to exploit this opportunity by offering that 'better deal'. Vitally, this is a deal that they at the very least aspire to be able to render permanent. After all, it is the purpose of insurgents permanently to displace the incumbent government. Courts that provide a solution for a few weeks or months are no use to farmers who need certainty to ensure proper planning for plantation and cultivation. This is beside the deeper question of ownership of important assets. Further, in the cases looked at here, there is little question as to the perceived procedural fairness involved. The purpose of those better deals was to displace courts that were not perceived as fair, or more plainly, that were out and out corrupt. By doing so, the insurgents acted not only to increase their own legitimacy but to increase the likelihood of their rule being permanent.

Acting to resolve such problems, in terms of passing and implementing laws, bolsters insurgent legitimacy. When the Taliban was in power from 1996 to 2001, it passed and implemented a series of land laws that 'benefited Pashtun tribals and remain popular and valid ... they are a key part of the Taliban's programme.'[51] At least of equal importance is the notion that judgements reached by Taliban judges will be enforced. For having an accepted legal code is one thing, but the utility of any legal system rests on the ability of those administering it to enforce its decisions. In the Ireland of the early twentieth century and Afghanistan today—and indeed in other working societies—formal dispute resolution is achieved through the institution of courts. In the early twentieth century, Arthur Griffith, the founder of Sinn Féin, said that 'it was the duty of every Irishman 'to carry every dispute to the arbitrators and obey the decision.'[52]

Griffith pointed out that such arbitration courts were in fact 'legal and their decisions have all the binding force of law when the litigants sign an agreement to abide by them.'[53]

Passing laws is one thing; adjudicating those laws in courts is another. Equally important, however, is the ability to enforce the judgements that such courts hand down. In all the cases mentioned above, from Mao's China to contemporary Afghanistan, a vital element and measure of shadow governmental control is the ability to settle land disputes and ensure that those settlements last and do not provide a medium for further internal conflict.

The purpose of this section was to show the potential of two aspects of civic life—corruption and the central one of land—to provide not only a cause for insurgents but also a vehicle for them to act as agents of dispute resolution. This is true whether in a Western setting, albeit agrarian, such as Ireland in the early twentieth century, or a tribal setting, such as contemporary Afghanistan. How insurgents actually carry out their dispute resolution role in the form of courts is the topic of the next chapter.

3

OFFERING A BETTER DEAL

INSURGENT COURTS IN THE TWENTIETH CENTURY

The idea of offering a better deal can involve all the functions of government. Insurgents can and do attempt to set up systems of education, health and basic social services. For example, during the 1990s, Kosovo separatists set up the 'Homeland Calling' fund whereby the extensive Kosovar diaspora were required to donate 3 per cent of their salary to the cause (peer pressure playing a major role). While some of this money was used to fund the purchase of weapons for the armed rebels, much of it went to provide a health and education system organised by the shadow government in Kosovo itself.[1] Most of the legal systems we will examine below formed part of a wider system of insurgent state services set up to replace incumbent state provision that was either not offered, insufficient or too dangerous to deliver due to insurgent threats.

There are no failsafe formulae for success. However, it is clear that the creation of a shadow state—with its attendant administrative machineries—is essential for the success of insurgencies in many situations. As outlined in Chapter 1, it is equally clear that a key part of any administration is the judiciary. As sociologist and economist Anne Marie Baylouny has written, 'authority is tied to the provision of substantive services to the population.'[2] However, courts have the potential to be far more than another social good provided by the insurgent government. While systems of taxation are often of a compulsory nature, the decision of whether to take one's dispute to a particular court depends on an assessment on whether that dispute will be fairly settled, and indeed on an assessment of whether the judgement of the court can be executed or enforced. The provision of an educational system, while it may be highly laudable (and indeed, in the long term, politically effective in terms of indoctrination), is not usually a competitive endeavour.

The importance of providing a legal service is that it is where the power of the government encounters one of its most rigorous tests. If it passes the test, resolves disputes in a manner that is perceived to be legitimate, the government and its judicial arm can be seen to have proceeded a considerable way down the road towards being seen as an effective government.

However, the delivery of a decision itself, even if delivered in a manner that is perceived to be procedurally fair, is of little or no use if it cannot be enforced. This in turn requires the presence of the implicit or explicit threat of the use of force to effect enforcement. This is as true in the United States, Canada and United Kingdom as it is in Afghanistan or Syria. For example, if a judgement is handed down to you against me that I am at fault in an accident and must pay you a sum of money, ultimately you must rely on my acceptance of the judgement's legitimacy. In other words, that I accept the authority of the court to deliver that judgement. However, that is not enough. The judgement that I owe you money is of little use to you if I do not pay. You must then take steps to ensure that someone enforces the judgement. In most countries where commonly understood ideas of rule of law apply, you will apply to the court to enforce the judgement, which may be done in a number of ways.[3] Ultimately, this may include simply taking property from me by force. The test of whether the government possesses the 'legitimate monopoly of force' is whether you resort to self-help, or whether you rely on the state or the government to do it on your behalf.

Any group of people can issue judgements. They are worth little, then, if they cannot be enforced. Now, there may be exceptions to the requirement for the use of force. Some authorities may possess sufficient capital in the form of legitimacy that no one would dare to challenge their authority by physical force or otherwise; I have in mind, for example, the effect that a fatwa (judgement) or pronouncement of a given religious authority may have. This is particularly relevant in the field of family law, where marriage, divorce and the bringing up of children are seen as matters for religious authorities.

Further, the enforcement of a judgement in itself may be of little value if it is unlikely to last. In the previous chapter, I mentioned that for a farmer in Afghanistan, or anywhere else for that matter, a judgement over a land dispute has to ensure that the farmer is in a position to plan. If there is a question over whether he will have ownership over land in six months' time, why bother to plant when his opponent in a dispute, or indeed the government and its officials, may receive the benefit? This is particularly important with vital assets such as land or land use. For example, let us say that you and I have a dispute over your ownership of a given patch of land (accepting that 'ownership' in the context of land is a very fickle concept). We agree to bring the dispute to an insurgent court, and you receive judgement in your favour. You will then make an investment in that land in order to cultivate or indeed build on it. It is vital to you not only that I accept this judgement and that it is enforced but that the judgement will last and will not be overturned by another authority. This will be one factor in the decision to go to the tribunal in the first place. There will be other factors: Will the court give a fair judgement? How much will we need to pay the judge? Are we likely to get a fair hearing? Is the judgement likely to be in our favour? However, just as important will be the element of final resolution. We will want the matter settled. Accordingly, we are not going to choose a tribunal that may be defunct tomorrow or whose judgement will neither be respected, nor complied with.

The significance of this is that, for those using this particular service, the criteria go beyond its immediate utility and reach into the future. The choice of an insurgent court is an indicator of confidence in the court's ability to produce a fair and legitimate outcome in a given dispute. It also implies an ability to enforce a decision and a certain level of sustainability.

As we will see below, there are many insurgencies where insurgent courts have not secured success. While possession of a working shadow state system, including a courts system, may not be sufficient for success, can the argument be made that it is necessary? To begin to attempt an answer to this, we now turn to the most successful of all insurgencies in recent history.

Ireland: 'The first modern insurgency'[4]

The Irish War of Independence (1919–21) occurred nearly a century ago. However, a study of the way in which this struggle was conducted in the realm of lawfare provides a highly instructive case study of how an effective insurgency can use justice to further its cause. The Irish were pioneers in exploiting weaknesses in the incumbent court system. We have already seen in the last chapter how land disputes are used to drive notions of justice and injustice in insurgences. The Irish revolutionaries, as well as using notions of injustice and illegitimacy as motivators, were also innovators in the use of their own courts as weapons.

In the words of insurgency expert Ian F. W. Beckett, the war was 'A true forerunner of modern revolutionary groups in terms of its politically inspired campaign.'[5] The campaign was sophisticated and multi-layered. Its military aspects have been looked at closely, and they may have influenced insurgent leaders as diverse as Ba Maw in Burma and Menachem Begin in Israel.[6] However, the lawfare techniques evolved during that conflict were arguably of equal significance to the military struggle. The system is well worth examining in detail.

The Ken Loach film *The Wind That Shakes the Barley* (2006) did not attract the approval of certain elements of the establishment. It was criticised for portraying the British as sadists and the Irish as romantic, idealistic resistance fighters who take to violence only because there is no other 'self-respecting course'.[7] That may well be so. It is also a picture of an insurgency from the insurgent's perspective—in this case, the IRA. One scene from the film presents a key element of the Irish War of Independence. In that scene, set in what appears to be a village hall or school, a court has been set up. Its function is not to decide the fate of traitors or collaborators. What is being decided is whether a particular debt should be paid. Putting aside the political aspect of this particular debt—it is owed to a loan shark who bankrolls the local IRA unit, which is trying to ensure that it is paid—this kind of case is the meat and bread of courts all over the world every day.

What is being depicted is an element of the IRA's campaign to establish and sustain its authority, its legitimacy as the sole government of Ireland.

The IRA's judicial strategy, 1916–22

As observed in Chapter 2, the 'arbitration courts' had been in operation since the late nineteenth century, and were successors to the Land League Courts. After the 1916 Easter Rising, the British (the Unionist forces) had instituted what amounted to martial law.[8] Insurgents who had been involved in the Easter Rising were tried under martial law at courts martial; fifteen were executed.[9] The effect of these executions, incidentally, was to turn much of the previously pro-government Irish population against the government. The use of courts martial was treated as an opportunity for Irish nationalist lawyers to challenge their jurisdiction and legality on the basis that the court hearings were wrongly held in secret.

In November 1918, elections took place throughout the UK. An overwhelming majority of Sinn Féin MPs were returned from Ireland, and these MPs decided to boycott the London parliament and set up their own parliament in Dublin, known as the Dáil Éireann (hereafter, the 'Dáil'—pronounced 'Daul'). Meanwhile, the nascent IRA had begun to intensify action against British security forces. Local initiatives had given rise to a new brand of locally organised land courts—a reaction to the wave of agrarian land disturbances, some of them acting 'in a haphazard and slipshod manner with grave possibilities of irregularity', according to the committee set up by the Dáil (itself, of course, a 'shadow' structure) to design a new courts system.[10] Following a relatively full assessment of the 'English courts' and the challenges of formalising the already existing insurgent courts, the Dáil announced the formation of national arbitration courts in August 1919. In due course, these became known as 'Dáil Courts'.

Setting up the new system was expensive, since all its participants were paid. In March 1920, it was assessed that the cost of the new system would amount to £113,000, a very large sum indeed for the time.[11] There was the full panoply of parish courts, with appeal lying to district courts and finally a court of appeal. A sense of legitimacy was fostered by the fact that judges at the parish courts were elected by those over whom they would minister. There was a scale of court fees, and all litigants had to sign a declaration that they would comply with the decision of the court and not submit to any 'enemy tribunal'.[12] Coupled with this, the campaign to boycott the Crown Courts gained momentum alongside a British effort to suppress the Dáil Courts by force.[13] The Dáil authorities acted quickly to deal with agitation over land issues by instituting dedicated Dáil Land Courts, although the speed with which the new systems were gaining momentum certainly surprised even Sinn Féin.[14] The new system of courts gained real purchase, especially when coupled with the effective withdrawal of the Royal Irish Constabulary from large parts of the country. At times, there were serious derogations from regular procedure; but these were at a local level, particularly in the comparatively radical south-west of the country, and were effectively a continuation of long-festering disputes.[15]

John Brayden, an Irish barrister who was fully experienced in the Crown Law, observed the proceedings of some of these courts and wrote about them in the *Journal of the American Bar Association* in 1920.[16] As far as can be determined, he himself was not a Republican.[17] He said that the Republican courts:

> endeavoured to provide 'an impartial justice and have surprised hardened Unionist [pro-British] practitioners by their willingness to decide in favour of an unpopular landlord against an unpopular tenant, when the facts called for such a decision.'[18]

Brayden goes on to describe a number of cases brought against those who might have been expected to gain little sympathy from a Republican forum. 'The Sinn Feiners have been able to organise their courts, equip them with judges, attract the confidence of litigants and secure obedience to their decrees.'[19] It is apparent that this was not an isolated assessment.

Not only was there—to a considerable degree, if not uniformly—what might now be called procedural fairness (or, more importantly, perceived procedural fairness), to the extent that, particularly in matters involving land, even Unionists, ideologically opposed to the Republicans, were often content to use the Dáil Courts.[20] The courts were able to enforce their decisions. As mentioned at the beginning of this chapter, the question of enforcement is vital. Brayden is pragmatic about the reasons for this: no litigant gaining a judgement from a Crown Court would be allowed to enjoy the fruits of that judgement in peace. If the litigant chose the Sinn Féin (Dáil) Court, 'she might live in peace'.[21]

The courts also dealt with criminal matters: 'the Sinn Feiners arrest men for every sort of criminal offence, try them in their necessarily strictly secret courts, and fine, imprison or deport as they please.'[22] Although these courts initially acted much as the arbitration courts had—which is to say essentially with the consent of the parties (the caveat being that there was much 'encouragement' not to use the Crown Courts)—in August 1920 the Dáil passed a decree giving coercive jurisdiction to the courts.[23]

By now, particularly in Nationalist areas, the courts had largely displaced the work of those of the British state. In the words of one contemporary, there had been 'a steady encroachment of Sinn Fein Courts on the constituted domain of law'.[24] Due to their increasing reach, they began to attract business from beyond the Nationalist community. Charles Townshend relates one Unionist landowner, Lord Monteagle, taking the view that the Nationalist courts had shown 'extraordinary fairness' and had been 'extremely just'.[25]

Barristers complained to Brayden that work in the state courts had dried up by late 1920, just at the time when the British armed forces were beginning to gain some grip over the military side of the conflict. By that time, a combination of perceived procedural fairness, the ability to enforce judgements, threats against those who continued to use Crown Courts (thereby breaking the boycott) and the destruction of courthouses had resulted in a situation where 'Sinn Fein justice was alone available; the King's writ had ceased to run; the Royal judges still went on circuit, but their courts, guarded by police and soldiers, were empty of litigants', who had by now transferred their cases to the Dáil Courts.[26] Echoing those complaints to Brayden, Conor Maguire, a future chief justice of Ireland, remarked in a radio interview that 'In the end, in 1919 we [the Dáil Court in County Mayo] took all the business of the county [civil] court. In 1920, we took all the business of the Assize [criminal] Court.'[27]

As Tyler puts it in *Why People Obey the Law*, 'A judge's ruling means little if the parties to the dispute feel that they can ignore it.'[28] Similarly, courts will not work if the staff or personnel in the procedure fail to attend. Witnesses were 'encouraged' to refuse to attend court hearings. Such encouragements included outright threats, such as a notice placed outside a court in Kerry stating that anyone who attended court as a witness that day would be shot. The court was adjourned. Attacks on courts and court officials were also common and a policy was announced that 'every person in the pay of England (magistrates and jurors, etc.) will be deemed to have forfeited his life.'[29] Concerted attacks on the court system were to have been part of a strategy following on from the failure of talks in 1921, and the order was not executed on a national scale as the talks succeeded. However, Austin Stack, the Sinn Féin minister of justice and home affairs, said in 1921 that efforts to 'empty the enemy courts' should continue during the post-agreement truce, but that it should be done 'unostentatiously'.[30]

Crown judges were always heavily guarded, but the more senior judges were rarely targeted. However, concerted plans were made to target these more senior judges if negotiation efforts during the truce of 1921 broke down. In any event, judges were often in sympathy with Sinn Féin aims. While threats contributed to mass resignations, the behaviour of elements of the British security forces, as well as the pervasive use of martial law, made a significant contribution as well. One magistrate resigned in August 1920, stating as his reason that 'His Majesty's government has determined on the substitution of military for civil law in Ireland.'[31] He was joined by 148 magistrates in that month alone.

At that stage, however, it might be argued that the British authorities had become the insurgents, as a new authority had established itself firmly, if not immovably. There was significant opposition, of course, from what might be termed 'legal vested interests'. In a letter to the *Times*, A.M. Sullivan, himself a barrister, though clearly sympathetic to the ideals of independence and highly critical of English rule, regarded Sinn Féin as a criminal society that 'bullied' litigants into submission; no barrister 'should soil himself by lending the sanction of his participation to the performance of a body which repudiates and denounces those principles of justice which constitute his creed.'[32] Despite the somewhat chaotic military operations of the time, a moderate Irish politician, Horace Plunkett, could say that 'Order is being preserved with increasing success by Sinn Fein'[33]—a remarkable judgement from a relatively conservative man. Independence was less than a year away (it came in December 1922) and the views of Sullivan, although by no means uncommon, were becoming irrelevant. One avowed Unionist summed up in *The Times* the effect of the Dáil Courts:

> An illegal government has become the de facto government. Its jurisdiction is recognised. It administers justice promptly and equitably and we are in this curious dilemma that the civil administration of the country is carried on under a system the existence of which the de iure government does not and cannot acknowledge and is carried on very well.[34]

The courts and the 'revolutionary legality' of the Nationalist judicial strategy had acted simultaneously to subvert the state order and strengthen the authority of the Dáil. A leading expert on the Dáil Courts, Mary Kotsonouris, herself an Irish judge, takes the view that they 'operated in an ordinary way and paralleled in their proceedings and procedures those of the courts they were intended to subvert. They were the promise and proof that the time for self-government had come.'[35]

In *Rebel Rulers*, Zachariah Mampilly provides the following hypothesis concerning insurgent behaviour: 'If an insurgency emerges in a state with high penetration into society it is more likely to co-opt pre-existing institutions and networks into its civil administration thereby improving governance provision.'[36] It is clear that his hypothesis is correct in the Irish case. Indeed, the same seems to be occurring in Syria, and did occur in Libya. In all these cases, as Mampilly posits, the state had a high degree of penetration into society. In Ireland, however, this was true to the extent that only a decade before the Irish War of Independence Ireland was, to all intents and purposes, a fairly settled part of the United Kingdom and its governmental systems (albeit with strong movements for devolution).

In the later conflict in Northern Ireland (1968–98), the Provisional IRA, the self-declared successors to the Irish Republican Army of the War of Independence, attempted a system of community justice, on a relatively local scale, in the housing estates and Republican communities of Northern Ireland.[37] Ultimately, the Provisional IRA's efforts at non-state justice failed to gain purchase. Despite the IRA's regular denunciations of the authority of the British crown in Northern Ireland, there was no effective overall civic strategy adopted by the Republicans of the late twentieth century. They set up no effective community-wide dispute resolution system. The acid test of such a system is not the number of kneecappings of petty criminals in Belfast housing estates, but rather the bodies to which litigants turn when they require adjudication of a legal dispute. In the Northern Ireland of the late twentieth century, the answer was that, whether a litigant was Catholic or Protestant, he or she would bring their dispute to the county court. Apart from the fact that the IRA of the time had nothing of the administrative or civic sophistication of their forebears, there was simply no way someone with such a dispute could assume that their judgements, even had they been made, would be lasting or enforceable.

The establishment of the Dáil Courts was only one aspect of a multidimensional legal strategy adopted by the Nationalists in the War of Independence. It was arguably the first such concerted strategy, certainly in recent history. It combined the use of courts to undermine the legitimacy of the state, those courts themselves acting as levers to increase the power and reach of the Dáil. In addition, they acted as indicators of that power and reach. The Nationalist strategy did not stop there, however. Certainly, the major element of the strategy comprised the Dáil Courts, but there was another dimension: using the Crown Courts to undermine their own legitimacy 'at home' in Ireland, in Britain, and indeed, with a rather modern-looking media strategy, abroad. In this, the Nationalists were probably the first successful practitioners of what was to become known as 'rupture strategy' (see Chapter 5).

In the words of Douglas Porch, 'each insurgency is a contingent event in which doctrine, operations and tactics must support a viable policy and strategy and not the other way around.'[38] What might have worked for Thompson in Malaya—however successful that British campaign was—might not work in another insurgency. This is as true for insurgents as it is for counterinsurgents: what may have worked for T.E. Lawrence (for he was an insurgent) will not have worked for Gerry Adams in Belfast.

Insurgent courts as lawfare

In his classic 1992 work *Guerrillas*, Jon Lee Anderson took the view that rebels use courts as 'revolutionary rehearsals of the exercise of the power they hope to wield one day on a larger scale.'[39] He visits several revolutionary movements: the Mujahedin of 1980s Afghanistan, the Karen National Liberation Movement, the Polisario Front of Western Sahara, the Occupied Palestinian Territory of Gaza and the Farabundo Martí National Liberation Front (FMLN) of El Salvador.[40] With the exception of the Polisario Front (see below), all these movements were involved in an active contest for territory and people with the larger and more powerful conventional forces of states, which were, if not necessarily strong, then at least as militarily capable as the insurgents. In other words, none of them securely occupied territory of their own for any length of time.

In addition, as Sandesh Sivakumaran writes, the Algerian insurgents of the FLN (Front de Libération Nationale) in the Algerian War of Independence ran courts, as did those of Biafra.[41] In today's insurgent world, the Marxist Naxalites of India, the Free Aceh Movement,[42] the Sierra Leonean Revolutionary United Front (RUF), the Kosovo Liberation Army,[43] the National Liberation Army (ELN) and FARC of Colombia, and the South Sudanese Sudan People's Liberation Movement (SPLM) (before winning independence)[44] have run courts of greater or lesser sophistication.

The FMLN of El Salvador provides a sound example of why such courts are set up. Jon Lee Anderson observed of them:

> it was necessary to impose order and discipline so that everyone, the guerrillas and civilians knew where the new boundaries lay. The FMLN moved swiftly implementing a strict system of justice ... mostly the system has worked and in marked contrast to the government forces the FMLN's combatants have earned a reputation for being well-disciplined.[45]

Anderson stresses that 'the administration of justice is a crucial aspect of [the FMLN's] revolutionary programme.' In other words, to some degree the nature of the justice imposed contributes to the strategic narrative of the movement. The case of the FMLN provides an instructive illustration of how justice was used to support a wider narrative.

The FMLN was essentially a classic South/Central American Marxist liberation movement. It was formed in 1980 and fought throughout that decade, before a ceasefire and its re-emergence as a political movement in 1991. Throughout its existence, the narrative of discipline and compliance with international law was a constant theme. In a book

57

published by the movement in 1988, internal discipline was stressed both nationally and internationally.[46] For example, when two wounded and captured US servicemen (the United States was heavily involved militarily in the Salvadoran Civil War on the side of the military government) were killed by an FMLN fighter, the FMLN declared that they 'admitted to what happened and said that those responsible have been charged with committing a war crime by violating the FMLN's Code of Conduct and the Geneva Conventions.'[47] A trial was convened that was open to international observers, who were not satisfied that the standards of fair trials had actually been met—for example, access to the identities of advocates and jurors.[48]

Speaking more generally about insurgencies, Kalyvas has pointed out that:

> [P]olitical actors face three distinct population sets: populations under their full control; populations they must share with their rival; and populations completely outside their control. These three situations constitute two general types of sovereignty: *segmented* and *fragmented*. Sovereignty is segmented when two or more political actors exercise full sovereignty over distinct parts of the territory of the state. It is fragmented when two political actors (or more) exercise limited sovereignty over the same part of the territory of the state.[49]

Among current insurgencies, segmented sovereignty might be epitomised by the Western Sahara Polisario Front.

In North Africa, the conflict over the area south of Morocco and now known as Western Sahara began in 1975 with the withdrawal of Spain, which handed the territory over to Morocco. A resistance movement was formed by the indigenous Sahrawi people that became known as the Frente Polisario. In due course, military pressure from the Moroccan armed forces drove the Frente Polisario from the physical territory of Western Sahara. Since 1991, when a ceasefire was negotiated with Morocco, most of Western Sahara has been under Moroccan control, although with a UN presence.[50] The Sahrawi Republic exists as a virtual entity now in eastern Algeria.

The Sahrawi Republic, run by the successors to the Frente Polisario, is, to all intents and purposes, a state with all the formal accoutrements, including a well-developed court system, with first instance, appeal courts and a supreme court. Like other states in exile, it considers itself to be the legitimate government of the entire territory of what is now

Western Sahara. Its court system is, at least formally, well developed and comparable in structure to any other state system in the region.[51]

The conflict between the communists of the New People's Army (NPA) and the Philippine government represents a useful example of what Kalyvas calls 'fragmented' insurgencies—wars where territory is actively contested. The NPA have been fighting since the heyday of Marxist 'people's movements' in the late 1960s. The foundation documents speak clearly of the need for courts to found the new state advocated by the movement. Such courts exist from the lowest municipal level to the higher political levels.

Arbitration courts exist at the *barrio* or local level. The Communist Party of the Philippines (CPP) has set up some local-level arbitration courts for which the guiding principle is asserted to be 'social justice'.[52] It is clear that the arbitration courts are competing, or are said to be competing, with the Philippine state courts on the basis that justice is cheap and quick.

Extensive reference in the documents of the CPP/NDA is made to cases brought in 'people's courts' against alleged criminals, some of whom had been acquitted for such matters as corruption in what the New Democratic Party of the Philippines (NFDP) calls the 'reactionary' state courts.[53]

The system prescribed by the 'Guide for Establishing the People's Democratic Government' posits three levels of courts—at the provincial, district and *barrio* levels.[54] A panel of three judges sits on minor cases, while a panel of nine judges handles major and complex cases, particularly those involving the death penalty.

While the operation of these courts has been extensive, and the CPP/NPA claims due process in its documents, the UN special rapporteur on extrajudicial executions at the time—the highly regarded Philip Alston—strongly criticised them, asserting that their system 'seeks to add a veneer of legality to what would better be termed vigilantism or murder.'[55]

Courts are also an indicator of the extent to which government might be failing. Nepal was the venue for one of the most successful Maoist revolutionary movements of the late twentieth and early twenty-first centuries. Beginning its armed struggle in 1996, in due course the Communist Party of Nepal—Maoist (CPN—M) took power locally in many areas of Nepal, eventually being permitted, following a ceasefire in 2006, to take part in elections. In 2008, it won a majority and took power.[56]

As in the Philippines, courts were developed nationally. As elsewhere, they were used as tools of control, indicators of power and a means of undermining government legitimacy. They were part of the wider administrative shadow state success of the Maoists throughout the Nepalese countryside, and exploited the failures of the state itself. As the BBC reported at the time, 'The Maoists regard their court system as the heart of their "People's Government", running in parallel with the official government through much of the country.'[57] An article in *The Economist* observed one such court handling dozens of cases a day: 'People's courts, which have mushroomed across Nepal in recent months, are only one sign that the country's Maoist rebels are getting more organised—and that the government is failing. While Judge Chettri passed judgment in a humble shack, Kohalpur's brand-new courthouse was closed for a two-week holiday.'[58]

Courts acted as an important element in the objective of filling a gap left not only by what was perceived as a corrupt and inefficient state, but by a hiatus in the armed struggle. As people awaited the outcome of a prolonged negotiation process towards the end of the insurgency, following the ceasefire 'the state was described as hardly functioning. Many policemen, for example, are sitting on their hands rather than enforcing the law until they see what kind of government will emerge.'[59]

Once again, by contemporary standards, these 'kangaroo-type court' procedures were rough and ready, with often only rudimentary procedural safeguards.[60] Judges were trained for only a few days, and many cases were simply considered to be a matter of 'common sense'.[61] The courts attracted a good deal of criticism from human rights groups and authorities—understandably so, given the savagery with which they dealt with those found guilty of crimes, with punishments often involving prolonged beating.[62]

By 2006, Maoist rebels controlled most of the Nepalese countryside. Following a ceasefire, elections were held and the CPN—M took power, in due course sharing that power with other parties.

All the above groups are either still in existence (in the case of the Karen National Liberation Movement, CPP/NPA and Polisario) or eventually took power (FMLN, CPN—M). On the other hand, the Tamil Tigers in Sri Lanka had perhaps the most sophisticated courts system of any insurgent group.[63] The Tigers developed a remarkably highly organised and apparently sustainable system including a comprehensive hierarchy of courts, fully articulated laws, law schools and a working constitution. However, they were defeated militarily: not by superior governance, but by superior firepower and the ability to apply intense coercive force. Whether in possession of 'segmented' or 'fragmented' control, it is difficult to see how the possession of a working courts system, however sophisticated and well developed, could change that dynamic. Having said that, even when the Taliban was under intense military pressure during the NATO campaign against them, as we will see in the next chapter, they still managed to retain a working judicial system sufficient to prove preferable to the governmental courts for which the NATO soldiers were ultimately fighting.

The legality of insurgent courts in international law

The message of insurgents comes across more easily in the international forum of lawfare if their own systems of justice are in accordance with international standards, and indeed international law. In his authoritative *Law of Non-international Armed Conflict*, Sandesh Sivakumaran takes a pragmatic view of such courts, believing that 'rather than ignoring them [the courts] or criticizing them … they may be utilized in order to aid enforcement of the law'.[64]

There are provisions in international law relating to insurgent courts, although they are minimal and to an extent ambiguous. Accordingly, there is controversy over what norms insurgent courts need to comply with under international law in order that they might be properly regulated—or, indeed, whether it is right in terms of international stability that they should be accorded any implied legitimacy by setting standards at all. Clearly, international legitimacy accorded by compliance with such standards can work in favour of insurgents. There is, however, another view, which may be characterised as the 'conservative view', which believes that to accord insurgent courts legitimacy might result in the undermining of international security.

Governments do not recognise their insurgents as combatants with legitimate objectives worthy of recognition. As Sivakumaran, says:

'There were very few conflicts in which the [insurgent] armed group was recognised as belligerent, thus bringing into play the law of international armed conflict.'[65]

Treating insurgents as belligerents clearly concedes to them a possibly critical degree of legitimacy. Instead, they are almost invariably treated as criminals worthy of prosecution and punishment under municipal criminal law. The essence of this approach is to ensure precisely that concentration of legal legitimacy in one authority—the so-called monopoly of force. To do otherwise would be to acknowledge that insurgents may have a practical claim to compete in legitimacy with the incumbent state as belligerents. Even if a state were to concede the question of belligerency, to do so would be to accord insurgents a status which, from the legal perspective, would take them out of the legal control of the counterinsurgent power.

The case for regulation of insurgent courts is founded on two legal documents. The first is the so-called 'Common Article 3' of the 1949 Geneva Conventions.[66] It is called 'Common Article 3' because it appears in all four Geneva Conventions as Article 3. The usual shorthand for it is CA3. CA3 is exclusively concerned with the protection of 'persons taking no active part in hostilities' in 'conflicts not of an international character'. As well as civilians, such persons are said to include 'members of armed forces who have laid down their arms and those placed *hors de combat* by sickness, wounds, detention or other cause.'[67] There is an overall obligation for such persons to be treated humanely.[68] As such, CA3 prohibits 'violence to life and person', the taking of hostages, and humiliating and degrading treatment.[69]

Crucial for present purposes is Article 3.1(d), which prohibits 'the passing of sentences and the carrying out of executions without previous judgment pronounced by a regularly constituted court affording all the judicial guarantees which are recognized as indispensable by civilized peoples.'

The important words here are 'regularly constituted court'. What constitutes such a court and the implications of such tribunals has given rise to much debate.[70] Two clear views have emerged in the discourse on this matter. Much of it has revolved around what a 'regularly constituted court' is in CA3. The arguments are long and complicated, and often turn on what intentions can be construed from the *travaux préparatoires* (initial debates and discussions) of Additional Protocol II (APII) in particular. The first view might be characterised as the 'conservative approach', and might be summarised as stating that to accept that an insurgent court can be 'regularly constituted' is to undermine international humanitarian law and could open the gates to great risks by conferring legitimacy on procedures that can never comply with international standards. As Parth Gejji says: 'At the end of the day, the real question is less a question of law than of policy: how much is the international community willing to risk in order to legitimize (and thus, hopefully engage) insurgent courts?'[71]

The other view may equally be summarised as taking the pragmatic view that such courts cannot be ignored: they will be constituted and, although they may provide an absolute minimum of protection, such protection is better than none at all. From the legal perspective, they say, had the drafters wished to exclude insurgent courts, they could and would have done so.

It is in places such as Afghanistan that, as Sivakumaran says: 'The concern of affording courts of armed groups a certain legitimacy and armed groups themselves some semblance of status also forms part of the explanation as to why the international community fails to engage with these courts.'[72] By way of illustration, there was no question whatsoever of the Sri Lankan government accepting a Tamil Tiger judgement on land while the conflict in Sri Lanka was active, whether or not such a judgement had been enforced and accepted by all concerned.

For the future, there is the question of the degree to which the international community will engage with insurgent courts. For many countries, this is more of a political than a legal question. There is, of course, also a 'de facto' element here that argues strongly in favour of greater engagement. As Sivakumaran says: 'Rather than ignoring them [courts] or criticizing them without offering concrete suggestions for improvement, the international community needs to grapple with them and consider how best they may be utilized in order to aid enforcement of the law.'[73] Notwithstanding the arguments of those who have been termed 'conservatives' here, there is surely a strong case to be made for international law according some form of recognition to insurgent courts.

These legal arguments concerning the extent to which insurgent courts are mandated under international humanitarian law have both historical and contemporary resonance. But they also tap closely into the question of legitimacy. The effect of the 'cloak of legitimacy' conferred on such groups as the Irish Republicans or the Tamil Tigers by virtue of their effective system of courts has already been remarked upon. That legitimacy would only be extended were the international community to accept such courts as having some legal validity.

The implications of developing a regularly constituted court go beyond maintaining law and order. For courts, as has been seen in this chapter, have roles that extend into every aspect of day-to-day life as regulators and validators of civil administration. The film *The Battle of Algiers* (1966) contains a brief scene where the marriage of two insurgents takes place in the presence not of a French notary, but of an FLN official. Courts are, of course, systems of dispute resolution. There is a structural impetus behind the development of such courts, as well as sound reasons to accord them some degree of international recognition.

Conclusion

Whether in north-west Europe in the 1920s, Algeria in the 1950s, El Salvador in the 1980s, or Nepal and Sri Lanka in the 1990s, or indeed in many other places, courts have played a vital role in shadow states and their struggle for legitimacy with their incumbent adversaries. Exploiting faults in formal governments, they serve to prise those gaps open even further, draining legitimacy from the state, and augmenting their own. Insurgent courts act both to measure and to cement that legitimacy, and may continue to work even when the military wing of the organisation is under great pressure.

It may well be that, for those who live in insurgent areas, their civic role as regulators is of equal importance in securing the legitimacy of the insurgent effort as is the military campaign itself. The comprehensive judicial strategy of the IRA would certainly indicate that this was so. We will see in the next chapter that the same is true in many parts of contemporary Afghanistan.

The insurgent courts we have looked at so far have developed within largely or entirely secular contexts. We now move on to examine the courts of insurgencies of the early twenty-first century. These are often avowedly religious in nature, but serve very similar purposes strategically.

4

CALIPHATES OF LAW

INSURGENT COURTS TODAY

'We aim to satisfy God, we don't care about international standards.'[1]

To some extent, justice is simply another social good, like the provision of health, education or welfare. Many insurgent groups provide such services as part of their aspiration to government. However, the provision of judicial services is of unique importance in that it serves to demonstrate the power and sustainability of an insurgency while furthering that power. We saw how rebels have done this in many places in the last chapter. Unlike the provision of other services, dispute resolution is often carried out as an explicitly competitive activity. As we have seen repeatedly above, to coin Kilcullen's term, justice is one component of competitive control.

The case of ISIS, which is examined later in this chapter, highlights the competitive nature of justice in insurgency. During the wars of the early twenty-first century, insurgent groups such as the Taliban, the various forms of resistance armies in Syria and other organisations such as the Union of Islamic Courts in Somalia have used courts and the provision of justice to further their causes. However, they have often done so not as some form of imposition upon an inert or subject population, but to a great degree to answer the needs of that population.

Their role, therefore, has been symbiotic. In other words, as in all societies, the requirements of the people dictate what the courts provide and the decisions and efficiency of the courts influence the behaviour of the people.

However harsh or repressive the terms of the legal settlement brought by such groups as the Taliban, they are all too often better than the alternatives, which may include no system at all. Two of the following examples, in Afghanistan and Somalia, have arisen in predominantly traditional rural cultures.

Ireland in the early twentieth century, whose insurgent courts were examined in the last chapter, was an integral part of a well-developed Western polity. By contrast, Afghanistan in the twenty-first century is an extremely poor, severely underdeveloped country in Central Asia. Yet insurgents in that country have used tactics similar to those once employed in Ireland to exploit their advantages in the operation of courts, in order to bolster their legitimacy and displace the incumbent government based in Kabul. Somalia's Union of Islamic Courts (UIC) filled a 'governance gap' left not by the absence of a working state but by the presence of rapacious warlord groups.

Syria, like its neighbour Iraq, was a relatively developed state and society where 'Islamic' justice of the kind now implemented by its rebel groups was largely unknown, at least in the cities. The first brief study will look at the Taliban, whose history goes back far beyond the current conflict.

Insurgent justice in 'ungoverned space': Afghanistan, 1979 to the present

In his seminal book *Guerrillas*, Jon Lee Anderson observed that 'If the Mujahedin are dominant in an area, their word is law. And this usually means Islamic law as interpreted by them and their mullahs.'[2]

He relates the setting up of a court in the Kandahar area by a shura, a council of elders, 'as a necessary alternative to the Afghan regime's own discredited judiciary [this shura] has come to exercise the Islamic authority throughout the province, underpinning the military authority of the Mujahedin at the same time.'[3]

It is all very redolent of today. Of course, what happened in Afghanistan also took place in many other insurgencies: what amounts to a shadow government was set up. Itinerant mullahs delivered judgements under a tree, not only on cases related to the war, such as the division of ammunition or the delineation of Mujahedin areas of control. They litigated thefts, adultery and murders. Anderson concluded his account of cases heard by mullahs in the district of Arghandab with words that may be seen as equally applicable to Taliban courts today: 'In Arghandab ... an Islamic land, the laws imposed by [the mullahs] are the ones the people have already learned to obey.'[4] Twenty years on, at the time of writing, Arghandab remains a district fiercely contested by government forces and the Taliban, with the Taliban clearly having the upper hand.

Mujahedin success in the field of justice provision has been inherited in full by the Taliban. After the Soviets left Afghanistan in 1989, a period of chaos ensued. This, at least in the south of the country, is said to have ended in 1996, when the Taliban came to power. If they have one unique 'selling point', insofar as one can distinguish the 'Taliban' from other more opportunistic groups in places such as Helmand, it is their provision of a justice system.[5]

Part of this is based on the Taliban's reputation from their period of rule, between 1996 and 2001. The Taliban's founding myth, as related by Abdul Salam Zaeef, the former Taliban ambassador to Pakistan, goes as follows:

> The founding meeting of what became known as the Taliban was held in the autumn of 1994 ... Mohammed Omar took an oath from everyone present. Each man swore on the Quran to stand by him, and to fight against corruption and the criminals ... The Sharia would be our guiding law and would be implemented by us. We would prosecute vice and foster virtue, and we would stop those who were bleeding the land. Soon after the meeting, we established our own checkpoint ... and we immediately began to implement the Sharia in the surrounding area.[6]

No name was chosen for the group at that stage. The next night, the BBC reported the birth of the new movement. This foundation myth may have some grounding in reality. Another version is 'that the Taliban were created by Pakistan's ISI [Inter-Service Intelligence] and trained in ISI camps.'[7] For present purposes, it is not important how the movement came into being, but rather how it constructed a narrative of justice, grounded in a myth, but one that is commonly felt to be true.

I was justice advisor to the UK security forces in Helmand in 2007. I recall speaking to a female member of the Helmand provincial council who said that she often felt regret as she walked past the town stadium where criminals and other alleged malefactors were punished under Taliban rule—frequently by death or amputation—but that 'at least we could walk the streets in safety then.'[8] As Kate Clark and Stephen Carter confirm in a study of justice in Afghanistan, 'current efforts by the Taliban to provide justice tap into the same deep desire for security and rule of law that helped attract the country to their rule in the mid-1990s.'[9]

When I deployed to Helmand in 2007, the Taliban already ran what seemed to be a relatively well-regarded system of courts. It was made clear to me very early on that the Taliban had been founded a decade earlier on a manifesto of justice, and it was a reputation that they were keen to maintain. As justice advisor to the UK mission in Helmand, I would regularly receive reports of what our rivals in the Taliban were doing by way of dispute resolution. In one case, a man was killed over a land dispute near Garmsir in the south of the province. He was arrested by police and given a short prison sentence of six months. The victim's family were not satisfied with this response, and after the man was released, they presented the case to the Taliban in Garmsir. The case was heard by four Taliban judges, with the accused present. The judgement was that the victim's brother should have the opportunity to kill the murderer. He did, and professed himself very satisfied with the outcome.[10]

Research at the time revealed that the Taliban of Helmand were operating a 'circuit court' system of four judges travelling the province settling cases. As the mission in Helmand matured, these were to become known as 'motorcycle courts'. The Taliban claimed to apply real justice. In addition to the fact that the official or formal system was widely perceived as moribund and corrupt, they asserted that the constitution as it now stands is simply un-Islamic. They would remove seventy articles from the constitution, not least because it implicitly excludes the harsher features of what they believe to be pure Quranic justice of the Hanafi school of Islamic law, informed by the extremist Deobandi (essentially Wahhabi) form of Islam.[11]

In another the application of what are wrongly regarded as the evidentiary rules pertaining to rape took an unusual turn: a woman was raped in the relatively remote Washir district. No recourse to governmental authority was available, so the case was taken before the Taliban judges. They ruled that the necessary four witnesses for a rape case were not available and, as such, no crime could be proved. The victim's family were unhappy with this and took matters into their own hands. They kidnapped the perpetrator and raped him themselves, and he in turn brought his own rapists before the Taliban court. The ruling was the same. He could produce no witnesses and therefore the crime could not be proved.[12]

The resident of Washir district who reported this case said that since the Taliban had arrived 'there had been no robbery or kidnappings. Indeed no crime.' The kind of justice offered by the state was not encouraging. It was clearly beset—indeed characterised—by corruption, incompetence and what might be described as pure criminality.[13] The Taliban had identified an important centre of gravity, a critical vulnerability, and attacked it. The narrative of Taliban justice is central to their success, as is the equally powerful sense of governmental injustice.

The Taliban's judicial strategy today

The Taliban's narrative of justice is prioritised by them as 'practically the only quasi-state service that they provide.'[14] It has been estimated that the Taliban justice system comprises around 500 judges, ranging in qualification from fully qualified religious scholars (called maulawis) to men with a local reputation for fairness.[15] They are reputed to be paid in the region of $250 per month, which is a good salary in Afghanistan.

The procedure involved in Taliban courts is full and comprehensive, but straightforward. Some of the following is drawn from a report based on extensive interviewing by a team led by Antonio Giustozzi.[16] The procedure used in Taliban courts is reported to be consistent nationally—from first instance courts (probably not unlike the 'motorcycle courts' mentioned above) to a Taliban 'Central Court' (Supreme Court), which in theory has its location in Helmand, but probably sits in Pakistan.[17] At first instance, a judgement can be delivered immediately, or it may take up to a month if further witnesses need to be called. As will be seen below, this compares favourably with the state court provision. The procedure itself requires no lawyers or specialist knowledge. It usually takes the form of a traditional Sharia court hearing, of the kind that has taken place in Afghanistan and throughout the Islamic world for centuries. This involves the parties being heard and the judges going on to call whichever witnesses they deem relevant. Judges will make their own enquiries. Critically, Taliban justice is not likely to involve anything like the same degree of payment of large bribes that is a major problem for the state courts.[18] Witnesses subpoenaed by the Taliban tend to turn up at court, out of fear, and torture may play a part in judicial interrogation.[19]

Punishments are seen as strict and based on traditional Sharia law, although there is doubt about the extent to which the condign *hudud* (amputation, stoning to death, etc) punishments are in fact used. Enforcement is highly regarded: a judgement in a Taliban court following a land dispute, for example, is in essence regarded as title to the land. Records are also kept of judgements.[20] The Taliban have what is called in Sharia law *tanfiz*—the ability to enforce.

As was observed in Chapter 1, legitimacy can be assessed as being at least in part a function of the adjudicative procedures being seen to be fair. This is partly based on the fact that the Taliban tap into societally acceptable norms of justice provision. They claim to base their judgements on the Sharia and their procedures are not seen as a departure from traditional Afghan judicial practice.

In a remarkable documentary film from 2014, the Afghan Danish journalist Nagieb Khaja (who also made *My Afghanistan*, discussed earlier) embeds with a Taliban unit in Charkh district, an area of Logar province just an hour's drive from Kabul.[21] In the second of the two-part series, Khaja films the procedure of one Taliban tribunal in the province. Two cases are seen to be litigated: the first concerns a widow being ejected from her home by her stepsons following the death of her husband; the second involves the settling of a debt. In both cases, it is clear that none of the parties had considered trying to settle the case using the state. The procedure was very similar to the informal Sharia hearings with which Muslims all over the world are familiar, and which are still common in Afghanistan, even under the state system. The difference between the government's system in the province and the Taliban's was twofold: first, as various local commentators said on film and as has already been observed, the Taliban system, while by no means incorrupt, is seen as far more trustworthy than the government's system; secondly, it is amply clear that any summons or judgement will be obeyed because it can be enforced. This aspect of enforcement is absolutely critical to a legal system becoming embedded into a society with the attendant advantages for the insurgent group providing it.

In addition, being a well-understood or at the very least basically acceptable procedure and its enforceability, the legitimacy of the Taliban's courts may in turn be countered by appropriate transparency and oversight of competing state systems. The Taliban are acutely aware of the competitive edge they have and the degree to which it depends on perception. Accordingly, great emphasis is placed on oversight. Internal oversight of the Taliban justice system is based initially on the appeals system, although doubts have been raised about its robustness, as people are said to be afraid to attempt to impugn local Taliban judges: 'Only those who were well connected with the local Taliban leadership were likely to feel that lodging a complaint against a verdict was a real option.'[22] Corruption is said to be a 'constant challenge'.[23] Supervision of judges who are not usually local to the areas over which they adjudicate is also exercised by the Provincial Military Commissions, which act to forestall problems connected with excessive familiarity with a given area, which can result in the temptation to take bribes from persons known to the judges concerned. Accordingly, judges are regularly rotated around districts, or indeed provinces. A comprehensive system of internal rules, known as the *Layeha*, govern (or are purported to govern) Taliban behaviour.[24]

Ever conscious of the reputational risks of corruption, Taliban counter-intelligence is said to be tasked with collecting information on allegations about corrupt judges. The assessment of Giustozzi and his fellow authors is that '[r]obust internal oversight appears to have always featured in the Taliban's judicial system since its beginnings; in a sense this is also the case of external oversight, whose effective weight seems to have been strengthening recently.'[25] That external oversight takes the form of measures ranging from the monitoring of rumours to the appointment of ombudsmen to deal with complaints against Taliban officials.

While maintaining a relatively close eye on their own image—just as the Irish Nationalists did—the Taliban discourage people from using the state courts. One state court judge in Wardak province, a contested area of the country, complained: 'I am constantly being threatened when I'm in my office, when I'm in my home or on the road. In areas where the Taliban have control, the people are basically barred from coming to the courts in the capital.'[26] It is clear that this is not an isolated instance, for several such cases have been reported in the south of the country, resulting in constant difficulty in recruiting qualified, willing staff.[27] Government prosecutors in Helmand are said to work with the express consent of the Taliban. For example, Jonathan Steele, in his *Ghosts of Afghanistan*, reports that the district prosecutor of Marjah (it is here that General McChrystal claimed to have installed a 'government in a box' in one of the many NATO campaigns in Helmand) 'is believed to have obtained clearance from the Taliban before taking up his appointment.'[28]

There are limitations to the Taliban's juridical success. They have achieved little penetration in the cities, and they are generally regarded by many as being too keen to rely on violence, or indeed the stricter end of the spectrum of Islamic justice.[29] Their reach is also limited to the Pashtun areas of the country—that area, in other words, where the insurgency is strongest. The judgement of Giustozzi, who has studied the Taliban for over a decade, carries a great deal of weight: 'Whatever individuals might think of the features of the Taliban's judiciary, the Taliban's success in bringing their judiciary to remote rural communities in thousands of Afghanistan's villages is undisputed.'[30]

The Taliban's justice efforts are well known and have deep foundations; indeed, it might be argued that they are a mature and developed form of judicial organisation, at least by Afghan standards. That notwithstanding, the Taliban's courts are seen as one part, albeit an important one, of the 'offer' they make to the Pashtun people. As with other insurgent courts over the last century or more, they act as a measure of legitimacy and reach as well as an instrument to extend and entrench that legitimacy. Further, they have clearly shown a high degree of adaptation to the need to be seen to have legitimacy not only in the eyes of their 'customer base' but also in the eyes of the international community with their *Layeha* code, which is seen as at least a gesture to international legal norms. Might it be that there is a long-term strategy in place to ensure some level of international acceptance, thereby contributing to their overall political aims?

Yet another insurgent group supposedly inspired by Islamic notions of justice made real efforts to entrench its authority. However, this one, in Somalia, defined and founded its authority on its ability to rule, or at least to provide some framework for authority, through courts.

Somalia: The case of the Union of Islamic Courts

Like the Taliban of Afghanistan, the Union of Islamic Courts (UIC) of Somalia was partly a reaction to rapacious warlordism.[31] Like the Taliban, its origins are controversial, as there is evidence for extensive Eritrean involvement in their foundation and initial success. What is certain is that their roots lay in the reaction to the chaos of the 1990s. In some areas, Sharia courts developed their own militias to protect themselves and enforce their rule. In February 2006, a group of eleven such militias came together to form the UIC and took the capital Mogadishu and much of Somalia's coastal region. By August of that year, the UIC had secured control over much of the country.

Their rule was ultimately short-lived. Ethiopia invaded Somalia, supported by the United States and other regional actors, and put an end to the UIC's de facto rule over large parts of the country, and particularly the major towns, in early 2007. Whether the UIC was in fact 'associated with Al-Qaeda' at the time it swept across the country is a matter of serious doubt.[32] What is certainly true is that its successor as a de facto aspirant regime, Al-Shabaab, which grew up in direct response to US actions, most certainly is.

Short-lived as a government though it was, what is interesting and significant about the UIC is that it crystallised the importance of dispute resolution in societies such as Somalia. 'The basic social fabric of Somalia militates against centralisation, and for this reason it is characterised by parochial or sectarian interests.'[33] For a short time, the UIC, if it did not quite transcend these interests, then it at least managed them for the clear benefit of a society that had been destroyed as a political entity for the previous sixteen years.

The genius, if it may be called that, of the UIC was that it combined Somali traditions of community justice (known as *xeer*) with Islamic legal practices.[34] The courts were the product of clan and Islam, two of the most important elements in Somali society. The Islamist ele-

73

ments in the courts did not have a particular agenda and the courts were not presided over by expert Islamic judges, nor were those judges supporters of any specific school of Islamic law. Their authority derived from the positions held in the relevant clans.[35]

In a Channel 4 documentary, Aidan Hartley reported that the UIC undertook:

> serious efforts to get the economy going again, arrested pirates, ended banditry, subjected pirates and bandits to Sharia. Sheikh Sharif [a senior leader of ICU] declared the waters of Somalia safe. Crime was severely curtailed with its attendant effects on security and popular consent. The courts handed down severe *hudud* sentences. Initially, the courts were localised and decentralised; this is not surprising. Every neighbourhood had its own court.[36]

The UIC brought basic social and Sharia legal services: 'UIC rule brought very tangible benefits to the population and gave the Islamists the aura of a national liberation movement; human security improved remarkably, as girls went back to school, transaction costs for business shrunk, entire neighbourhoods were thoroughly cleaned and Mogadishu's streets became safe again at night.'[37]

Governance was mainly confined to the provision of dispute resolution and the enforcement of decisions. While some courts were connected to jihadists, many centred on the various clans. All the courts, of whatever clan, answered to a Supreme Council. At the very least, they were seen to have provided security in a country where none had been available, save localised gang governance by warlords. 'They restored peace for the first time in 15 years', and as a result began to garner support from business and hitherto unaligned clan leaders.[38]

But it lasted only six months. Benefits that were clear to Somalis were less than attractive to US and Ethiopian interests. One clan, the Darod (one of the five dominant Somali clans) had become influenced by jihadism and had declared war on Christian Ethiopia. The internal politics of the Al-Shabaab movement and its allied groups are very complex and far beyond the scope of this book.[39] Nonetheless, what is a matter for debate is the extent to which the reaction on the part of the United States and its failure to understand not only the internal dynamics of Somalia but also the intense and ancient rivalry of the 'Highlanders' of Ethiopia and Somalia made the situation worse.

Ethiopian fear of jihadist influence in its Somali region resulted in a full-scale invasion of Somalia by Ethiopia, supported by the United States. This brought the end of the UIC and led Somalia into clan-driven political chaos. In turn, the situation was made worse by the greatly increased influence of Al-Shabaab, which continues today throughout much of Somalia, especially in the south of the country.

Contemporary Syria

In the intense and savage Syrian Civil War, it is difficult to gain any real idea of how insurgents operate in any given area. This is a far more dangerous area for academics and journalists to work than Afghanistan. Necessarily, then, any account of Syria's insurgent courts must to a certain extent be rather impressionistic. This is especially the case when we come to look briefly at the most notorious of all insurgent groups of the last few decades. Turning first to more moderate courts, and keeping in mind that 'moderate' is most certainly a relative term in today's Syria, a *New York Times* article in May 2013 reported that: 'The court system serves as a prime example of the contest for a postwar Syria. As crime has proliferated after government control vanished in many areas, Syrians clamored for security. Rebel leaders, particularly Islamists, responded by opening dozens of courts.'[40]

In doing so, the rebels were responding to a need for security following local conflict, itself against the background of an intense civil war. It is instructive that once an element of control had been established, the first impulse, at least in this case, was to set up dispute resolution mechanisms—courts.

The first such courts in Aleppo were run by a group of former judges and lawyers calling itself the 'United Courts Council', according to a 2013 news report on CNN,[41] or the 'United Court of the Judiciary Council' (al-mahkama al-muwâhada lil-majlis al-qadhâ'i). The television report gave the impression of a relatively normal operation, complete with a notary service. The chief prosecutor, a former professional, described the court as an emergency measure. The cells contained members of the Free Syrian Army, supposedly incarcerated for war crimes. One inmate blithely remarked that he had tortured a regime officer to death. One judge says of his work, 'we believe that this will prepare us for the day the regime falls, for then there will be anarchy.'[42] The impression given by this report is very much of a simple renaming of jurisdiction, with much the same procedure and personnel, of the kind seen in Libya or Iraq, rather than of a revolutionary court. Indeed, the legal code used is the Unified Arab Code (al-qânûn al-'arabî al-muwahhad), developed in Cairo in 1996 by a group of Arab jurists.[43]

I observed a similar dynamic in Benghazi and Tripoli during the Libyan revolution of 2011–12. In both Benghazi in the early days of the revolution, and later in Tripoli, the state courts worked much as they had during Qadhafi's time. The same procedures were adopted and the same laws were used—based on post-colonial Italian and French models. Judges assured me that minimal disruption was taking place to normal judicial activities, and the only major controversies concerning reform revolved around details, albeit important to lawyers, of the Criminal Procedure Code.

As of 2016, there is insufficient information coming out of Syria to determine whether anything remains of the United Courts Council in Aleppo. Nonetheless, we know enough to be able at least to identify relevant hypotheses. Was this the 'shadow state' at work or is this the reflection of a normal human impulse to provide a sensible and accepted form of dispute resolution, doing exactly what the prosecutor said above—providing an antidote to anarchy? Do we see in this court the formation of a social contract in action? Or is the case simpler than that, merely the continuance of a necessary social good? Was there anything insurgent about this court at all?

In the latter part of 2013, a French TV station filmed an extraordinary fifteen-minute piece on four courts in Aleppo that had been set up by the Jabhat al-Nusra rebel armed group (which has since been renamed Jabhat Fatah al-Sham: 'Front for the Conquest of Syria') supported by an Islamic police force, which tried those suspected of involvement with regime forces.[44] It is not clear whether this system eventually replaced or complemented the United Courts Council, perhaps in another part of Aleppo, but it was clearly a different kind of court. Named the 'Legal Committee' (haî'at ash-sharî'a), it had been operating since April of that year, complementing, but not necessarily competing with, the jurisdiction of the United Courts Council.[45] The reporter in the documentary states that these courts, established in February 2013, are 'at the centre of the new Islamist power'.

The chief judge, who went by the *nom de guerre* Abu Suleiman, was 'on a mission to install the foundation of an Islamist society in the city.'[46] As interesting as the interviews with the main players may be, it is the backdrop and some of the vignettes that are most striking. The court has the appearance of any such institution in the Arab world, with a stream of investigations being carried out by 'prosecutors' in busy offices, with witnesses waiting outside and men with rifles wandering the corridors. However, the differences are more striking. Adultery is one of the charges regularly litigated. No lawyers are allowed, as strict Sharia posits no formal role for legal representatives. A looter is interrogated while having the soles of his feet beaten with a cane; a man is questioned, threatened and beaten on camera for allegedly allowing his son to join Assad's army; a captured Assad soldier is freed in exchange for some valuable tactical intelligence and a fine of $500; another is transferred to the Supreme Court for judgement and possible execution.

In its Jabhat al-Nusra iteration, the court was providing a basis for Islamic society—or, as otherwise framed, forming an ideological basis for a new polity. There are cosmetic similarities to the courts that preceded it, although the founding norms are entirely different. Whereas the United Courts Council uses secular law, with a leavening of Sharia, as is common in Arab societies, the Al-Nusra court is an avowedly Sharia court, with none of the accoutrements of civil law. There are no lawyers, and the judges seem to act not in accordance with any form of due process but according to their own views of what Sharia is. Nonetheless, with a clear structure formed of district and appeal courts, this is a system that aspires to legitimacy and longevity.

As of late 2013, these two jurisdictions seemed to be coexisting, albeit very uneasily. In late 2013, it was reported that:

> The Legal Committee is accusing the members of the civilian administration of being bad Muslims—a strong argument in a time of jihad—while the institutions attached to the Coalition [United Courts Council] consider their rivals incompetent. Last August, men from the Legal Committee even encircled the United Court for one day until they were forced to retreat by the Free Syrian Army combatants closely related to the civil institutions.[47]

Given the fluid situation in Syria, there can be no doubt that matters have moved on since late 2013. There was clearly a threat emerging from a group even more radical than Al-Nusra (which for some time was an IS franchise in Syria) and its close allies.[48]

A 'Caliphate of Law': the 'Islamic State' and its courts

In her essay 'ISIS' Social Contract', Mara Revkin, an Arabic-speaking scholar of law and insurgency, explicitly outlines a renegotiation of the social contract by the so-called Islamic State (IS)—an organisation that she has called a 'Caliphate of Law.'[49]

> When ISIS captures a new area, its first priority is to win the trust and co-operation of civilians … it offers civilians a social contract that provides three main categories of benefits: justice and accountability, protection and services … it is important not to discount the relative legitimacy of ISIS governance compared to equally bad or even less desirable alternatives; a repressive dictatorship.in Syria, sectarian politics in Iraq or rule by rival armed groups such as the Free Syrian Army.[50]

At the outset, and as something of an aside, it is worth asking the question whether Islamic State constitutes an insurgent entity at all. There is no question that it is insurgent in that it acts in direct opposition to established governments. Like many insurgent entities, it is something entirely different. In that sense, though, it has much in common with other insurgent groups holding territory such as the Tamil Tigers. Commentators are as one in stressing that IS attaches a great deal of importance to its ability to establish and enforce its authority and provide social goods. Further, if nothing else, Revkin points out that IS presents itself as better than what went before.[51] They are not generally corrupt by our standards or indeed the standards of many Iraqis or Syrians in that they do not exchange money for judgements. This is not the commonly seen aspect of IS rule, at least in Western media. In her book on IS, *The Islamist Phoenix: The Islamic State (ISIS) and the Redrawing of the Middle East*, Loretta Napoleoni quotes an insurgent who deals explicitly with the question of perspectives:

> You look only at the executions, but every war has its executions, its traitors, its spies. We set up soup kitchens, we rebuilt schools hospitals, we restored water and electricity, we paid for food and fuel. While the UN wasn't even able to deliver humanitarian aid we were vaccinating children against polio. Its just that some actions are more visible than others.[52]

In Napoleoni's words, IS has 'assimilated some of the characteristics of the modern state, such as domestic legitimacy gained by a rough social contract.'[53] All writers are very clear that the appearance of governmental propriety is stressed, in much the same way as the Taliban operates its *Layeha* system examined above. It purports to establish a relationship between the government and the people that is based upon accountability and Islamic justice, according to which the caliph himself can be removed.[54] Against a background of serious instability that has persisted for over a decade in some places, this attempt to develop some form of social contract is very attractive to many Sunni Muslims.[55] As journalist Aaron Zelin put it in a June 2014 article in *The Atlantic* on the 'softer' aspects of its rule, 'IS is able to offer a semblance of stability in unstable and marginalized areas, even if many locals do not like its ideological program.'[56]

A major part of that programme is the IS judicial system. After an initial crackdown on its supposed enemies, Mariam Karouny writes that IS began 'setting up services and institutions—stating clearly that it intended to stay and use the area as a base. "We are a state," one commander in the province said. "Things are great here because we are ruling based on God's law."'[57] Karouny writes that some Sunnis who had worked for President Bashar al-Assad are said to have stayed on after they pledged allegiance to IS. 'The civilians who do not have any political affiliations have adjusted to the presence of [IS], because people got tired and exhausted, and also, to be honest, because they are doing institutional work in Raqqa', said a Raqqa resident opposed to IS.[58] This would appear to buttress, in Napoleoni's phrase, that 'rough social contract'.

Experienced analyst of Syrian affairs Charles Lister affirms that 'the implementation of a strict form of sharia law is clearly central to IS's governance.'[59] While March and Revkin have produced some excellent research on the structure of IS's judicial system, its purported legal foundations and procedures, details of the running of these courts are far sparser than for the Afghan Taliban given the security situation in the country.[60]

However, as with Jabhat al-Nusra and Taliban courts, some evidence is available in the form of television footage. This in itself may indicate an important factor in the priorities of IS. They have shown themselves to be highly adept in using social media. Nowhere is this more apparent than in a documentary programme produced by Vice News on the emerging and intensely controversial state. The documentary, called *Inside the Islamic State*, in part follows the work of the 'Hisbeh', the Islamic police in Raqqa, in mid-2014.[61]

The Hisbeh call their approach 'positive intervention'. In the documentary, one of the members of the Hisbeh states: 'We aim to build an Islamic state in all aspects of people's lives.'[62] An important element of that control is the work of the courts—or the part of the courts that the IS media officer who accompanies the Vice News crew allows them to see. The courts are based in the old court building of Raqqa, and cases are brought and registered in much the same way as in any Arab state court. Indeed, the building and routines as seen in the documentary are similar to those seen in the Al-Nusra courts. This is not surprising, of course, given that both groups were using Syrian state court buildings. While the documentary shows the results of a murder trial in the form of a crucifixion, it also makes clear that most of the court's work concerned arbitrating minor disputes. The court clerk to Judge Abu Al-Bara'a, named 'Haidara', is interviewed: 'The court has returned rights to the people after the oppression they suffered under the regime's courts.'[63] It is explained that there are specialist judges for 'all kinds of cases'.

A particularly jarring moment comes when 'Haidara' is asked: 'Does this court meet international standards?' To which 'Haidara' answers: 'Of course not; we aim to satisfy God, we don't care about international standards.' The court, as portrayed in the documentary, was full and, as in Aleppo, busy and visually very similar to courts in any other part of the Arab—or indeed civil law (as distinct from common law)—world.

The accounts above are gleaned from the media. All of the journalists were escorted by press officers, with the IS media officer becoming the star of the documentary. The appearance of order, administration, accountability and legitimacy is more important than the reality, which is at best relevant only to the city's population. That these programmes were made at all is testament to the importance of this impression being made on target populations. Patrick Cockburn, a veteran journalist on the Middle East, sums up his impression of the way IS uses the media: 'Followers of ISIS continually flood Twitter with pictures of the bodies of their enemies, but they also use the medium to show functioning hospitals and a consultative administrative process.'[64]

Mara Revkin has opened another window into what is happening in Syria by conducting extensive interviews with refugees and defectors from the IS. She describes in detail the purported foundations of their rule and the laws and regulations they apply to their subjects. Like the Taliban's *Laheya* code, IS claims that it regulates the conduct of its fighters and applies some form of Islamic humanitarian law. Such rules set down the supposed standards required for lawful killing, enslavement or indeed rape.[65] It seems that their system is regulated by a form of hierarchy, at the top of which is the 'Shari'a Council' to whom each governor of a province (or *wali* of a *villayet*) answers. These governors oversee local Sharia Councils, which in turn supervise local courts. Judges themselves are subject to discipline, particularly if they stray from the acceptable line. One judge 'disappeared' in the Syrian town of Deir Ezzor because he objected to the torture of prisoners.[66] Needless to say, IS also runs prisons.

Once again, it seems that Islamic State provides a relatively good service for those who require dispute resolution. Revkin told me about a man in the Al-Bab district of Aleppo who was impressed by the way in which a land dispute was settled by IS courts even though the decision went against him. The man, 'Bassam', now living in Turkey like so many former subjects of IS, told Revkin that it would have taken years to resolve the matter in the Syrian state courts before the onset of the Civil War; it was 'the efficiency and professionalism of the process' that was important to this litigant. In this way legitimacy may be acquired, if not retained.[67]

It seems that IS also uses its courts in an attempt to project territorial as well as psychological influence. It has a court in Arsal in Lebanon, for example, outside IS control.[68] There, away from the capabilities that IS has in the way of enforcement, this court acts as something of an arbitration tribunal for those who submit themselves to it.

Revkin takes the view that once IS becomes 'the new normal', their appeal starts to fade, as comparisons are no longer made with the previous rule of the Syrian or Iraqi state. As observed above, the issue of comparison is important as IS courts appear to act in a way that is broadly considered to be professional by comparison with what went before. This is a factor that is constantly referred to by all those who have researched IS and their courts. Rather, as time goes on, people often by now inured to the harshness of IS rule begin to object to the cost of the services being supplied.[69]

At the time of writing, it seems unlikely that IS will itself be accepted as a legitimate state, and even less likely that the judgements of its courts will be regarded as having legal integrity in any future settlement mediated by any form of international community.

One can expect that IS will collapse either from its own corrupt inconsistencies, military pressure or popular dissent of one form or another. Beyond their activities, one day there will be an end to the Syrian Civil War more widely. When that comes, there will need to be a reordering of the legal ecology in all parts of Syria. This will require deep thinking from jurists of all traditions, and especially jurists in the Islamic tradition. It will require a judicial strategy of unprecedented proportions.

Efforts are in motion to begin this process. The World Bank has begun a project to look at the acute and chronic legal problems that will follow the Syrian Civil War, not least of which is the status of land ownership.[70]

Sharia, insurgency and security

In his survey of how Sharia law developed and how it works in many countries today, British barrister Sadakat Kadri argues that the extreme manifestations of Sharia are an innovation. During the 500 years of the Ottoman Empire, for example, during which Islamic law was regularly implemented, there is only one recorded case of someone being stoned to death. Far from being a harsh system of desert discipline, Sharia law 'was the touchstone of right and wrong, and its guidance enabled humanity to enjoy God's bounty without guilt.'[71] Throughout many parts of the world, Islamic law is seen as a moderate and just way of resolving disputes. In other words, in many places the idea of Sharia is comforting. At its best, it offers clear, procedurally fair legal solutions, the legitimacy of which, being divinely ordained, is absolutely crystal clear.

Against the background of acute instability and conflict, however, Sharia has been 'shrunk to meet the needs of the moment', supplying people's most basic needs.[72] One relatively westernised Helmandi lady told me in 2007 that she sometimes wished the Taliban were back, so that at least she and her family could walk the streets of the provincial capital Lashkar Gah in safety. She was not alone in that view. Similarly, the Union of Islamic Courts was seen by some as a reaction to the rampant warlordism of the time. Without basic security, no other quality of life is possible, wherever one happens to live. Shrinking to meet the needs of the moment is one thing, but perversion of the kind found in some of Islamic State's jurisprudence is another.

5

DISRUPTIVE LITIGATION

Rupture strategy

We turn now to how insurgents might use counterinsurgent (or 'incumbent') courts to their advantage. Insurgents often use courts to challenge the right of their accusers to try them. The most famous incident of this kind took place in 1649. The English Civil War was over, and the leader of one of the parties to that war (fought to a very great extent over the issue of the source of legitimacy—parliament or king), King Charles I, was indicted and tried for the crime of high treason. He answered the indictment as follows:

> Now I would know by what authority, I mean lawful, there are many unlawful authorities in the world, thieves and robbers by the highways, but I would know by what authority I was brought from thence, and carried from place to place, and I know not what: and when I know by what lawful authority I shall answer [the charge].[1]

At this point, the former head of state was no longer in a position of active authority, even though he still claimed such authority. As such, at the point of his trial, it could be said that Charles was himself an insurgent.

The well-known and controversial French lawyer Jacques Vergès called this the 'rupture defence': 'so that when the judge says "You're French", the prisoner says "I'm Algerian"; the judge says "You're in a criminal conspiracy", the prisoner says "I'm in the resistance"; the judge says "You committed murder", he says "I executed a traitor". From then on no dialogue is possible.'[2]

Vergès developed this form of lawfare in Algeria in the late 1950s when he earned a reputation for uncompromising criminal defence of men and women suspected of involvement in attacks on French interests, including terrorist attacks. He encapsulated his approach in his 1968 book *De la stratégie judiciaire*.[3] The book sets out a way in which insurgents use courts against the established order. Vergès himself, who died in 2013, was a radical lawyer, well known for his support of causes highly unpopular in the West, such as Palestinian guerrillas and the Khmer Rouge, as well as Nazis indicted in France for war crimes committed in the Second World War.

De la stratégie judiciaire is a review, with historical and modern examples of techniques that can be used in court by insurgents. The author writes that: 'In terms of political (legal) defence, there are always two methods. The compliant strategy (Dreyfus, Challe) or the "rupture strategy" (Socrates, Jesus). The first endeavour to save their lives; the second to win their cause. The novelty of today is that they can also save their lives.'[4] The idea was based on the astute observation that 'by nature, the prosecution is conservative.'[5]

Irish insurgents combined both approaches when it suited them. 'When the defendants were brought before the court, they refused to recognise it, stating that they were soldiers of the Irish Republic and denied the right of a foreign tribunal to try them.'[6] As was discussed above, they then took to the offensive in the very courts whose jurisdiction they denied. The same approach was taken by IRA prisoners in the 'troubles' of the late twentieth century. At least one judge at that time took the view that Mr Justice McGonigal, a judge in the Diplock Courts (judge-only tribunals), set up to avoid 'jury-tampering' 'would show grudging respect for those IRA men who refused to recognise his court, regarding them as behaving like proper soldiers.'[7]

When done skilfully, this form of defence makes the courtroom part of the battlefield. Vergès' first major case, the Bouhired trial, illustrates this. Djamila Bouhired was accused of planting a bomb that killed eleven civilians in a cafe in the European quarter of Algiers in 1956 (an event depicted in the film *Battle of Algiers*). In 1957, she had been captured and allegedly tortured; in July 1957, she went to trial for murder. She was defended by Jacques Vergès. The usual defence strategy in such a case might be to attempt to undermine the prosecution case by challenging the integrity of the evidence, the intelligence upon which it was based or the conclusions of the forensic experts. If there was a confession, that too might be challenged (in Bouhired's case, there was no confession). Alternatively, it might be possible—in the event that the prosecution's evidence was overwhelming—to negotiate a favourable guilty plea. Again, in Bouhired's case, a conservative defence approach might be to agree a plea of guilty on the basis that the death penalty would not be imposed. Vergès would have called this the *défense de connivence*—a collaboration defence. He took the view that Bouhired's trial should not be a 'play for sympathy as left-wing lawyers advised ... from the murderous fools who judged us.'[8]

Vergès took a different approach. He attacked not the evidence, or indeed the police or security forces; he attacked the court itself. He refused to acknowledge that the bombing of the cafe was a criminal offence and accused the court of being complicit in the army's *corvée de bois* (woodcutting; a euphemism for torture) tactics. Jacques Derrida called this a 'radical contestation of the given order of the law, of judicial authority and ultimately of the legitimate authority of the state that summons his clients to appear before the law.'[9] Vergès took the view that another role rupture strategy plays is to highlight the arbitrary nature of the relationship between accused and accuser.[10]

This strategy, in purely legal terms, is unlikely to work as a judge is unlikely to find in favour of the insurgent. Indeed, in the case of Djamila Bouhired, the result—from the narrow perspective of the trial itself—was conviction and a death sentence. The sentence was never carried out and Bouhired would eventually marry Vergès and become a senior member of the government of independent Algeria. But from the perspective of the insurgent campaign in Algeria, the Bouhired trial was a triumph: Vergès had succeeded on the international stage in changing the narrative from the French story of a savage terrorist attack into his version of an illegitimate state engaged in the oppression of a legitimate struggle. That he had done this through the medium of a trial is testament more to his courage than his originality.

Other critics have suggested that not only were Vergès and the rupture strategy not original but also that it amounted to nothing more than a 'rehashing of the "tu quoque" argument advanced by the defendants at Nuremburg and that it was very much a tactic of its time in terms of the effect it had.'[11] They say that Vergès was employing a tactic advocated by Lenin, among others, who said that Bolsheviks accused before courts should 'defend their cause not their freedom ... [and] address the masses over the heads of the judges.'[12] As contemporary journalist Ted Morgan, who had been present in Algiers throughout the war, points out, it was not only the 'masses' to whom Vergès was appealing; his target was also the elite of metropolitan France.[13] Certainly, the Bouhired trial was very much of its time, set as it was in the context of a war of liberation in an age of wars of liberation. With its use in the Bouhired trial, Vergès made the term rupture strategy part of legal vocabulary, even if only in a fairly rarefied area of practice. Vergès was content, as well he might have been, to acknowledge that he was not the first to use this tactic.[14] As he himself said, it was a strategy used by Jesus and Socrates. The denial of the court's right to sit in judgement is only part of the strategy, however. Without a public hearing, there is simply no point in using rupture strategy. The essence of the strategy is intimately connected with ensuring that the message of the cause is reinforced, while simultaneously undermining the legitimacy of the state. As such, it is as much a strategic communications tool as it is a legal one. Indeed, on purely legal grounds, the technique rarely succeeds, save on its own terms.

Rupture strategy in the Irish War of Independence

As demonstrated in Chapter 3, the Irish Nationalists of the War of Independence (1919–21) were the masters of a multifaceted judicial strategy. Apart from their use of courts to undermine crown legitimacy, they instinctively understood Vergès' point that choosing 'rupture' opens the possibility of 'turning the tables, even if you lose.'[15] When it suited their purposes, the Nationalists were happy to use the Crown Courts—the judiciary of their enemies—for their own purposes. If matters went against them in those courts, this could be presented as an example of corrupt justice; if the court decided in their favour, the case could be presented as vindicating the case that had been brought, and thus presented as a victory. Either way, their position was bolstered.

While the default position for those IRA volunteers before Crown Courts was to deny the authority of the court to try them, a draft general order of IRA command stated that 'open permission is granted to all members of the army charged before enemy courts on charges involving the penalty of death to enter into a formal defence if they so desire.' However, permission was not extended to 'men taken in open warfare', for whom a legal defence might be evidentially difficult, as to do so would involve the pointless expenditure of legal fees 'much needed for other matters.'[16]

The courts were also used for civil cases against the crown in the event that property was destroyed or damaged in the course of raids or action by crown forces. These would be made under the Criminal Injuries (Ireland) Act (1919). Indeed, awards were made by Crown Courts in favour of next of kin of persons killed. Senior Republican figures were perfectly prepared to bring such actions. Judgements in favour of such litigants were used in propaganda efforts.[17] This in turn assisted in efforts to ensure that the message of the rebellion was sustained and extended, particularly in the United States, but also at home. Every effort was made to hobble crown forces through Crown Courts. Using coroners' inquests into those killed by British forces was a particularly effective tactic. The first, and arguably most celebrated, case concerned the inquest into the death of Thomas Ashe, who died after a failed attempt to force-feed him when he was on hunger strike in 1917. The jury's verdict condemning the government's treatment of Ashe and censuring the British authorities was nothing less than a propaganda triumph.[18] It was the first of many such coroners' verdicts that went against the crown. These courtroom victories were given great prominence in Nationalist media, with stress being placed on the argument that the verdicts reflected all the worse on the British by virtue of the fact that the juries were 'selected and summoned by the police'. Adverse verdicts were either not reported or were presented as instances of bias.

In one case, an attempt was made in the Crown Court to stop police raids on Sinn Féin's pamphlet printing house. Although the case was eventually lost, 'we had got our objective in the breathing space created and our literature was made available.'[19]

The link between these cases and the media was critical. The Nationalists were fortunate to have the remarkable Erskine Childers (author of the famous pre-WW1 novel *Riddle of the Sands*, and British naval hero) as the Dáil's director of propaganda, with the declared aim of ensuring that 'the matter of propaganda abroad would be on a much wider scale.'[20] Childers also edited the *Irish Bulletin*, distributed in Britain, Ireland and the United States. The *Bulletin* regularly reported courtroom victories and criticised defeats as examples of 'corrupt British justice', echoing *avant la lettre* Vergès' view that even in losing, the tables could be turned. Childers and his team ensured that the message of the Nationalist courts' fairness was carried nationally and internationally, with foreign journalists being granted access to the underground tribunals by the propaganda department of Sinn Féin.[21]

Rupture strategy today

Rupture in its traditional form, as espoused by Vergès, is still used by lawyers. The legitimacy of the military commissions used to try Al-Qaeda and other terrorist suspects was a particular issue throughout the decade-long saga after they were instituted by President George W. Bush in November 2001. In the first major account of the US Military Commission procedures, *The Terror Courts*, Jess Bravin relates that in the chaotic arraignment hearing for the alleged 9/11 conspirator Khalid Sheikh Mohammed in May of 2012, the defendant's lawyer, David Nevin, struck at the core of the controversies by challenging the right of the court to exist. He 'questioned whether by wearing a judicial robe [the Commission's military judge] Pohl had prejudged one of the central issues "the legitimacy of the structure of the court itself," something that had never come up in any case in Nevin's career.'[22] Nor, one expects, in the careers of the other American lawyers or judicial officials in the room.

In some contemporary judicial discourse, the idea of rupture has undergone something of a renaissance. The idea of 'immanent critique' has arisen, where, rather than the submissions of a party, judicial activism has resulted in insurgent ideas having real effect in the form of court judgements. For example, in one judgement of the Indian Supreme Court, which arose out of the Naxalite insurgency in India, the court stated that 'what we have witnessed in the instant proceedings have been repeated assertions of inevitability of muscular and violent statecraft.'[23] This judgement concerned the activities of a particular group of counterinsurgent paramilitaries, the so-called Salwa Judum, composed of 'Special Police Officers' (SPOs), which amounted to groups of armed tribal youth. These were conscripted into the service of the counterinsurgent state government.

An action had been brought by three claimants alleging widespread violation of human rights by the state authorities. In its judgement, the Supreme Court drew on academic works critical of globalisation and essentially took an approach remarkably in line with much of the theoretical framework advocated by counsel for the claimants. As a commentator on this case put it, 'the court thus positions the rights to equality and dignity in opposition to capitalist development imperatives ...'[24]

Indian academic Brenna Bhandar argues that this case is significant because it shows the continuing potential of political shifts originating in judicial authority: 'a strategy of rupture might involve an exposure of the contradictions that inhere in colonial capitalist legal orders that eviscerate the potentiality that rights hold to enable individuals to live lives free of fear, violence and exploitation ... through the act of judgement.'[25] One is tempted to state that the 'might' in that characterisation is the key modifier. She is undoubtedly right, though, when she says that 'it is clear that an independent judiciary does have the power to disturb the monopoly of violence exercised by the government and to transcend this disturbed framework by offering a radically different interpretation of security and freedom.'[26] Courts in a free society have the potential to achieve even more than this. The question as to what social, psychological or political forces ensure that this potential is rarely, if ever, exercised lies beyond the remit of this book. While Bhandar argues that this is an example of 'rupture', a case could well be made that it was an instance of 'disruptive litigation'.

'Rupture' and transparency

The rupture strategy, as described and practised by Vergès and epitomised by the Irish judicial strategy, may have been effective in both Algeria and Ireland. However, the strategy is of little use in the absence of two important factors. If, for example, an accused person in an Iranian or Russian state court is accused of terrorism, will gain no publicity if he denies the authority of the court to try him and attempts to subvert that court. The response of those authorities may simply be to close the courts to public access and deny the accused any form of publicity. Further, the decision of the court in such societies may have little in common with notions of fair trial: the trial is likely to be more in the nature of a production line than an examination of the factual and legal issues surrounding the accused's alleged crime. There needs to be an element of basic notions of rule of law, as well as judicial professionalism. In other words, in order to work, the 'target' court needs to operate in an environment approximating to Western notions of rule of law. This was the case in both Ireland and Algeria—at least to the extent that the rhetoric of the law was complied with to some extent. In order to have purchase, notions of 'using the courts against themselves' must have a degree of credibility. In such circumstances, the claims of courts to professionalism and compliance with legal norms should have some basis in fact, or at least perceived fact. It may be worth mentioning at this point that even martial law courts in democratic countries may display such characteristics. As David Foxton points out in his *Sinn Féin and Crown Courts*, there was a sense of 'punctilious legalism' alongside brute force in the British approach in Ireland.[27] One leading defence lawyer for IRA volunteers, Tim Healy, had a high regard even for the courts martial officers in Ireland, who were considered to be relatively fair: 'As a rule, courts composed of officers of the British Army make a fine tribunal.'[28] Few would consider attempting the rupture strategy in a closed court presided over by judges employed only to process convictions, or indeed a court martial composed of military officers in an operational zone.

Secondly, rupture strategy requires the voice of rupture to be heard by an audience outside the courtroom. This requires a degree of media access and freedom. Indeed, it is at such media that rupture strategy is aimed. Once again, to refer to Rupert Smith's characterisation of contemporary war being a form of theatre, a theatre needs an audience, and with the rupture strategy that audience has to be in the form of media. Ted Morgan, an American journalist reporting from Algiers at the time of the Bouhired trial, wrote that Vergès 'had little concern for the truth': he was 'playing to that part of public opinion in France that had turned against the war.'[29] This was certainly true, but that was exactly the point. 'Truth' was secondary at best: Vergès' purpose was to advance a cause, and playing to the 'home front' was one way of doing so. And that depended on having an audience that was supplied by the international media. In today's terms, his actions would be considered an effective information operation.

As well as being tools of government and insurgency, courts may also be platforms for political declarations. Castro's 1953 speech, 'La historia me absolverá' (History will absolve me), was made in open court.[30] It is still regularly quoted in Cuban society today. Similarly, all of Vergès' most famous trials took place with a full media presence. Rupture, and indeed a wider judicial strategy, is and must be part of a strategic communications strategy, and for it to have a place in such a strategy, there has to be a means of propagation. Such a narrative will, in its essence, act as a foil to the counterinsurgent story of adherence to human rights, due process, and so on. It is this that will feed into the idea that the insurgent offer is one that is fair.

Rupture is a complement to the development of insurgent courts, which were looked at in the last two chapters. As insurgent courts undermine the legitimacy of state courts in the domestic realm, while promoting their own legitimacy, rupture attacks that legitimacy from within the courtrooms of the state. Cogently and professionally conducted, and in the right context, it can play an important part in insurgent judicial strategy. As was stressed in Chapter 3, the Irish Nationalist strategy in 1919–21 amply demonstrated the potential of an insurgent judicial strategy.

Disruptive litigation

If lawfare is the means by which 'law is used as a means of achieving military objectives', 'disruptive litigation', like 'rupture', is a weapon within that realm of warfare.[31] Disruptive litigation can be defined as 'the use of court decisions to influence the conduct of strategy or operations in war or conflict.' There are two categories into which such litigation (defined here as the conduct of court proceedings) might fall. The first is hostile disruptive litigation; the second is non-hostile disruptive litigation.[32] The difference between the two lies in the intent of the litigant or claimant. Hostile disruptive litigation has the intended effect of disrupting counterinsurgent operations. Its non-hostile counterpart may have the effect of doing so, but the intent is not present. The latter, as will be seen, has been common over the last decade, particularly in the context of the conduct of the wars in Iraq and Afghanistan. Orde Kittrie has used the term 'compliance-leverage disparity lawfare' for this form of litigation. He defines it as 'lawfare designed to gain advantage from the greater influence that law and its processes exert over an adversaries'. He sees 'battlefield lawfare' as a 'subset' of 'compliance-leverage disparity'. Those terms have not been used here, as it is by no means clear whether 'disparity' is involved in this form of lawfare. As we will see below, Kittrie's book has looked at the litigation used by Hamas and other insurgent groups. He sees 'battlefield lawfare' tactics as designed to achieve two objectives: first, to cause the adversary to restrain their use of military force, and second to erode public and international support for the adversary's position.[33]

In his essay on Chinese lawfare, Dean Cheng outlines some scenarios whereby a Chinese legal campaign using US courts, which he calls 'offensive lawfare', could work:

> The most obvious such measure would be the filing of a variety of legal motions in American courts aimed at delaying any American intervention. These motions could be filed in response to a host of issues, ranging from the War Powers Act to the right to mobilize various American resources. More subtle actions could include legal action related to environmental or labor law—areas that, while not directly related to foreign policy and national security, could still have an impact on US military operations.[34]

Cheng's predictions in the context of international conflict, with respect to lawfare, have yet to be fulfilled. In a conversation with me, however, Cheng went further:

> Imagine the case of a US Navy carrier group approaching Taiwan during a crisis. What better way of disrupting its command structure than, say, removing the admiral by means of false criminal or civil accusations, generated by Chinese agents in the US? Images of child abuse, for example, planted in his personal computer. At the very least, the enemy could hope for his peace of mind disturbed. Even better, he might be summoned back to the US. Either way, the operational efficacy of the admiral could be seriously damaged at minimal cost.[35]

The scope of such potential operations is almost unlimited, provided the resources and will are present.[36] However, within the context of insurgent warfare, there is evidence that the kind of hostile disruptive litigation to which Cheng has drawn attention has in fact been used.

In a paper presented to the Fort Leavenworth School of Advanced Military Studies in 2010, Juan Padilla, a Colombian officer, wrote about a well-known Colombian court case. [37] The case derived from a famous incident in the conflict between the Colombian government and various insurgent groups and drug cartels in the 1980s. In 1985, a group from 'M-19', an offshoot of FARC, raided the Palace of Justice in the capital Bogotá and took 300 people hostage. An attempted rescue mission by Colombian security forces resulted in ninety deaths. The commander of the operation was one Colonel Alfonso Plazas Vega. In 1986, the Supreme Court investigated the incident and determined that the actions of the security forces and of Colonel Plazas were within proper bounds, and that culpability lay with M-19. In 1992, convictions were obtained against the M-19 leaders of the operation, although all avoided prison terms. Some subsequently entered politics. Twenty-five years after the incident, Colonel Plazas had retired from the army and been appointed by President Álvaro Uribe as director of the Narcotic Enforcement Office. Padilla says that he achieved great success in that role.

In 2005, proceedings concerning the raid were reopened and Colonel Plazas, who was by now running for Congress, was detained. Pending resolution, he remained in detention and was no longer eligible for political office. Padilla's case is that, by means of politically inspired litigation, Plazas had been removed from the fight against narcotics and insurgency in a democratic country. Whatever the merits of the case, Padilla claims that an effective fighter against insurgency and terrorism had been removed through legal means. [38]

There is clearly a line to be drawn between cases of supposed 'hostile disruptive litigation' and the more common allegations and litigation of abuses by security forces of the kind extensively dealt with in the aftermath of the 'Bloody Sunday' events. [39] Equally clearly, the real motives of claimants in cases of hostile disruptive litigation may only become clear years or even decades later; for if they were clear at the time, it is unlikely that courts would entertain their claims. It is vital, generally, that such motives are concealed. There are occasions when there is no such attempt. For example, credible media reports assert that Hamas has made attempts to secure British lawyers to ensure the arrest of Israeli military and political leaders should they ever visit the United Kingdom.[40] In all such cases, the effect of such actions is two-fold. First, a successful case might remove inconvenient or effective leaders from the enemy incumbent's order of battle. Second, whether or not the legal action is won, there is significant strategic communications value in simply the fact of having brought the case. By engaging British lawyers in the manner alleged, Hamas succeeded in raising the profile—and possibly the credibility—of their cause.

Inadvertent disruptive litigation?

In many cases, it is difficult to disentangle the motives of litigants from the arguments in the cases themselves, or indeed from the effects those cases might produce. The well-known human rights case of *Ireland* v. *UK* arose out of the use of interrogation techniques by British forces in Northern Ireland that allegedly amounted to torture.[41] As well as reaching back to the early days of the Northern Ireland campaign, the consequences of this judgement and the facts that gave rise to it remain relevant today, not only in the development of British policy on inter-rogation—which it directly continues to affect—but in the framing of British counterinsurgency in the contemporary context.

As an example of lawfare—conflict in the domain of law that directly affects the conduct of operations, the legitimacy of those operations and, further, the legitimacy of the counterinsurgent cause—no case has had more impact. It set the tone for discourse on British counterinsurgency specifically. It also provided much of the background to the even more critical discourse surrounding UK and US activities during the Iraq and Afghanistan wars of the early twenty-first century. However, the litigant in the case was the Republic of Ireland, not a combatant. Nor was it particularly sympathetic to the political aims of the Provisional IRA, whose alleged members were the internees subject to the torture and ill-treatment that was the crux of the case. Was this 'litigation warfare'? Was it disruptive litigation? In one sense, it was. The intent was surely to stop the ill-treatment of detainees that the Republic of Ireland claimed as citizens. However, the intent was not to impede the aims of the UK's security forces, let alone advance those of the IRA.

No state entity will bring cases in the UK against, for example, the Taliban for actions in Afghanistan. And even were they minded to do so, the chances of any judgement being enforced would be nil.[42]

From the conceptual perspective, such actions tend to erode incumbent legitimacy. In his review of Stephen Neff's *Justice in Blue and Gray* on the use of law in the US Civil War, Alan Kaufman writes that:

> Law becomes a strategic partner—a lubricating oil smoothing accomplishment of national security objectives—when it produces a perception that military operations are, or even that the war itself is, legitimate and therefore righteous and supportable. Law becomes the *enemy's* strategic partner, however—that is, creates friction in the other direction—when it produces the opposite result. This is so because law in war operates on, against and within all three aspects of what Clausewitz once called the 'paradoxical trinity' of which war is composed: the people, the commander and his army, and the government.[43]

On occasion, the 'friction' produced that might benefit the 'enemy' may be initiated or indeed created by parties not directly involved in the conflict. Typically, since 2001, such people have often been anti-war activists or human rights campaigners. Certainly, in the Iraq and Afghan cases in the UK, referred to above, this has been the case. The view taken by some US observers is that within the context of the 'war on terror'—'in grim reality, a prolonged, worldwide irregular campaign'—these actors have had some success.[44]

According to Mark Holzer 'During the past decade the United States and its citizens have been subjected to numerous legal actions in European and domestic courts that appear to be aimed at negatively impacting the United States' ability to fight Islamic extremists.'[45] There may be some confusion, to put it mildly, between the effect and the intention. The effect of litigation aimed at curbing bomb attacks (be they 'drones' or other delivery systems) by US military assets, for example, including Special Forces, may well be to 'negatively impact' the vast capabilities of the US military machine. In most cases, the intention is rather to act to enforce what proponents might argue were, until the last decade, well-accepted tenets of the law of the use of force. While some may characterise such an approach as 'abuse', others would see it as the exercise of litigation to entirely appropriate legal ends.[46] For example, when Italy indicted CIA officers for kidnapping, allegedly for the purposes of rendition, was this a legitimate action by a state in support of its security and legal integrity, or an attack on the US capability to fight terror?[47] While the result might be to blunt the discretion of US military commanders—in that case affecting their ability to kidnap nationals of another state from the streets of a third (and allied) country without reference to that state—that is not the intent.

By the same token, is the use of the Alien Tort Claims Act, which has been used to sue for 'victims of Palestinian terrorist organizations' in Israel, a restriction on the discretion of other countries to use torture?[48]

Non-hostile disruptive litigation and the US home front, 2001–14

Even 'exogenous' counterinsurgency campaigns are not confined to the borders wherein the military interventions take place. There is a long history of counterinsurgencies being fought and won in the countries of the intervening states themselves. Vietnamese General Giap said in an interview that 'the [Vietnam] War was fought on many fronts … the most important one was American public opinion.'[49] More recently, in his memoirs, the former UK chief of the General Staff, the professional head of the British Army, said: 'Losing popular support at home is one guaranteed way to lose a counterinsurgency campaign, as the Americans discovered to their cost in Vietnam.'[50] The home front has been a vital part of the counterinsurgency campaigns of the early twenty-first century.

This has involved many layers of discourse and argument, ranging from the polemic to the academic. From the UK and US legal perspective, the courts have provided a forum for some of the controversies surrounding the wars in which both states have been involved. In the United States, the matters litigated (and which have entered or influenced public discourse on the war on terror) have largely concerned questions surrounding detention and interrogation, and the extent to which American courts have jurisdiction over such matters. There has been particularly intense litigation over the detainees in Guantanamo Bay, many of them Taliban or other insurgents. The cases brought in the so-called 'military commissions' were frequently hobbled by the use of torture and mistreatment.[51] This has had an effect on the stories told of the wars, with allegations made in court providing excellent copy for the media in the context of portraying the campaigns in a negative light.

A series of legal cases concerning both the Iraq campaigns of 2003–11 (for the British) and the Afghan campaign of 2001–14 casts light on the approaches taken. They further highlight the importance of having a legal strategy.

General Michael Dunlavey, commanding officer Joint Task Force 170 Guantanamo Bay until November 2002, conflates the cases ostensibly brought to enforce constitutional liberties with the activities of 'terrorists.' 'When it is about protecting rights, we have to come up and develop a way to deal with terrorists who use the legal system against us.'[52]

He was referring to the Hamdan stream of cases in the US Supreme Court, which imposed serious restrictions on the jurisdiction of the military commissions set up to try alleged Al-Qaeda operators in the US naval base at Guantanamo Bay, which has been described as a 'legal black hole'.[53]

Another perspective is that, if the United States and its allies complied with international law, then they would have far fewer problems. Critics see the United States as the leading proponent of lawfare, and that lawfare cuts two ways. Rather than the United States being the victim of lawfare, it is a leading practitioner. Writing in *The Guardian*, one Pakistani scholar, Ahmed Dawood, points out that the US:

> Military prowess is not enough in this age; and the United States knows it. America's 'other army'—its less visible but equally potent cadre of skillful lawyers (in government and even in private practice)—dutifully got busy crafting appropriate international law narratives for the War on Terror. They realized that winning the battle for defining 'legality' on the world stage was critical. Until you build the capacity to counter the dominant account and promote competing interpretations of what is 'legal' in international law, you will continue to be outwitted in international affairs, not just on the battlefield.[54]

Dawood identifies here the link between law and narrative. Such narratives do not operate only on the international level. Insurgencies are at least as concerned to capture and dominate domestic narratives of legitimacy by using, among other tools, the law and courts.

It has been said many times that the revelation of the torture at Abu Ghraib was the 'US Military's most serious setback since 9/11', a thought echoed by David Kennedy, who said it was 'a military defeat'.[55] Kennedy may well be right, but the setback was not legal—except insofar as the activities forming the basis of the setback happened to be illegal (torture being a crime in the United States). The few criminal prosecutions brought as a result of these crimes attracted far less attention than the iconic photographs of the abuse at the prison. The setback was presentational.

Non-hostile disruptive litigation in the UK: the Iraq and Afghan cases

The treatment of detainees in Iraq by UK forces has been controversial from the outset of the Iraq War in 2003. The death in custody of Baha Mousa in 2003 led to a series of investigations, trials and inquiries.[56] In terms of litigation and its feedback into operations, two cases dominated the discourse. The first was that of Mazin Al Skeini and others who were shot dead by a British patrol in Basra in August 2003. The other was that of Hilal Al Jeddah, a prisoner who sued the British government, alleging mistreatment at the hands of UK soldiers during his detention for over three years in a UK military detention facility in Basra.[57]

A further matter concerned Hamid Al-Sweady. This was a rather different kind of case, wherein it was alleged that prisoners taken by British soldiers after a battle were tortured, killed and their bodies mutilated. It became the subject of an inquiry.[58] The Al Skeini and Al Jeddah cases established that the British authorities were legally responsible, under the European Convention on Human Rights and the Human Rights Act, for those killed or detained. Neither the detail of the judgements nor the legal reasoning behind them is immediately relevant for present purposes. However, these judgements had military and political effect, in that first they altered the parameters within which military operations take place, and second, to some degree they shifted the debate from the political purpose of the missions to the manner in which they were conducted, with intense press focus on the behaviour of UK forces.

A similar effect can be observed in another stream of cases, brought in the civil courts of England and Wales by Maya Evans, 'a peace campaigner opposed to the presence of UK and US armed forces in Afghanistan.'[59] These concerned the allegation that the transfer by UK forces of detainees captured in combat to the Afghan authorities for trial was unlawful, as the detainees were thereby exposed to torture, ill-treatment and unfair trials. It was decided in these cases that the safeguards introduced by the British were adequate, although barely so. A further case was brought in 2012 by Serdar Mohammed, a detainee captured by British forces and transferred to the Afghan authorities, who allegedly tortured him.[60] This case was brought on much the same grounds, and the information provided indicated that the safeguards were most certainly not adequate.[61]

In all these cases, much effort was made by the British authorities to make sure that the matters being litigated were brought under provisions that would ensure that the proceedings were secret. In one of the cases, it was stated that: 'The importance of the case lies not only in its subject matter but in its implications for security in Afghanistan and the effectiveness of UK [counterinsurgency] operations there.'[62] There is no need to discuss here the extent to which the judgements (which, it is fair to say, largely favoured the accounts given by the UK authorities) were informed more by a desire to ensure the continued 'effectiveness of UK operations' than by a willingness to cease handing over detainees to a regime with a highly questionable human rights record (and specifically to the Afghan Intelligence Service, the NDS).[63] However, what is clear is that, once again, the effectiveness of operations was perceived to be at stake. As a result of these cases, much effort was expended by UK personnel in Afghanistan, and it is apparent that there was a real concern to ensure compliance with relevant legal strictures.[64]

These cases are not to be confused with the category identified as hostile disruptive litigation of the kind described above, envisaged by Dean Cheng and indeed carried out by Colombian insurgents and others. The litigants in such cases fully understand that their role is often as unwilling participants in the conflict, not as active supporters of one side or the other—and certainly not as combatants. However, in bringing actions in courts, they know that 'the audience are not just the people in the war zone, nor even the population of all the belligerent states, but the court of world opinion.'[65]

As such, they instinctively understand that perceptions are at least as important as the outcome of the cases they pursue.

I must be clear here, the litigants are not themselves insurgents. Nor do they necessarily adopt the views or objectives of the insurgents in

Iraq or Afghanistan. Nonetheless, as one solicitor involved in the Maya Evans cases acknowledged: 'There is a political purpose behind this litigation. What gets us up in the morning is the prospect of making change ... I had a concern about the military not operating under law. It's all about government operating under law.'[66] While the objectives of those involved in such cases may not be to affect the operational effectiveness of UK or allied forces on the ground in the operational zones of Iraq or Afghanistan, the result is that they do.

It should have come as no surprise to the British government that detention in Iraq and Afghanistan became a 'live issue'. Yet it is clear that even in 2012, when the Evans litigation was brought before the courts, no policy or strategy was in place. As pointed out above, Kennedy observed of the scandal of torture and abuse of prisoners at the US-run Abu Ghraib prison near Baghdad that 'the whole episode was clearly a military defeat.'[67] The same argument can surely be made of the British experience, albeit at a far reduced level of global impact.

'Legal feedback': disruptive litigation and the effect on operations

A 'targeting meeting' is a regular occurrence in modern warfare. It is usually composed of representatives of all those involved in the planning and execution of missions to destroy, kill or capture enemy 'assets', be they human or otherwise. Such meetings will generally include the 'kinetic element' of warfare—those who will actually conduct the mission; there will be intelligence officers to brief the meeting on what is known about the target; there may well be a 'psyops' (psychological operations) officer to look at the media or 'info ops' (information operations) potential that may be inherent in the mission. There may be a civilian representative to analyse the political impact, if any, of destroying or killing the target. At all such meetings, however, in the twenty-first century the one certain presence will be the lawyer, who will be trained and qualified in the operational law referred to above: in other words, the application of the laws of war (*ius in bello*) to the operation itself.

A NATO military intelligence officer gave me his account of one such targeting meeting in Afghanistan. The purpose of the meeting was to assess certain individuals for kill or capture raids. When the agenda reached a particular individual, the psyops officer said that, rather than killing or capturing him, another way of dealing with the target might be to put about rumours concerning his sexual proclivities. At this point, the legal advisor stated that this might contravene the local law on slander, or indeed the law of the country or countries in which the officers were carrying out a mission. The commander of the unit tasked with kill or capture then asked whether it would be permissible to kill the target. The legal advisor is said to have stated that there was no reason why he could not be killed. The officer did not tell me what was actually decided.[68]

That the law influences the day-to-day conduct of counterinsurgency operations is nothing new. What is relatively new is the effect of the potential for litigation and the use of courts in the home countries of counterinsurgents who are foreign to the country in which they are operating. This litigation has had a feedback effect on the conduct of operations in such places as Iraq and Afghanistan.[69] Since 2001, this has been particularly evident in the treatment of prisoners and the use of interrogation.[70] This has been a major issue for counterinsurgents endogenous to the insurgencies (i.e. not foreign, such as those in Northern Ireland or, arguably, the French in Algeria).

There is no doubt that there was a feedback effect from the Maya Evans stream of cases for UK forces and operations in Helmand. Such feedback not only had an effect on military operations. As one of the British civilian justice advisors in Helmand explained to me:

> the resources devoted to anti-terrorism prosecutions on the civilian side, a key part of the detainee pipeline, did suggest that this was in part prompted by judicial challenges at home. It seemed to me that such resources ought to have been deployed far earlier, with a far more strategic look at the detainee pipeline at that stage.[71]

Those comments explicitly demonstrate the effects that litigation can have on how counterinsurgent forces actually carry out their operations. This in turn highlights the need to make certain strategic decisions at an early stage in the conflict with respect to legal issues that are likely to arise.

Insurgent disruptive litigation at the strategic level

The option for insurgents to use the courts of an incumbent government, the counterinsurgent authority, against the government may only be open in societies where there is some measure of democratic transparency. In cases where courts are simply rubber stamps for the government, there is little or no scope either to adopt a rupture strategy or the approach that I have called here disruptive litigation. It is difficult to imagine, for example, Chechen rebels being given an opportunity to grandstand in the way that Vergès did in Algeria. The idea of suing a Russian Army unit for the cavalier use of force or bringing allegations of a breach of the Russian Constitution or international law with respect to its detention or interrogation practices would be given similarly short shrift. However, in an increasingly globalised world, using litigation to further the interests of insurgent or rebel groups may become an ever more attractive prospect. For example, over the last twenty years the London courts have been used as the forum for oligarchs and other interests, state and personal, to bring libel actions. The reason for this is that these people believe, probably rightly, that they may receive a sympathetic hearing and that cases are likely to be decided upon the law, which until very recently was highly skewed towards the interests of the aggrieved claimants in such cases. These wealthy individuals and interests were commonly perceived to be using the London courts as proxies to pursue their political enemies. Many of these were NGOs or the proprietors of small newspapers who could not afford to hire the extremely expensive lawyers needed to defend cases.[72] Choosing courts upon criteria related to whether they are likely to be sympathetic is known as 'forum shopping'. Such an activity is not limited to quasi-criminal, commercial or media interests.

In his *Lawfare: Law as a Weapon of War*, Orde Kittrie details many examples of US, Israeli and Chinese state use of courts as instrument of achieving political ends—as weapons, in other words.[73] However, his most extensive study is reserved for the various manifestations of Palestinian interests, particularly Hamas and Palestinian NGOs. Here we see forum-shopping and indeed the use of democratic and transparent tribunals in action.

Two particular examples are significant. The first is the well-organised and prolonged campaign surrounding the behaviour of Israeli forces during the 2014 Gaza War. This took place at several levels, ranging from the use of Israeli courts to the engagement of UN agencies to corroborate claims by groups including Hamas. Among Israel's responses, Kittrie lists changes to battle tactics, expanding the role of lawyers and enhancing Israeli investigations into alleged war crimes by its troops.[74]

At the wider strategic levels, there is an ever-present drip of threats of legal action against Israeli officials on the basis of universal jurisdiction with respect to various alleged war crimes. Some countries accept that a breach of certain international conventions (the most prominent of which is the 1982 Convention against Torture) in one country provides the basis for criminal convictions in another.[75] The most prominent example of the use of universal jurisdiction was the arrest in the UK of General Pinochet in October 1998 following an indictment issued in Chile for, among other crimes, torture. The case became a major *cause célèbre*.[76] When conducting this form of disruptive litigation, it will serve those advising insurgent groups to ensure that forum-shopping results in the best possible result. Such a result might not take the form of a legal 'win' in court; however, whatever the result, it is highly likely to serve to damage the public image of the 'target'.

Perhaps the best contemporary example of this kind of lawfare is the regular effort by pro-Palestinian activists to have various Israeli officials arrested for alleged war crimes on visits to some Western countries. These efforts are invariably unsuccessful, but they do serve the purpose of continuing to damage Israel's public image.[77]

These cases and many others highlight the potential and achievements of disruptive litigation. In so doing, they point the way for future insurgent groups and rebel authorities to the possibilities offered by courts in potentially sympathetic countries or indeed adversary courts, provided of course that they are essentially democratic in nature.

The Colombian army officer quoted above, Juan Padilla, starkly states the case for increased awareness of future lawfare:

> Democracies must understand holistic lawfare as a growing approach for contemporary confrontation in order to creatively improve their own mechanisms to counter it. After all, lawfare is going to be increasingly used by adversaries as it is becoming an essential feature of twenty-first century conflicts to the point that perhaps in Clausewitzian terms, it can best be described as a 'continuation of war with legal means'.[78]

Having examined the various options open to insurgents, both on the battlefield and upon the territory of their adversaries, we now turn to look at what measures counterinsurgents can take to resist insurgent lawfare.

6

COUNTERINSURGENT DILEMMAS

HINTS FROM HISTORY

'He lives in a land with a settled social system, where life is secure and where the rights of property are protected by laws which are obeyed. But his opponent has grown up in very different conditions. He has been accustomed, like his fathers before him, to look upon might as right and to trust to his own right hand for safety amid the turbulent surroundings in which his lot is cast.'[1]

The fiction of 'ungoverned space'

Some societies display few of the attributes of 'rational legal' government. Indeed, 'ungoverned' or 'alternatively governed' space may be rather more the norm than the exception, as 'the dominance of the Westphalian [i.e. the Western model of the] state in governance provision has steadily eroded since the end of the Cold War.'[2] Societies such as this are often characterised as 'ungoverned'.

To governments dominated by the rational Westphalian state legal paradigm, such areas are seen as threatening, particularly against the background of the perceived growing threat of terrorism, which is often considered to centre itself in such areas. As Anne Clunan and Harold Trinkunas have put it: 'it is normal to expect that all states will perceive ungoverned spaces as threatening, even if they contain no threats.'[3]

Many of the West's recent military engagements and its parallel civilian efforts have been predicated upon preventing the emergence of ungoverned space into which terrorists might fit. The essence of this idea was summarised well by the former British foreign secretary, Jack Straw:

> [Places like] Somalia, Liberia and Congo invoke the Hobbesian image of a 'state of nature' without order, where continual fear and danger of violent death render life nasty, brutish and short ... As well as bringing mass murder to the heart of Manhattan, state-failure has brought terror and misery to large swathes of the African continent. And at home it has brought drugs, violence and crime to Britain's streets ... We need to remind ourselves that turning a blind eye to the breakdown of order in any part of the world, however distant, invites direct threats to our national security and well-being.[4]

We may put aside for the moment the fact that the attacks on Manhattan were carried out largely by Saudis who had trained in the United States as well as Afghanistan for an operation planned to a great extent in Germany. Nonetheless, the kind of approach espoused by Straw has had considerable scholarly support. For example, in 2007 the RAND Corporation produced a book on the topic, which took the following view: '[U]ngoverned territories generate all manner of security problems, such as civil conflict and humanitarian crises, arms and drugs smuggling, piracy, and refugee flows. They threaten regional stability and security and generate demands on US military resources.'[5]

Whether or not those demands on US military resources are self-generated depends to some extent on whether the authorities controlling the US military accept the premise that ungoverned space necessarily equates to a threat to the international order and national security, a calculation beyond the scope of this book. The RAND report discusses in detail several areas of the world perceived to be ungoverned spaces: those areas taken together constitute a considerable portion of the earth's surface.[6]

Each of the extensive chapters in that report was written on the understanding that military intervention may be required. Much of the strategy of US defence policy over the last two decades has been predicated on the need to control such spaces. An entire 'command' of the US armed forces—Africa Command—was created explicitly to deal with the supposed risks attached to sub-Saharan governance.[7]

Casually linking failed states to a story of terrorism and global instability is a further step, and many commentators have argued strongly against taking it.[8] Aidan Hehir adopts a methodologically similar approach to RAND of surveying a large selection of countries, but comes to very different conclusions. He sees 'no causal link or pronounced correlation between failed states and the proliferation of terrorism or between democratization and the negation of terrorism'.[9] Instead, he sees the kind of assertion represented above as a 'façade erected not because of its accuracy but because of its rhetorical impact.'[10]

The question of whether there is in fact any ungoverned territory in the world is itself problematic. In speaking about Afghanistan, military historian Robert Johnson could have been discussing any one of several similar environments:

> The absence of Western state structures of governance in large swathes of the tribal areas should not be conflated ... with the absence of governance. Depictions of the frontier as a lawless land of endless feuds and bloodthirsty tribal raids owe more to Victorian romanticism than to objective reality.[11]

De facto governments do of course exist in areas frequently claimed as ungoverned spaces. There are also the 'differently governed spaces', such as Somalia, parts of Afghanistan, Pakistan and Africa. The fact of their being 'differently governed' should not necessarily imply the necessity of intervention of any kind. There are other forms of ungoverned space. For example, so-called 'feral cities', even in some Western countries, offshore financial markets or marginally regulated reaches of the internet.[12]

The reality is that a 'variety of non-state actors, including insurgent organizations can and do control the fate of civilian communities for substantial periods.'[13] The extent to which the solution is the application of the seventeenth-century European (Westphalian/Hobbesian) state structure outlined in Chapter 1 is not clear. As summarised by Christopher Clapham:

> The problem of failed states is most basically about whether the grafting of such states ... onto unpromising rootstock can be made to take—even with the various kinds of fertilizer provided by the international system in

the form of universalist ideologies, incorporation into the global economy and the provision of diplomatic and military support.[14]

This chapter will seek to demonstrate the truth of that statement, with particular reference to the provision of what in the West is called 'dispute resolution'. Differently framed, it will seek to show the inherent weaknesses in the way lawfare is conducted in ungoverned space at the 'operational level', look at how it has been done in the past and offer suggestions for further consideration as to how it might be done better in the future.

I argue here that the central idea of failed states is flawed. Afghanistan was regarded as a failed state from 1994 to 2001. Yet, as will be seen, thirteen years of state-building have rendered it (by one measure at least) the least governed society on earth.[15] However, even in Afghanistan, the problem was not that the country was 'ungoverned' (which it most certainly was not). For the international community, the problem was rather by whom it was governed.

The fear of ungoverned space is new. For over a century, the challenge of such places was seen as just that, a challenge, not as a source of existential fear of the ungoverned. Such ungoverned spaces, as Johnson pointed out above, are anything but ungoverned. The problem is that they are not governed by centralised government; instead, they exhibit a characteristic to which such central governments have an aversion, pluralism.

The challenge of pluralism

The perceived problem of having more than one legal or dispute resolution system in the same area, and perhaps one far removed in nature from the state system, is known as 'legal pluralism'. We briefly touched upon it in Chapter 1. Some theorists regarded 'legal centralism'—the idea that one, usually state law, 'is and should be the law of the state, uniform for all persons exclusive of all other law and administered by a single set of state institutions'—as a counterpoint to pluralism.[16] Others see legal centralism as 'a myth, an ideal, a claim, an illusion.'[17] As discussed in Chapter 1, the fact is that there are multiple sources of dispute resolution in all societies.

There is a vast amount of literature on the topic of legal pluralism, which is essentially considered to be a discrete field of the anthropology of law. However, it is only in the last decade that attention has been directed at its role in conflict and post-conflict situations. Yet while the term and the academic discourse are relatively recent, the study and practice of rule in pluralist society can be identified as far back as 1772. In that year, a regulation of the East India Company provided: 'In all suits regarding inheritance, marriage, caste and other religious usages and institutions, the laws of the Koran with respect to the mohamedans [*sic*] [etc.] shall be adhered to.'[18]

During the imperial period in India, from roughly the 1750s to the 1940s, in order to retain a modicum of order in colonial territories with apparently multiple sources of legal power, there was an awareness of the need to ensure that conflict was kept to a minimum. For over a century, there was extensive discourse and writing on how colonial administrators should deal with the challenges of what is now called 'customary law'.

In the colonial era, the imperial powers sought to maintain effective rule (or rule that was effective enough to maintain authority) over huge areas through the use of a small number of administrators with minimum effort in terms of the imposition of 'formal' judicial (or indeed other) governmental functions. Many of the lessons identified by such regimes as the British, French and Ottoman Empires have been forgotten in recent counterinsurgency campaigns, which have focused more on formal structures, at the expense of more effective 'light touch' informal provision. We will see the effects of this in Chapter 8.

The essence of the technique became known as 'indirect rule', which

> came to require that indigenous law [what might now be called 'customary law'] be discovered, written down and made available for implementation. The assumption was that 'native law' could be recorded as a set of rules about how social life should be ordered and then applied by magistrates in the settlement of disputes.[19]

This technique was used in almost all the areas of Africa and Asia governed by the British and the French.

The key work on 'indirect rule', written in the early twentieth century, was Frederick Lugard's *Dual Mandate*.[20] This book is a long discourse about the nature of the imperial task, particularly in Africa, based on a deep and long engagement as a colonial administrator—

mainly, but not exclusively, in West Africa.[21] Indirect rule, as outlined in the book, amounted to devolved authority at the political level.[22]

Lugard states that '[p]rinciples do not change, but their mode of application should vary with the customs, the traditions and the prejudices of each (administrative) unit.'[23] There has been much debate as to what jurisprudential or moral value should be placed on this approach. One highly regarded commentator characterises it thus: 'The "customary law" recognised in colonial legislation and applied in the new "native courts" was a tendentious montage. Insecurely linked to the past, it was a system supportive of colonial rule entrenching elders over juniors, men over women.'[24] While indirect rule was indeed a matter of ad hoc improvisation, it made 'a virtue of necessity'.[25] It was realised that there was simply no practicable alternative.

There are considerable dangers in overemphasising the British imperial experience or indeed its success. As senior World Bank official and academic commentator on development and law, Doug Porter, puts it, the Dual Mandate model of customary authority, with its inherent emphasis on the 'recognition' of local authority, 'constituted a single model of customary authority across Africa that mirrored images of traditional European monarchy and patriarchy.'[26] He points out that 'this model came to grief' when it encountered such fiercely autocephalous non-state societies such as the Yoruba and Ibo.

This may indeed be so. In addition, it was the case that unpalatable societal norms were entrenched and minorities subjugated—things that today are utterly unacceptable. However, what indirect rule also did (albeit drawing a virtue from necessity) was to maintain a modicum of control, and indeed retain a modicum of acceptability, so that insurgencies were not able to get the necessary purchase in terms of legitimacy to sustain themselves. For the subjects of these systems, the organically developed dispute resolution systems suited them, or perhaps more pragmatically, suited the interests that might otherwise be tempted into rebellion. The tension between quixotic maintenance of firmly held (if metropolitan) ideals and strategic objectives was almost always resolved in favour of the latter in the British imperial project. It is true, as sociologist Boaventura de Sousa Santos has said, that 'there is nothing inherently good, progressive or emancipatory about legal pluralism.'[27] Nonetheless, the same might be said of legal centralism. For the strategic purposes of fighting an insurgency—or indeed preventing insurgency, as the British and French colonial authorities wanted to do—the only question that mattered was 'does it work?'[28]

It was not only European imperial rulers who arrived at versions of indirect rule. In Ottoman Albania, particularly in the north, the customary law known as the Kanun Lekë Dukagjini was deeply embedded in the culture and society.[29] This system was founded on notions of honour and was similar to that found in contemporary Pashtun Afghanistan. There was a sense of Islamic polity, at least in those areas where Albanians were Muslim (by no means all of the country).[30] However, despite the largely hands-off rule of the Ottomans, they did take exception to the blood feud, which, according to some commentators, claimed up to 19 per cent of male deaths and certainly constituted the major single cause of death for young males.[31] But there was little that could be done about it. The tribes of northern Albania in particular were regarded as almost impossible to control. It was the same in Yemen, where notions of blood feud and revenge were far stronger than centralising Ottoman governance and law. The Ottoman form of governance in such places was minimalist. It relied on the co-optation of local elites. There were concerted efforts to eliminate the old ways of the Kanun during the reign of King Zog in the 1920s and 1930s, accompanied by the deployment of some Western police experts.[32] But this had little success. When the communist government took power in 1945, there was a largely successful effort, accompanied by extensive repression for many years, to extend the control of central government, including criminal legal jurisdiction, over the previously ungoverned space of Albania, particularly in the north of the country. It remains questionable whether the Albanian state has purchase there even today. I worked in Albania for several years, and even by the somewhat flexible standards of Albanian governance, the north of the country remains a serious problem.

In his survey of nineteenth-century Ottoman governance in Yemen, Thomas Kuehn relates how: 'Ottoman administrators came to insist that because of their 'backwardness' the locals had to be governed according to their customs and dispositions.'[33]

The Ottoman approach to ungoverned space was consequently very similar to the ideas implemented by British administrators. There are interesting cognates in the way that, after a long period of trial and error, Ethiopia has, for the moment at least, settled upon a system of de facto indirect rule, at least over much of its territory without significant negative consequences. The exception may be the difficult Somali Region.[34] This is an area described by one commentator as 'a shameful stain, the poison at the heart of the Horn of Africa.'[35] It has remained in a state of almost constant low-level insurgency for decades.

The ideas of indirect rule, then, are still very much alive. For them to succeed, in the words of a leading contemporary commentator on law and insurgency: 'The implicit bargain struck between the center and the communities is that the local actors recognize the authority of the central government and the central government grants the local actors considerable autonomy.'[36]

For that to occur in turn requires a relatively strong local polity, secure enough in its independence to ensure an adequate degree of obedience, and compliant enough with the centre to ensure minimum interference. It requires personnel who are intimately familiar with local norms and practices. This is particularly the case when those actors are themselves foreign. The exogenous ruler can himself become a cause of insurgency, which is the main problem in the Somali Region, for example, where there is a strong dislike of 'highlanders' who are Christian and Amharic-speaking rather than Muslim and Somali-speaking,

The politicals

The British and other colonial powers administered these policies through the locally appointed political officer. In the British and French cases, these men were carefully selected from an academic and often military elite.[37] On occasion, they might be picked from native leaders who had received a Western education.[38]

In his work on contemporary interventions, Rory Stewart counterpoints the experience of today's inheritors of the tradition of the 'politicals' of the Indian civil service. He relates the career of John Lawrence. Having studied Indian languages and literature in India for three years, he was given his first posting in the service—to Delhi, where he served for sixteen years. 'He spent that posting taking measurements in agricultural fields and hearing domestic court cases in local languages.'[39] His next fourteen years were spent in the Punjab, involved in all matters of governance. His bailiwick included the 'frontier'. 'He came from a system whose career structure repeatedly rewarded experience in country and promoted people who had served in remote posts and displayed detailed knowledge of specific cultures.' Lawrence was by no means an isolated example.

Stewart contrasts such expertise with a contemporary equivalent he met in Afghanistan:

> He, like most international civilians, was an expert in fields that hardly existed as recently as the 1950s, and which are hardly household names today: Governance, gender, conflict resolution, civil society, and public administration. They were not experts on gender and governance in Afghanistan; they were experts in gender and governance in the abstract. They had studied 'lessons learned' by their colleagues in other countries and were aware of international 'best practice'.[40]

There is a risk of orientalism. It has been alleged that the views of some historians on the prowess and efficacy of the 'politicals' have been clouded by established views. The military historian and sceptic of any notion of a consistent theory of counterinsurgency, Douglas Porch, suggests that the knowledge of many of these politicals amounted to 'parachute expertise', applying imported imperial 'best practices', which generally consisted of alternating between bribes and severe repression, rather than being grounded in true cultural fluency.[41] This is corroborated to some extent by Christian Tripodi, arguably the leading scholar on the history of the politicals on the North West Frontiers of India.[42] None of the much-trumpeted 'cultural fluency' exonerates the politicals of the charge that their actions often in fact amounted to 'imposing incomprehensible decisions on the locals behind an imaginary facade of cultural knowledge'. The same applied, he says, to the French 'bureaux Arabes', who were working under similar doctrines to the British in their North African possessions.[43]

According to Porch, 'Knowing the country might translate into nothing more than superficial platitudes that more or less mirrored the racism and integral nationalism of the age.'[44]

As Porch concedes, though, the aim and purpose of the politicals was, in essence, not to act as exemplars of culturally assimilated experts or anthropologists of their day, but to 'keep a lid' on violence and disruption.[45] There can be little doubt that they tended to succeed in that aim, at least at the tactical level. It should also be said that their cultural expertise was not intended to work only one way. Many of them, indeed the great majority, were former army officers, and part of the trouble they often had with their former military colleagues was in mediating the ways of the British and British Indian armies to the 'natives'. The same applied vice versa, it must be said. In other words, their cultural knowledge of their own side—with its limits and advantages—was at least as important as the (admittedly often somewhat romanticised) expertise concerning 'their' tribes. Porch's criticisms have force, but perhaps while others have romanticised the role of the politicals, there is little benefit to be derived from denigrating what were (as few could deny—not even Porch) highly qualified men, expert in their fields.

One such was the original 'hearts and minds' advocate, a man who had lived most of his life in Victorian India: Robert Sandeman.[46] During his time as District Officer and subsequently Chief Commissioner (a role very similar to Regional Governor), he extended the rule—or, to be precise, influence—of the Raj into Baluchistan. The technique he developed became known as the 'Forward Policy'. Previously, this had been somewhat discredited after the disastrous defeat of the British Army in the defiles between the Khyber Pass and Kabul in 1842. Sandeman devised a more subtle way of extending and maintaining control. Using a judicious combination of pay-offs and occasionally force, he extended British rule deep into Baluchistan, rejecting entirely the old attitude of the 'Close Border', which meant defending only the borders and making no effort to extend either them or British influence. Nowadays, the method of rule might be described as 'soft touch', as there was little attempt to supplant local governance or laws. Sandeman took the view that British interests and secure borders depended more on ensuring friendly neighbours than on threatening neutral or hostile ones, and conquest by military force was simply not going to achieve that.

The Sandeman system seemed simple:

You made friends with the tribes, you dealt with them through their chiefs, you paid tribesmen to patrol your communications, you adhered to tribal custom and settled disputes by *jirgas* and not through law courts. You tried to solve all problems peacefully, but you kept an effective military force ready and visible; and from time to time you extended your control by the construction of roads and forts.[47]

Olaf Caroe, another British political officer, once claimed that 'The Raj ticked because on the whole the people recognised the administration liked the people.'[48] While now that claim may seem somewhat simplistic and perhaps even quixotic, it was based on many decades of hard-earned experience. One aspect of Porch's criticism does, however, hit home and has resonance today, when matters of intelligence and their application to Afghanistan in particular are concerned:

As the Raj grew, information became mangled, fragmented, dated, increasingly esoteric and useless as it passed through congealed layers of bureaucracy. While the Mughals [the previous ruling dynasty in India] had used information to inform power, exercise moral suasion and increase legitimacy, the British operationalised it in the police and army.[49]

In other words, damagingly, intelligence began to be seen as a matter relevant primarily to day-to-day security rather than a longer-sighted strategy. The importance of wider knowledge and awareness was under-prioritised and continues to be under-prioritised.[50]

Colonial legal solutions

In some ways, the foregoing discussion is concerned at least as much with governance as it is with lawfare. That experience of the politicals fed into profoundly informed debate on how 'indirect' the British policies should be. This debate, of which Lugard's *Dual Mandate* was an African expression, was especially fierce around the borders with Afghanistan. Much of this was occasioned by the legal means by which the Pashtun people govern themselves, based on the code that defines them, the Pashtunwali. There was no role for the state in this code. It certainly did not accept the basic tenets of British or Western law, whose central pillar is that it is for the state, not the individual, to correct criminal wrongs. Pashtunwali sees no role whatsoever for the state.

The Raj dealt with this in legal terms: not by trying to impose an alien way of thought, but by accepting that it was not going to change and incorporating it into its own law, in the Frontier Crimes Regulations

(FCR), which allowed the tribes themselves to deal with crimes. This framework still exists today, albeit not without considerable controversy. The cultural supremacism we see today in the form of legal centralism was, to all practical purposes, virtually absent.

The FCR went through several iterations (in 1873 and 1876) before being redrafted in 1947, prior to the independence of India and Pakistan. As matters stand, constitutionally the president of Pakistan has direct executive authority, which is exercised though political agents, direct successors of the political officers of the Raj.[51] Indeed, the agents were directly subordinate to the very few political officers. At the time of the Raj, the agents were almost always ethnically Indian (although most of them were from what is now Pakistan). This ensured a relatively smooth transition of authority in the tribal areas.

The FCR comprise lengthy and complex provisions, but may be summarised as permitting tribal authorities in tribal areas bordering Afghanistan to dispense justice in what outsiders would call criminal matters in a manner that those across the border and working for the international community would call 'informal'.[52] Because there is no separate category of 'crime' in Pashtunwali, the FCR rules often adjudicate in other disputes as well, by way of *jirga* [tribal council]. This is to say by means of *jirgas*. Those decisions are reported to the political agent for validation and approval. The FCR are the subject of constant criticism by Pakistani courts and NGOs for their failure to conform to any notion, national or international, of human rights standards.[53] This has been the case for decades.[54] For present purposes, what the FCR do is allow government to ensure some form of oversight in territories that have defied such oversight for centuries and continue to defy it today in Afghanistan.

Two points arise out of the FCR and their application. First, they are founded on well over a century of negotiation, both literal and military, learned discussion and debate, and hard practical experience. This system is not burdened by any difficulty arising out of what legal development practitioner Thomas Carothers has termed the 'problem of knowledge'—a misunderstanding as to the basic legal infrastructure.[55] However beset they may be by other problems concerning human rights, the FCR have been shown to function.[56]

This somewhat basic discussion of pre-1947 British practices on the North West Frontier of the empire has two purposes. First, it illustrates a central argument of this book, namely that dispute resolution is fundamental to governance. The primary role of the political was to mediate disputes. The central debate of the Frontier—'forward' versus 'close' policies—revolved around how governance should be exercised. The solution arrived at was what amounted to a modified 'close' policy, for the simple reason that it proved impossible to extend state structures, beginning with courts, to those frontier areas.[57] The only part of the Sandeman system in Baluchistan that did not comfortably translate to the Pashtun lands was the gradual extension of forts and military infrastructure.

Similar approaches were taken to the continuation of indigenous legal practices throughout the British imperial project. In Sudan, for example, the analogue to the FCR was the Chiefs Courts Ordinance of 1931.[58]

This followed the Civil Justice Ordinance (1929), which had similar effect. Rather than attempting the task of imposing a 'state' legal model, it accepted the authority of the Customary Courts of Sudan. There was a qualification to this acceptance: 'The Chiefs' Court shall administer the Native Law and Customs prevailing in the area over which the Court exercises its jurisdiction provided that such Native Law and Custom is not contrary to justice, morality or order.'[59]

The Chiefs Courts Ordinance was 'the most important legal milestone in Sudanese history in the North as well as the South', setting the tone for the approach to be taken in all parts of Sudan.[60] Although repealed in 1977, after Sudanese independence, the central importance of customary law was recognised by the People's Local Courts Act (1977). In South Sudan, the 1929 Civil Justice Ordinance was absorbed in its essence into the New South Sudanese legal system with the introduction of the Local Government Act (2009), which codifies the role and function of customary courts.[61] At the time of the British occupation of Sudan, there was no significant resistance after 1900, and therefore little or nothing in the way of insurgency. It is argued here that the fact that there was no attempt to impose state forms of justice and governance on a society that centred on customary justice may have played a role in ensuring that there was no such insurgency, as the added *casus belli* of imposed rule was not present. To that extent, what was in fact an exogenous government could credibly take the form of an endogenous one. As anthropologist of law Simon Roberts puts it:

'What was perhaps distinctive of the British colonial project was the concurrent imagination and reconstruction abroad of a metropolitan legal order *and* the making of explicit arrangements for the qualified survival of local governmental arrangements and normative orders.'[62]

South Sudanese academic Francis Deng has observed that the years since British rule ended have brought incremental Islamisation, civil war and intense, continuing conflict. Nonetheless, the legacy of the Sudanese version of the Dual Mandate in the south of the country remains strong.[63] He quotes a senior South Sudanese judge, Biong Mijak Deng: 'The first colonialists—the British—were to some extent more lenient, merciful and sympathetic to our traditions than our second colonialists—the Arab, Muslim minority clique based in the capital Khartoum. I for one thank the British for protecting our culture, identity and customs.'[64] That statement is clearly rather loaded with presumptions and the legacy of recent conflict. However, Deng makes it very clear that customary law in Southern Sudan has retained a strong influence in the country, despite the years of conflict.

From the above, it may be clear that developing and operating such a legal or judicial strategy requires a fairly deep knowledge of the environment in which the insurgency is taking place. This might be characterised in military terms as 'intelligence preparation of the battlespace'. This is exactly the form of knowledge possessed by many of the politicals of the British imperial effort. The case being made in this chapter is not a moral defence of colonial Dual Mandate thinking. Nor does it advocate a particularly positive approach to the imperial legacy. Rather, it aspires to demonstrate that in some areas the Dual Mandate approach, as adopted in various forms by governors of ungoverned space, acted as a means of preventing insurgency, and indeed as a counterinsurgency weapon, devolving as it did a great degree of practical authority to deeply embedded and arguably legitimate institutions.[65] The exercise of such authority would be far more likely to fit any notion of 'fair procedure' than an imposed system.

Notwithstanding Porch's points outlined above, it is true that many advisors or politicals, at least when compared with those deployed on today's operations, were knowledgeable and aware of the environment within which they worked and their approaches represented a real effort to innovate and adapt to their environments. However, a case can be made that Stewart's complaint about the supposed 'generic' knowledge of current 'experts' might also be relevant to imperial administrators.

In his study of the British experience in administering Iraq in the early twentieth century, *Inventing Iraq*, Toby Dodge expresses great reservations about the capabilities of such administrators: 'Inserted into an unfamiliar society and charged with building the institutions of a modern state, British colonial officials had little choice but to strive to understand Iraq in terms that were familiar to them.'[66]

What is particularly interesting about this observation is that it might almost have been made about contemporary stabilisation officers and officials. Dodge's point is that many of the colonial officers carried their experience of India with them to Iraq: 'The general influence of colonial India on those serving in Iraq is hard to over-estimate.'[67] They did so, Dodge argues, with extremely damaging effect, particularly with respect to the way they imported ideas and approaches concerning land tenure and law. As briefly noted in the previous chapter, this laid the foundation for problems in land tenure that persist to this day. Such experience as British Indian administrators had was no more applicable in post-Ottoman Mesopotamia than it was in Victorian Britain.

As observed above, other commentators have attacked the characterisation of these officers as highly effective operators. Nonetheless, the Pakistani, West African and Sudanese experiences tend to show that the solutions arrived at, admittedly after many decades of controversy, were and are sustained in their essence at the very least to some extent today. Why this may be is beyond the remit of this book; however, though as individuals these officials may have had their faults, at least the corporate knowledge of the institutions they served was very great. Furthermore, there was clearly an element of trial and error that took place over many decades in all imperial possessions, and this institutional learning fed into the legal approach taken to support the aims of the missions. This applies particularly in areas where the counterinsurgents are of the same nationality and background as the insurgents.

7

TWENTIETH-CENTURY COUNTERINSURGENCY JUDICIAL STRATEGY

THE BRITISH EXPERIENCE

In his *War and Law*, David Kennedy describes war as a 'legal institution'.[1] By that, he means that the conduct of war and war itself take place in a legal environment: 'Law itself may also be an instrument of policy, on a continuum with war—different means to the same end.'[2] The conduct of war is heavily regulated, and law is a constant influence on participants in warfare. Jose Padilla, who is quoted in Chapter 5 above, makes the same point. It is that insight that informs this book: the idea that law itself and the practice thereof may play a part analogous and complementary to armed force—in other words, as another weapon in the arsenal of the combatants. It is this idea that forms the core of the concept of lawfare. The previous chapter looked at the lessons that were and indeed still are available from the nineteenth and early twentieth centuries to counterinsurgents engaged in attempts to deal with challenges to the state system. This chapter takes that forward and looks at how counterinsurgency theory—known as 'doctrine'—sees the use of courts and justice in insurgency. Given the foregoing, it is remarkable how little of the imperial experience seems to have been permitted to survive.

Orthodox counterinsurgency doctrine

Since the large-scale interventions in Iraq and Afghanistan, insurgency and its counterpart counterinsurgency (hereafter abbreviated to 'COIN') have been at the forefront of discussion of military matters. Many books have been written, websites set up, long-out-of-print texts about previously forgotten campaigns have again been sent to press and commentaries have been penned.[3] Very many PhD theses have been produced.

The entire corpus of US and UK counterinsurgency doctrine is concerned with insurgency in countries other than the UK or the United States. Insurgency is something that happens elsewhere.[4] There is little hint in either definition of military forces dealing with internal subversive violence such as the Northern Ireland campaign, which took thirty years to resolve. The predicate of both is that US and UK forces will be engaged in putting down, or helping put down, insurgencies that either arise from or are incidental to 'interventions'. This in turn is known as 'third-party' or 'exogenous' counterinsurgency.[5]

The approach any government takes to defeat an insurgency depends on the character of that government. However, as commonly understood, the term counterinsurgency has developed something of the nature of a doctrine based around the extensive literature on what might be termed 'population-centred counterinsurgency'.

It has been claimed that 'about 80 per cent of all conflicts since the end of the Napoleonic era have been insurgencies or civil wars.'[6] There have certainly been a great many 'savage wars of peace', a term coined by Rudyard Kipling, incidentally, in his poem 'The White Man's Burden'.[7] Counterinsurgency expert David Kilcullen points out that:

> that most of these conflicts involved what would now be called guerrilla conflict, stability operations and post-conflict nation building. since the mid-19th century, in fact, the United States has been drawn into literally dozens of small wars and irregular operations.[8]

British doctrine

Much of what has been called here 'orthodox' counterinsurgency doctrine is founded on supposed British successes in the wars of imperial retreat of the 1950s. It was in the 1950s that the British reinforced their reputation in fighting the wars that were to become known as insurgencies. One author has referred to this as the 'high period of British counterinsurgency'.[9] These campaigns took place as the British were withdrawing from empire. There was little room in them for the kind of approach outlined in the last chapter.

One scholar of British counterinsurgency, Colonel David Benest, says that 'there is no comparable history of counterinsurgency anywhere in the world to match that of the British record.'[10] If by 'comparable history' he means experience, there can be no doubt that this is true. But whether experience has translated into expertise and success is a different matter.[11] Until the recent campaigns in Iraq and Afghanistan, British expertise in such matters was taken for granted. As one of its own doctrinal documents put it, the British Army 'has much to teach a world increasingly challenged by the problem of internal war.'[12] Has it anything to teach about the application of law in the pursuit of legitimacy?

From the accession of Queen Victoria in 1837 to her death in 1901, the British Army fought no fewer than 250 campaigns, large and small.[13] Since the Second World War, Britain has fought a great many more wars: at least one credible study has suggested that it has fought more conflicts than any other country in the world.[14] As for the results, the British Army (like most professions) loves keeping score: in the post-war period, the British have been involved in no fewer than seventy military campaigns (by no means all of them wars) of varying sizes, eighteen of which may be classified as 'counterinsurgency' actions. The Army Staff College handbook on counter-revolutionary warfare gives the tally as seven successes, three partial successes, five failures and one draw (plus two more recent wars ongoing).[15] Many of these struggles were rebellions by people who did not wish to be ruled by the empire. 'So perverse is mankind that every nation prefers to be misgoverned by its own people than to be well ruled by another', as one of the empire's leading generals, Charles James Napier, put it.[16]

In the early twentieth century, the British fought dozens of small campaigns, with greater or lesser degrees of success. They developed techniques that were to become the keynote of a 'British way' of counterinsurgency. These ideas revolved around a strong degree of civil–military cooperation and respect for a basic level of rule of law. It was 'not the annihilation of an enemy but the suppression of a temporary disorder, and therefore the degree of force to be employed must be directed to that which is necessary to restore order and must never exceed it.'[17] In essence, this was 'minimum force'.[18] These ideas were developed further in the 1930s, with the publication of a range of books on suppressing rebellion, notably Charles Gwynn's *Imperial Policing* (1936) with its focus on minimum force, and H.J. Simson's *Rule and Rebellion in the British Empire* (1937), with rather more of a stress on the use of force and the enforcement of law.[19]

In his study of UK counterinsurgency doctrine, Colonel Alex Alderson reviews how the UK military framed its thinking over the century or so before the Iraq and Afghanistan wars of the early twenty-first century.[20] It is striking that there is a consistency of rhetoric concerning the requirement to comply with legal strictures in 'low-intensity' military operations. Alderson affirms that legitimacy and minimum necessary force 'are critical to the British approach to counterinsurgency and have underpinned it since *Duties in Aid of the Civil Power* was published in 1923.'[21] That publication was the first of several official or semi-official doctrinal guidance documents produced between the First and the Second World War.[22] All stressed minimum force, subordination to the civil power and the necessity of compliance with the law, all to ensure the maintenance of support and legitimacy.

Unfortunately, in none of the doctrinal documents or founding texts did there seem to be an indication of what legitimacy actually meant. Even in the British doctrine that supposedly governed the operations of the early twenty-first century, the 2001 edition of 'Counter Insurgency Operations', as Alderson points out, 'legitimacy *per se* is not explained at all, neither is the need for British forces to safeguard their own legitimacy through their conduct, nor the evident problems of maintaining, if not re-building legitimacy faced by a government dealing with an insurgency.'[23]

There has been extensive questioning of the extent to which there was in fact any working system of transmission of doctrine in the UK's 'small wars'.[24] If in fact doctrine was not consulted, and instead there was a rather more informal transmission of 'institutional knowledge' of the kind promulgated by John Nagl in his *Learning to Eat Soup with a Knife*, it might be asked whether the many writings on British counterinsurgency doctrine could be characterised more as rhetoric than as guidance. In a study of recent military campaigns, *British Generals in Blair's Wars*, Hew Strachan points out that 'doctrine may exist, but that does not mean that it is read.'[25]

In his study of British counterinsurgency doctrine Alderson identifies only rare and fleeting mentions of justice in UK military doctrine before its recent redrafting.[26] As part of what he calls the 'expanding torrent' of realisation that fighting insurgency might require cogent doctrine going beyond the fighting of insurgents, he identifies the 1969 edition of the British Army's *Counter-Revolutionary Operations* as an indicator that the complexity of the insurgency problem was being realised and considered. Unfortunately, the 'justice sector' is aligned in importance with freedom of expression, religion and amnesty plans.[27]

The British Army Field Manual Volume 1 Part 10, better known as *Countering Insurgency*, is reluctant to address justice in any more than terms that are of little practical consequence. Although an entire chapter is devoted to 'counterinsurgency and the law', most of that chapter deals, rightly, with the basis for intervention (*ius ad bellum*), status of forces agreements, and domestic frameworks.[28] The bulk of the chapter is concerned with the laws and rules of war, such as those relating to the use of force,[29] rules of engagement,[30] types of armed conflict,[31] discipline and detention,[32] and the questioning of prisoners.[33] Internal matters such as the duties of a military legal advisor (LEGAD) take up most of the rest of the chapter.[34] There is a short paragraph on 'rule of law'—but it is of no practical use in terms of the expression of any awareness of the importance of justice.[35] A mere nod is given to analysing 'the perceptions and experiences of local people, particularly the poor, women and marginalised groups'. In practice, no LEGAD will ever analyse anything of that nature. There are few LEGADs on operations who have the time for such matters, or indeed the experience to undertake them.[36]

Another 'doctrinal' document, this one directed at civilian development, JDP 3–40 *Security and Stabilisation: The Military Contribution*, is a substantial document.[37] It displays an awareness of the dangers attendant upon allowing insurgents to grab the initiative in the justice sector. Indeed, it quotes an article written by the present author concerning Taliban courts and the effective competition they offer to corrupt state systems.[38] The manual takes a realistic approach to justice reform, recommending that government efforts should focus on building on existing systems, rather than on inventing new and probably impracticable (not to say inappropriate) structures: 'By building on existing structures, the expansion of governance is more likely to succeed than a system imposed by outsiders.'[39]

With the exception of the UK's JDP on stability operations, there is no mention in the tactical doctrine of the pragmatic necessity of addressing the reality of existing systems and of reflecting on any threat they might present to the mission. One overriding principle—familiar to anyone in any field of international assistance, or indeed any doctor—is (or should be) 'do no harm'. For aid workers, this precept is absolutely central. That 'doing no harm' is a lesson to be drawn from history is explicitly stated in a short but excellent account of British counterinsurgency practice written to supplement JDP 3–40 for the Ministry of Defence by retired Colonel Michael Crawshaw.[40]

COIN (the shorthand used for 'population-centred counterinsurgency') methods are predicated on the idea, now called the 'population-centred approach', that the 'people are the prize'—as if they are the subject of a sporting contest.[41] They are, of course, not a 'prize', inert and without autonomy; they are the environment within which, by definition, 'wars among the people' take place. They live and breathe and have their being. They are dynamic agents. This was one of the central notions behind the Dual Mandate outlined above. Taking the perspective of a COIN advocate, albeit within a contemporary framework, Kilcullen sees the 'people' as manipulators of the counterinsurgent:

> We think of the population as lacking in agency … nothing could be further from the truth; not only are non-combatant civilians in these environments extremely active and highly influential, but they are in many cases masters of manipulation and experts in leveraging the presence of rich, ignorant and gullible outsiders in order to get what they need, outsmart their rivals and survive another day.[42]

This is entirely right. Yet the 'people' are curiously absent from much formal military and academic discourse on insurgency, save as an abstract entity or as 'extras'. This is crucial when matters of justice are concerned—and particularly judicial systems that may not accord with Western paradigms.

Kitson's dilemma

In a seminal essay on lawfare and counterinsurgency, Thomas B. Nachbar questions whether the law, or mechanisms of justice, can be used by counterinsurgents to promote legitimacy, or whether it will necessarily be perceived as unfair and will thereby undermine legitimacy.[43]

In his *Low Intensity Operations*, a work written during a sabbatical from military service at Oxford University in 1970 that synthesised his experiences into what amounted to a doctrinal treatise, General Frank Kitson looks at the dilemmas presented by the use of justice as a weapon:

> Broadly there are two possible alternatives, the first one being that the law should be used as just another weapon in the government's arsenal and in this case it becomes little more than a propaganda cover for the disposal of unwanted members of the public. For this to happen efficiently, the activities of the legal services have to be tied into the war as discreetly as possible … the alternative is that the law should remain impartial and administer the laws of the country without any direction from the government.[44]

For governments concerned with the conduct of operations within a legal framework, this is an exceedingly difficult balance to strike. As will be seen below, Kitson's dilemma was extremely familiar to those closely involved in counterinsurgency operations in the 1950s.[45] David French quotes the assistant secretary at the Colonial Office with responsibility for Palestine in 1946:

> The plain truth to which we firmly shut our eyes is that in this emergency Regulation Detention Business [essentially authorising arbitrary arrest and detention] we are taking a leaf out of the Nazi book, following the familiar error that the end justifies the means (especially when the means serve current expediency).[46]

This line of argument is perennial, especially in times of stress or perceived stress. There is a long line of legal decisions dealing with this issue. The most famous of these judgements was delivered by Lord Atkin in 1941, in the case of *Liversidge* v. *Anderson*, with the often-quoted lines:

> In England amidst the clash of arms the laws are not silent. They may be changed, but they speak the same language in war as in peace. It has always been one of the pillars of freedom, one of the principles of liberty for

which we are now fighting, that the judges ... stand between the subject and any attempted encroachments on his liberty by the executive, alert to see that any coercive action is justified in law.[47]

What is rather less well known is that Lord Atkins was in the minority in the case concerned; the majority judgement of the court went against him. More recently, Israeli Supreme Court Judge Haim Cohen summarised a similar point for Israel:

> What distinguishes the war of the State from the war of its enemies is that the State fights while upholding the law, whereas its enemies fight while violating the law. ... There is no weapon more moral than the rule of law. Everyone who ought to know should be aware that the rule of law in Israel will never succumb to the state's enemies.[48]

As an instructive example of the tensions inherent in the dilemmas facing a fully engaged counterinsurgent state, we turn now to the approach taken by the British in the 'high period' of counterinsurgency, during the withdrawal from empire.

The 'classic period' of counterinsurgency

The British withdrawal from its global empire with its many 'small wars' rarely involved the imposition of martial law (i.e. rule by military authorities.) The sources of the British approach to legislation in insurgency may be found in the idea that while 'British domestic law did not recognise a state of siege, British Colonial Law did.'[49] Rather than institute states of martial law, the British colonial powers, and indeed (as will be seen) eventually the domestic government in Northern Ireland, developed a system of 'emergency powers'.

French has looked closely at the legal framework behind Malaya, and indeed Kenya and Cyprus. He identifies a 'pyramid of committees' as the chosen mechanism.[50] He points out that the legal basis upon which most of the actions described above were taken was the Emergency Powers Order in Council (1939), which granted colonial officials very wide latitude of action. Although, between the wars, the British had relied upon what amounted to martial law, during the 1930s, partly as a result of events in Palestine, there was an extended shift towards moving judicial authority closer to civilian control in the form of so-called emergency regulations.[51] This culminated in the Emergency

Powers Act (1945), which itself evolved out of a long line of Orders in Council that largely dealt with the insurgencies in Palestine in the 1930s.[52] The situation was later summarised by the governor general of Malaya, Sir Henry Gurney: 'In Palestine ... the Emergency Regulations were continually being added to and tightened up, so that at the end it might almost have been said that the whole book of regulations could have been expressed in a simple provision empowering the High Commissioner to take any action he wished.'[53]

While delegating all power to the discretion of the high commissioner may have been lawful in the strictest sense, it can hardly—at least by today's standards—be described as in accordance with the rule of law.

The Emergency Powers Act (1945) itself derived from a 1939 Order in Council, which provided for a colonial governor to enact measures that might well be regarded as arbitrary and oppressive. In cases of 'public emergency':[54]

'The Governor may make such Regulations as appear to him to be necessary or expedient for securing the public safety...'[55]

There then follows a list of actions that may have to be considered, including detention and expulsion of suspects, sequestration of property, summary suspension or indeed application of any law, and the trial and punishment of offenders.[56] Such powers could be delegated to any person by the governor of the colony, and such powers as were declared in force were not to be restrained by pre-existing legislation.[57]

Rather than rule of law, this may be described as an example of arbitrary rule, and the point was appreciated at the time. There was considerable discomfort expressed about these provisions. For example, it was suggested that the existence of the original enabling 1939 Order in Council should be kept secret.[58] Indeed, the fact that the enabling instrument (which is passed by the Privy Council and does not require parliamentary approval or even scrutiny) was an Order in Council rather than a statute in 1939 says something about such unease.[59] This discomfort clearly subsisted after the war, when the provisions were placed on a statutory basis. In a 1950 note by Arthur Creech Jones, the colonial secretary, clear reluctance is expressed about the propriety of introducing emergency powers: 'I must emphasize the necessity of adhering as far as possible at which an emergency has to be declared, to the normal principles of English Law by which the rights and liberties of the individuals are maintained.'[60]

In using these provisions, versions of which were brought into force in all Britain's counterinsurgency operations of the 1950s, it could easily be argued that any semblance to the rule of law was thereby removed.

One of the founding documents of the idea of British counterinsurgency is *Defeating Communist Insurgency* (1966) by the former minister of defence of the Malay Federation during the 'Emergency' Robert Thompson.[61] In one of his often-quoted precepts of counterinsurgency, Thompson comments that: 'The government must function in accordance with law'.[62] Thompson's views concerning the importance of adherence to the law and the consequences of failure to do so are very clear: 'If the government does not adhere to the law then it loses respect and fails to fulfil its contractual obligation to the people as a government.'[63]

This message is as relevant today as it was in the 1950s. After his time as minister of defence in Malaya, Thompson spent some years in Vietnam as an advisor to the United States. He recalls: 'I remember saying to General Khanh, then Prime Minister to Vietnam, that when I heard of a case of a peasant suing the government for a buffalo killed by the army during operations and being paid compensation, we would be winning the war.'[64]

Thompson is less insistent on the necessity for security forces to be accountable for their actions, but the point is made.[65]

Strategy, narrative and legal legacies

There were great differences between the British counterinsurgency campaigns. In Malaya, there was a clear strategy that evolved from well-defined political directives. At the outset of his time in Malaya, the High Commissioner General Gerald Templer made it abundantly clear that he required guidance from government, specifically Winston Churchill (the prime minister of the day), as to exactly what the strategic objective was: 'I am not at all clear as to what [the UK government] is aiming at from the political point of view … I must have a clear policy to work on.'[66]

Templer received a detailed and clear reply in the terms he had requested, outlining the policy of the government for the development of a Malay nation, with full citizenship, 'partnership' and democracy for all its races.[67] This required the defeat of communist 'terrorism' and a 'worthy and continuing British involvement in the life of the country'. This constitutes what would now be called a 'desired end-state'. The commitment to independence bled any form of legitimacy from the Malayan Races Liberation Army, beyond its appeal to those of a Marxist inclination. At an early stage in the campaign, there was a strong insistence that 'the civil courts functioned ... although we were of course at the time introducing all the emergency regulations and so on, most of which were very tough ... all crimes would go through the civil courts.'[68] This was the key point from the perspective of the ideas expressed in this book; *there was a judicial strategy.*

The framework in which these courts operated is of crucial importance, as it marks the difference between what were essentially formally 'civil' courts and courts that in fact operated as arms of the security forces. This is of far more than conceptual or theoretical importance, as it plays into legitimacy.

As David French points out, the fact that the British very much tended towards security and away from basic human rights is painful for those, such as Thompson, who stress the need for counterinsurgency to remain within legal boundaries. The truth is that there is no doubt whatsoever that had the methods employed by the British in Malaya or Kenya been employed in Europe at any point over the past sixty years, they would be characterised as deeply oppressive, howsoever backed up by 'legislative' provisions. Indeed, in more recent years, the 'enormous resettlement programme' in Malaya would simply be labelled as 'ethnic cleansing', as would the activities authorised under emergency powers in Kenya.

As French asks, 'if it is legal, was it also legitimate?'[69] This distinction between legal and legitimate is a trope that plays out in many (or perhaps even most) insurgencies. Despite the relatively liberal approach in Malaya (relative to Kenya), the fact remains that the use of emergency powers amounted to a gap between the British rhetoric of remaining under the rule of law and the reality, which was far more than, as Strachan has put it, 'the firm smack of government'.[70] In terms of rule of law, it is instructive that the UK entered what are termed 'reservations' to relevant human rights instruments, specifically the Geneva

Convention Article 68, forbidding the execution of civilians by military courts. Indeed, the 1949 Geneva Conventions were not ratified by the UK until 1957.[71]

Recognition of, and obedience to, law—the nearest approximation to the practical demonstration of loyalty (as we saw from the writings of Tyler in Chapter 1)—derives at least in part from the willingness of those people subject to a law to see that law and its enforcement as legitimate, rather than from their fear of what the law might do to them if they transgress. The subject will ask 'Is the procedure fair?' when assessing legitimacy. Enforced compliance is always possible, as several oppressive regimes have shown, even in insurgencies.[72] But this is not legitimacy, and is arguably unsustainable.

The various wars fought by the British against different resisting peoples have left a legacy, often of bitterness. This has certainly been the case in Kenya, where legal actions are still being taken by hundreds of Kenyans—to the continuing embarrassment of the British government, which has spent a great deal of time and money trying to suppress the records of misdoings.[73] Only one such case has been brought in Malaya, concerning the alleged massacre of rubber plantation workers by a unit of the British Army at Batang Kali in 1948.[74] The Batang Kali incident has carried forward to the twenty-first century and at the end of 2016, when this book was written, shows no sign of going away.[75]

In neither Malaya nor Kenya were the insurgencies the British faced sufficiently developed, and nor were those insurgencies allowed to develop sufficiently to put into operation their own competing systems of justice to challenge for legitimacy. In neither place did the British courts face any competition as working dispute resolution systems acting within a political sphere. There were no Malayan Peoples' Liberation Army (insurgent) courts as accepted arbiters of civil or criminal disputes, or at least there is no record of such courts. The same applies in Kenya. In both cases, the military campaign was against guerrillas who enjoyed no outside support, had little training and found themselves challenged by comparatively well-developed military systems and very hard pressed. In neither theatre was there space for an alternative or shadow government to grow and establish an alternative source of legitimacy. In Malaya, the foundations laid by the British colonial administration have provided the basis for Malaysian legal approaches: 'In many ways, the 1948–60 Emergency set the pattern not only for the conduct of future Emergencies but even in some respects for what became regular laws.'[76] This was as true in Palestine and its successor state, Israel, as it was in Malaya.[77] One might argue that the British judicial strategy in its approach to Palestine was the grandfather of Israel's today.

Counterinsurgent justice at home: The 'Diplock Courts'

The insurgencies of the 1950s were part of a general retreat from empire for all European colonial powers, including Britain. Far closer to home, another conflict, more ancient in character, had flared up again, with a civil rights movement in Northern Ireland being co-opted by insurgent groups, as a result of a combination of opportunism by those groups and serious misjudgements on the part of the British government. The British, in essence, faced a similar dilemma 'at home' in Northern Ireland as they did in their overseas insurgencies: namely whether to stick strictly to the law of the land or to do 'whatever works'. The problem with the latter approach was that, in the United Kingdom itself, the British authorities faced a far more developed legal and media ecosystem.

By 1972, the political and military situation in Northern Ireland had deteriorated to such an extent that direct control from London was imposed on Northern Ireland. Previously, the province had been governed by a government in Belfast that the predominantly Catholic minority Nationalist community regarded as sectarian. One of the first tasks of the new government was to reassess the effectiveness of the courts system. The highly controversial system of 'internment' had been introduced to offset the difficulties caused by gaining credible witness testimony. Accordingly, a commission headed by a leading judge, William Diplock, concluded that for certain 'scheduled offences' (connected with terrorism) the right to jury trial would be abolished.[78] Diplock summarised the risks as follows: 'The main obstacle to dealing effectively with terrorist crime in the regular courts of justice is intimidation by terrorist organisations of those persons who would be able to give evidence for the prosecution if they dared.'[79]

Due to the clear risks of intimidation of jury members within a highly charged political and military environment, it was 'therefore necessary to consider whether any changes can be made in criminal procedure which, while not conflicting with the requirements of a judicial process, would enable at least some cases at present dealt with by detention to be heard in courts of law.'[80] Certain 'scheduled offences should be [tried] by a Judge of the High Court, or a County Court Judge, sitting alone with no jury, with the usual rights of appeal.'[81]

Criticism of the new courts began as soon as the first announcement of the conclusions of the Diplock Commission.[82] To some extent, the establishment of the courts played into the hands of the insurgent IRA, and this was almost inevitable. The human rights implications of having state-appointed judges as deciders of fact were clear, and human rights organisations were equally clear in their condemnation.[83]

Though it is not at all clear what alternatives the British (or indeed Lord Diplock) had to establishing such courts, short of internment, from the strategic perspective the courts played well in the context of the IRA's 'Long War' strategy.[84] This aimed at making the province ungovernable except by what the IRA called 'Colonial Military Rule'. The way was clearly open for the IRA and its supporters, highly capable strategic communications operators, to make the claim that the Diplock Courts were essentially a quasi-colonial imposition; in so doing, they denied the Courts' legitimacy. To that extent, the IRA operated the rupture strategy initially advocated by Vergès in Algeria. In due course, the courts became a key stake in negotiations to end the conflict, and they were abolished in July 2007.[85]

In some ways, the Diplock Courts were 'cousins' of the courts of the various British counterinsurgency campaigns of the 1950s. They decided cases under what amounted to emergency regulations, although they themselves were not emergency tribunals as such (still less military tribunals). Arms of the state in one sense, they were to some extent instruments for 'the disposal of unwanted members of the public', as Kitson would have it. In one sense, that is the function of all criminal courts. The issue here is not one of function, but rather one of fairness.

There is no doubt that the courts played an essential role in providing some oversight for the activities of the security forces (as did the courts in Malaya), since there were many acquittals. Criticisms of the Diplock Courts equate the lack of a jury to a lack of fairness. But it is worth observing that most legal systems in the world function without juries, and often in a way that is accepted as fair by many of those subject to their jurisdiction. There is evidence that, in effect, if not in form, the Diplock Courts were essentially a hybrid of the adversarial (in that there were prosecution and defence lawyers playing highly active roles in the proceedings) and the inquisitorial (where the judge takes the leading role—the so-called 'civil' or 'continental' system).[86] As in those civil systems, judges took an active part in proceedings. It is also fair to say that there are few allegations from independent critics to be found of bias on the part of judges in such trials.

Whether or not the Diplock Courts did in fact offer due process and fair trials is of secondary importance. The problem they created was not necessarily that they were unfair, but that they were perceived to be unfair. As we saw in Chapter 1, there is considerable evidence to suggest that it is the perception of fairness that supports legitimacy, and that perception is itself fed by, and in turn feeds, a wider narrative. This in turn opened space for the state's opponents to dominate the narrative aspect of the legal battlefield and adopt what amounted to a rupture strategy. That it was not expressed as such is neither here nor there; this is what it was.

While it may be that the introduction of the Diplock Courts was to some extent inevitable, given the degree of jury intimidation, it is clear that the legitimacy of the state was undermined by the way in which emergency legislation cut into well-entrenched ideas of rule of law. Space was opened for nationalists to hold sway. Courts were seen by the 'target community'—the Nationalist Catholic community of Northern Ireland—not as independent safeguards of their rights, but as the arm of the state. Once again, this was rupture strategy in operation.

This was clearly the case in all of the theatres here, with the possible exception of Malaya. That is not to say that the courts in Malaya were not arms of the state, or that the courts in Northern Ireland were supine. Neither of these assertions is correct. In fact, despite perceptions, it can readily be argued that the Diplock Courts were not simply an inert arm of the executive, but a function of a democratic judiciary; the best that could be done in the circumstances. However, that was not the perception; and in counterinsurgency, as current doctrine has it, perception is (almost) all.

8

COUNTERINSURGENT JUDICIAL STRATEGY TODAY

'And most difficult of all they came armed with laws and regulations which had not necessarily any relevance whatever to the standards by which a Pathan society lived.'[1]

The last two chapters looked at the experience of one counterinsurgent state, the United Kingdom, summarising the extensive doctrines, strategies, controversies that applied to its various conflicts. This chapter will show that none of that was consulted or considered in any way relevant when the UK began its counterinsurgent operations in southern Afghanistan. Much of that experience was admittedly irrelevant, as with almost all theory in connection with conflict, and particularly insurgencies, it is contingent on circumstance. General rules are thin on the ground. Malaya and Northern Ireland were often taken to demonstrate that without further effort British expertise in counterinsurgency was world-leading. This idea was comprehensively knocked down in Iraq, where the UK's contribution to any civilian role in its area of operations in Basra was nugatory. It was knocked out in Helmand, where there was an extensive civilian effort.

Chapter 4 looked at the Taliban's judicial strategy and the extent to which it appealed to Afghans. To a very great degree, this was due to the nature of the Afghan government. As Sarah Chayes is quoted as saying in Chapter 2, the Afghan state, which the international mission

was in the country to protect, was little more than a 'vertically integrated organised crime organisation.' A mafia, in other words. The
extent to which the mission in Afghanistan was bereft of a judicial
strategy (some may argue any kind of strategy) might be illustrated by
a short vignette. In mid-2007, I was appointed by the British government to be the first justice advisor for the UK mission in Helmand—
Provincial Reconstruction Team (PRT). Much of this chapter explicitly
draws from the UK experience in Helmand. It must be remembered
that there were thirty-two PRT's, each run by a different country, each
with different priorities, and few if any of them paid the slightest
regard to the Afghan central government. The UK PRT had a well-
developed and funded justice programme. It must be remembered
though that it was not the only one. That said, it is worth reiterating
that there was no national justice strategy being applied.

I had several briefings before deployment, some being more useful
than others. The most senior official to speak to me was high up in the
Cabinet Office, and I saw him in his plush office overlooking Downing
Street in the heart of London's government district. I asked for some
guidance on the approach the government expected to be applied to
justice in Helmand. Was there to be a focus on traditional systems, customary law or indeed the state system? His answer was brief but to the
point: 'Your job is to offer the people of Helmand a better deal.' Excellent
advice as far as it went. The problem was that I had never been to
Afghanistan, spoke none of the languages and had but the haziest idea of
how justice was provided in the country. I was far from alone in that,
which brings us to the first problem of contemporary counterinsurgency
judicial strategic reality. The 'problem of knowledge'.

Rule of law and the problem of knowledge

Countering the work of insurgent justice is now essentially a civil role.
The nature of courts and the enforcement of law should not and does
not fall within military duties or military expertise. We saw in the last
chapter that there is a strong body of thinking and practice in the provision of judicial services by counterinsurgents. Today, however, the field
is dominated by ideas of 'rule of law development'. A key problem is
that ideas developed to assist peaceful construction of state-centric

systems may not be appropriate for suppressing or undercutting insurgencies in highly fractious states with strong traditions of pluralism.

Rule of law development was a well-funded and fashionable development activity from the 1970s to the 1990s, with much work done particularly in Latin America. It was with the fall of the Soviet Union and the consequent opening up of the former satellite states of Eastern Europe that the field really began to expand. In some ways, the golden age of rule of law development was the 1990s. During this period, there was a rapid evolution of ideas as it became clear to many practitioners that simply transposing apparently successful Western systems on to evidently unsuccessful 'eastern' justice systems was not working. Even in countries with strong European legal traditions, it became clear that there was more to this task than cutting and pasting constitutions or, even worse, systems of litigation and justice. It was, in fact, entirely analogous to transplanting organs without troubling to assess such matters as blood group.

In the former Soviet Union itself, this idea of simple transplant caused lasting damage, with US-style property systems, ultimately derived from medieval English landlord and tenant law, being applied in Russia, a country itself with a legal tradition equal to any other. As experience began to grow in the late 1990s, a more nuanced attitude began to take root, with far more attention being paid to the traditions of the countries themselves. The idea of the 'cookie-cutter approach', applied to Russia for example, as an actively destructive mechanism began to take hold. Rule of law justice development providers 'do not have much interest in non-Western forms of law, in traditional systems of justice, or, in the case of some American rule of law experts, even in civil law.' The result is the 'cookie cutter syndrome'—a 'breathtakingly mechanistic approach involving drafting, construction and training'.[2] In recent interventions, matters have not improved: 'practices ... have come to have an almost template-like quality'.[3]

One of the leading theorists and practitioners of rule of law development is Thomas Carothers, who took the view that 'law is not just the sum of courts, legislatures, police, prosecutions and other formal institutions with some direct connection to law'; it is also a 'normative system that resides in the minds of the citizens of a society.'[4] This is as true, incidentally, in the United Kingdom as it is in Afghanistan. It is surely the case that most disputes are resolved before they ever get near the courts, through negotiation or compromise.

Fashions in 'rule of law'

In a 1998 essay in *Foreign Affairs*, Carothers observed: 'One cannot get through a foreign policy debate these days without someone proposing the "rule of law" as a solution to the world's problems.'[5] Yet over the decades it has become very clear that there is little agreement on what 'rule of law' is, although there has been rather more, paradoxically, on how it should be imposed. What 'rule of law' is and its rationale depends to a large degree on who you are. For those who place stress on commercial development, particularly market advocates, rule of law must promote market ideals, such as sanctity of contract and property. One leading advocate of this is Peruvian activist Hernando De Soto: 'Simply put, formal law is the foundation of the market system, essential to the development of corporations, limited liability contracts and an adequate business environment.'[6] It has 'become a new credo in the development field that if developing and post-communist countries wish to succeed economically they must develop the rule of law.'[7]

For human rights activists, rule of law is necessary and should be founded on the basic principles to which most Western societies are contracted. This approach focuses on the need for due process, equality before the law, accountability, and so on. The focus for human rights advocates is safeguards against executive power.

There is another perspective, in no way recent: what might now be called the 'security' perspective. Within counterinsurgency operations, this is usually packaged under the catch-all shibboleth of 'security sector reform', within which 'rule of law development' is, in practice, subverted to the extent that police and security apparatuses are given the preponderance of attention, often at the expense of the mechanisms necessary to make those apparatuses work in a way consistent with traditional counterinsurgency principles. For example, when I was sent to Helmand as justice advisor while it was under a 'rule of law' flag, the funding and strategic approach, insofar as there was a strategic approach, came from the counter-narcotics programme.

Most rule of law specialists are lawyers. The significance of this is that 'lawyers often have relatively formalistic views of legal change and are slow to take up the developmental, process-oriented issues that have come to inform work in other areas of socioeconomic or sociopolitical change.' The assumption among lawyers newly involved in the field, understandably perhaps, has been that 'if we build it they will come'.[8] Carothers coined the phrase 'problem of knowledge', and identified several ingredients that would ensure the failure of rule of law development to meet its objectives.[9]

First, there is the inherent complexity of rule of law development itself. In any society, the theory and practice of law and legality, or of the settlement of disputes, is intensely complex. That complexity is all the greater when the requirement is to attempt to reform the rule of law—or, as we will see in Afghanistan, to create it in another country. This is the essence of the closely related second problem: the particularity of legal systems, in that most mature systems have evolved organically over many years, sometimes centuries. Such evolution cannot be replicated in a few years.[10]

Third, there is an acute problem of institutional learning. The British armed forces differentiate between a lesson being learned and one being identified, and this distinction is as evident in the rule of law world as it is in the military. The difficulty of institutional learning is compounded by the regular turnover of positions and personnel. In turn, this has a tendency to produce staccato and inconsistent approaches.

Fourth, there is the problem of a lack of applied research: those who write on this topic, says Carothers, have tended not to have been practitioners. Finally, there is the problem that most practitioners in rule of law development have tended to be lawyers, who are trained and conditioned to take formalistic and process-oriented approaches to almost any question. Even the most broadminded and informed theorists and practitioners make deeply cultural assumptions, and this is as true of lawyers as of any other profession. Supplementing that problem, there are the internal tensions of assistance missions themselves, which may contain members with little experience of legal or any other form of development work.

These complexities may have contributed to a 'template' approach to rule of law development. In a landmark essay, Stephen Golub summarised the problem as follows:

This 'top-down', state-centered approach concentrates on law reform and government institutions, particularly judiciaries, to build business-friendly legal systems that presumably spur poverty alleviation. Other development organizations use the rule of law (ROL) orthodoxy's state-centered approach to promote such additional goals as good governance and public safety. The problems with the paradigm are not these economic and political goals, per se, but rather its questionable assumptions, unproven impact, and insufficient attention to the legal needs of the disadvantaged.[11]

As will be seen, ten years after those words were written, this is the dominant approach to counterinsurgent lawfare in insurgency zones.

Current military counterinsurgent justice doctrine

Military lawyers have become heavily involved in the rule of law development world, particularly, but not exclusively, in operational combat zones. Rule of law became something of a fashionable additional construct to the counterinsurgency campaign in Afghanistan in 2009. Handbooks were drafted and printed.[12] 'Rule of law green zones' were proposed and a 'rule of law ambassador' appointed.[13] Vast resources were ploughed into this activity, which acquired a far higher profile in the overall effort. A 'rule of law field force' was developed, with a highly conservative approach to rule of law and a strong adherence to the rule of law orthodoxy.[14]

The US 'Rule of Law Handbook' was produced in at least two editions.[15] This is a comprehensive guide for judge advocates of the US Army who are to be deployed on 'rule of law operations'. As an introduction to legal systems that such officers may encounter, it is indeed a comprehensive guide. There are extensive sections on 'key players in rule of law' and 'fiscal considerations' (the systems used by US government agencies). There are 'theatre-specific' sections on Iraq and Afghanistan. There is little, however, on the challenge posed by insurgents and their own countervailing courts systems; nor, interestingly, is there any extended reference to other US doctrines on insurgency, particularly FM 3–24 (necessarily the 2006 edition),[16] with its extensive focus on legitimacy. The result is that there is little linkage between the rule of law element of operations and the rest of the counterinsurgent effort. Overall, the handbook is a straightforward military restatement of civilian rule of law development ideas, with a strong emphasis on Golub's rule of law orthodoxy. The effects of this are illustrated by the huge effort to provide justice in Afghanistan. Here, counterinsurgents were engaged in a struggle to counter the Taliban's 'offer' on justice, which was well-developed and culturally apposite.

Counterinsurgent judicial strategy in Afghanistan

Traditional counterinsurgency of the kind practised in Afghanistan and elsewhere over the last decade has seen justice as part of the entire governmental 'piece': as simply another form of service provision by the government, and one that fits within another huge construct, the security sector. As this book attempted to demonstrate in Chapter 3, insurgents often see justice as rather more than that: they see it as a key part of their project to insinuate their control into the society they aspire to rule.

The problems of culture and knowledge are multi-layered and wickedly complex. This is true at the most basic level of 'cultures' and the assumptions carried within them—the imperium, so to speak, of anthropology and, in military terms 'human terrain'. As Carothers points out, however, those cultural assumptions can go deeper. It is here that we get into the deep waters of jurisprudence and the analysis of legal systems. For present purposes, we need not wade out too far into those waters.

As seen above, the Western rule of law paradigm is based around some apparently anodyne and straightforward ideas. In most state-based systems, these are, at the very least, a recognisable aspiration. Unfortunately, in practice the ideal of an independent and impartial tribunal is far from common. Indeed, east of Vienna it is far more the exception than the reality, with judges and courts being bywords for corruption and venality, and all too often regarded as part of the problem of crime rather than an element in its solution.[17]

As I mentioned in Chapter 2, no one with any serious experience of law reform almost anywhere east and south of Vienna is unfamiliar with judicial corruption, often of a most blatant nature. In Afghanistan, one of the three or four most corrupt countries in the world, matters are even worse.

Once ensconced in the army base in Helmand's capital Lashkar Gah, the work began of providing what I took to be the 'better deal' for the people of Helmand. Every day, I would conduct meetings with judges, NGOs and police officers. Sometimes, those meetings would take place in our offices in the Provincial Reconstruction Team headquarters in Lashkar Gah. On most days, we would venture out, accompanied by a team of 'close protection officers' (heavily armed bodyguards) to court offices or police stations. It should have been pretty clear how matters stood after my first meeting with the chief justice of the province. The good judge handed me a picture of his son, resident at that time in Saudi Arabia, and suggested I might find him a place in law school in the United Kingdom. Even had I been inclined to attempt to do so, this might have been very difficult as the young man could speak no English. 'Very good Arabic though', said his father.

As time went on, it became very clear that, even by the standards I had become used to in south-eastern Europe or the former Soviet republics the justice sector, if it could be called that, was in a very poor state indeed.

A senior UN official of my acquaintance has spent two decades as a legal and justice reform advisor in many countries and has most recently spent five years in Afghanistan. He described to me the reality of Afghan judicial life:

> Much of Afghan life is regulated by what we might call corrupt mechanisms. There are four kinds of 'corruption': simple greed, family connections, friends, networks of other kinds. This is their life, everything comes through these networks. It was, of course, the same in Western countries for centuries. However, our system has evolved to a state where all these types of, in our term, 'corruption' have been privatised, devolved to a state or eliminated. Afghans rely for protection on family and tribe; that's what matters.[18]

As the official put it, 'this is their life'. Sure, money was commonly exchanged for legal favours, as it was elsewhere. That was one thing; it was to be expected. However, when I came across the arrest, detention and sentencing to death of men to ensure the transfer of valuable property (in this case part of a town marketplace) to judges and prosecutors, this I had not come across before. It was in effect a kidnap racket being run by the judiciary. This would not be countenanced even in many of the states of the former Soviet Union. Each case succeeded the last in what seemed to me to be appalling injustice to ordinary people.

The general view taken was that the government system, insofar as it is present at all, was moribund, expensive, slow and almost totally corrupt. The formal justice system in Helmand was what might be termed a 'legal fiction'. Throughout huge swathes of this province, it simply did not apply at all. Over a period of four years before 2007, the provincial court convicted only seventy-five persons for serious crimes. Several of these were released in any event on the payment of bribes for 'recommendations'. For a population of nearly a million, either this represents an extraordinarily low rate of commission of serious crimes or the formal system is missing something. There is no question that the great majority of Helmandis had little truck with the government criminal justice system for the very good reason that it was chronically corrupt. As for the police, they were just as bad.

The problem here was not 'this is Afghan society, this is how it is'. Any country in conflict for four decades, with a fragmented, indeed shattered society, still in a state of active and lethal daily conflict will have such problems. This, it might be argued, is one reason why the rule of law approach was structurally and conceptually unsound, designed as it is to develop societies where there is an implicit contract between people and government, or at the very least the possibility of such a relationship. In a society at war, taking the nation-building/stabilisation approach is akin to attempting to put up a tent in a storm and calling it a town hall. The case of Major Jeffrey Mullins, outlined in the excellent US Manual for Rule of Law development, provides a granular example of how very difficult, indeed impossible this may be.

'If we build it they will come': the case of Major Mullins

Major Jeffrey Mullins served as judge advocate for the 101st Airborne Division's 4th Brigade Combat Team from March 2008 to March 2009.[19] The Brigade Combat Team was deployed to Regional Command East and based in the Afghan province of Khost. As a military lawyer, Mullins' role was slightly different from the usual operational legal attachment. It is normal on operations for military lawyers to be confined to advising commanders on the legality of their units' actions. This can take many forms: an operational lawyer is often concerned with the legality of the application of armed force in combat, advising on targets and, on occasion, the degree or even type of force that might be legal. There are usually tetchy issues connected to detention practice or policy. British operational lawyers, for example, spend a great deal of their time writing reports on whether particular use of force has been justified.

Major Mullins' role presumably included all these tasks. Additionally, he was specifically deployed in support of the counterinsurgency mission of his brigade, as part of the International Security Assistance Force (ISAF). They perceived their task in classic counterinsurgency terms, to separate the insurgents from the population. This was interpreted as requiring the brigade to 'support the Afghan government in a manner where the Afghan leaders were at the forefront.' Mullins was granted authority to 'move out aggressively' in developing his 'rule of law' programmes. On the third day of his fifteen-month deployment, he left his base on a convoy to see for himself what he describes as 'one of the largest rule of law programmes ever initiated in Afghanistan'—the Khost Law Centre, set up as a 'one-stop shop' for judicial and legal services.

Mullins regarded the Khost Justice Centre as his highest-priority project: 'it was the most necessary of the "rule of law" projects. Insurgents need to be prosecuted and convicted if guilty. Judges and prosecutors need a safe work environment where they are not gunned down walking to work. Afghanistan needs provincial level justice centers in each province.'

'This became my pet project', Mullins states. After some difficulties gaining approval from the Afghan and US authorities, Mullins began his task. It was agreed that this was to be an entirely Afghan-run operation, once it was constructed. The US military would have no involvement whatsoever. The project was briefed to Afghan national legal figures in Kabul, including the attorney general and the director of the Supreme Court. It took several months from the last of these meetings for the Afghan figures, in Mullins' words, to 'contemplate the memorandum of agreement that had been presented to them.' There were serious problems with coordination of almost every organisational matter, ranging from which department would fund the running costs, to who was responsible for the security of judges. It seems that these questions were in due course resolved.

One other issue, typical of the practical problems that arise late in such projects, was that there was no well. The Americans solved this problem quickly. In December 2008, the formal agreement handing over the centre to Afghan control was signed. This was now an official Afghan judicial compound: 'The only problem is, no-one is using it.' With a candour quite extraordinary in what amounts to a military manual, Mullins reflects on the failure to make this flagship development work:

> Failing to use the Khost Justice Center has a cost that goes beyond the wasted time and resources that went into building it; building the justice center and not using it is likely worse than not building it in the first place. If, even with a safe, secure location for prosecutions, insurgents are still not being prosecuted, the insurgents have won.[20]

This whole exercise was a testament to the sheer determination and moral courage of Major Mullins and his staff. As the major himself acknowledges, it was in all likelihood wasted, as so many exercises in determination and moral courage were in Afghanistan. This approach to nation-building in general and counterinsurgency lawfare in particular was common in Afghanistan and, indeed, to the extent that there was any attention given to the role of courts, in Iraq as well. One of my priorities in Helmand, like Major Mullins, was to build a courthouse. It took several months to discover that there was already a courthouse, constructed at great expense by the US mission that had preceded our own in the province. Sadly, much of it had fallen down due in part to the chief judge's insistence on having an extra floor built for his personal use. In due course, the courthouse was rebuilt and put into use.

A tactical lawfare perspective: the case of Helmand, 2006–14

Against that background, dispute resolution was going on every day. However, the people of Helmand were not choosing the state courts that we were working hard to try to entrench. When the British arrived in Helmand in 2006, there were at least five different entities providing dispute resolution in Helmand and the rest of southern Afghanistan.[21]

1. The Afghan government's formal judicial system (judges, prosecutors and other Ministry of Justice staff), including *Hukkuk*—a state-funded system of mediation and settlement, largely using Islamic Sharia law as its foundation. It is often the first port of call for those in dispute.

2. Afghan government officials (usually the district governor [DG] and district chief of police [DCOP]). These officials act to resolve disputes in a similar way to elders.
3. The tribal elders themselves, in the form of *jirgas* or *shuras*. It was this system that was used in the dispute over the treatment of people by police officer 'Khan' (see below). They use Pashtunwali and its procedures to ground their decisions.
4. The mullahs, in their *de officio* capacity as interpreters of Sharia. This is the traditional method used in Afghanistan for the resolution of legal disputes. Disputes are settled using much the same procedure as that used by the Taliban. This system, however, like the Pashtunwali, has fallen into disuse, as traditional society has fragmented due to the constant wars, which have resulted in a constant flow of refugees.[22]
5. The Taliban, who, as has been seen, have taken advantage of the weaknesses of the other forms of justice provision.

People who required their dispute to be resolved might pick one of these methods. This approach is called forum-shopping. An illustration of forum-shopping in this kind of legal and judicial environment is illustrated by the example of 'Abdul' a case I dealt with in Helmand in 2007. 'Abdul', an employee of the British Mission, found himself in a dispute with his mother-in-law, who had formed the view that he had kidnapped his own wife (her daughter) by virtue of having failed to pay the full bride price.[23] In fact, the woman concerned was mentally ill and had forgotten that Abdul had in fact married her daughter and paid the bride price some months previously. She reported Abdul to the local Afghan National Police checkpoint in Lashkar Gah, alleging kidnap and rape. The checkpoint commander, 'Khan' and several of his men apprehended Abdul, and over several hours beat him, causing acute pain and some internal and external injury. 'Abdul' reported the matter to the police training unit of the PRT. They considered that the matter would provide a good test case for a police complaints procedure they had instituted as part of their reform programme.

The perpetrator (the checkpoint commander) requested the intervention of a group of elders from his own tribe and that of 'Abdul'. The group, or *shura*, met and discussed the case, suggesting that the police commander apologise. 'Abdul' was told that the formal system suggested by the foreign police advisors was inappropriate. He accepted, as he was absolutely bound to do, that he had to let the matter rest and withdrew his formal complaint.

It was made very clear to him that if he elected to pursue this matter through formal channels his life would be threatened. In view of that, and not wishing to move to Pakistan, 'Abdul' did not proceed any further with his complaint. 'Abdul' states that he would not have begun to consider reporting the matter to the police had he not been an employee of the PRT and supported by police mentors.

'Khan's' checkpoint was regarded by the people living near it as a serious menace. 'Abdul' was one of many who had been dealt with in a similar fashion. As a postscript, the perpetrator of this beating, 'Khan', was killed along with six other policemen (he was the main target of the killing) some three weeks later. It is said that local people were supportive of this killing.[24]

No doubt many such cases were brought to a similar conclusion. This one did not, at least as reported, involve the Taliban in resolving the dispute, though it was resolved in a violent manner. However, it was clear to all concerned that the state authorities, with whom 'Abdul' was working, were not considered to be the appropriate forum. One reason for this was that the matter was well suited for resolution in the traditional way. For this was not simply an example of what in the West might be called 'mediation': it represented Pashtunwali at work. All participants in the process were clear as to the procedure and what each party would be required to do. The politics of the perpetrators, insofar as they may have had any, were not relevant. Of rather more importance were their utility in resolving disputes.

However, 'Khan' was killed. He was killed not by the other party in the dispute, or at least there is no evidence that he was, and there was no subsequent blood feud; he was killed, along with his team of Afghan National Police, by the Taliban. Interestingly, as an aside, an Irish police officer serving with me observed that 'this is exactly what would have happened in Cork in 1921.'[25] Here, the Taliban were seen as enforcers, and their action was popular because they had removed a threat to the local people—and indeed probably to local commerce.

In her review of the informal justice sector in Helmand, Kate Fearon, my successor as justice advisor, points out that: 'Not only do the five justice providers [listed above] regularly engage in dispute resolution by themselves, but also it is more common than not to find *combinations* of these five involved in any given dispute.'

David Kilcullen, has said that: 'We can beat the Taliban in any military engagement, but we're losing in Afghanistan not because we're being outfought but because the Afghan government is being outgoverned.'[26] He's absolutely right about that, as at the time of writing in late 2016 this remains the case. The most evident manifestation of that is in the field of dispute resolution. However, it is clearly the case that the Afghan government is only one of several players. Western culture is heavily influenced by the classical idea of a government having a monopoly of force. Accordingly, the government or the state is seen as the de facto, or perhaps default, dominant source of power and consequently justice provision.

In societies such as the Pashtun, this is not the case. Power and the legitimacy to settle disputes do not necessarily—or even usually— derive from the state. However, nor is there always, as Fearon suggests, a single direct competitor. Rather, the situation may be characterised as a market, where, for some purposes, a dispute may be settled by the Taliban—a matter concerning land, perhaps, since in some provinces (as we saw in Chapter 4) a Taliban judgement has the effect of title. For a divorce case, however, the forum of choice may be the mullahs' courts in local mosques. The situation is not one, therefore, of binary conflict. One difficulty faced by counterinsurgents has been excessive adherence to the Western, urban notion of rule of law, as described and defined above. It might well be argued that a major error of Western intervention was to identify legitimate courts with state courts. The assumptions of the mission were invalid and this was based on a lack of relevant knowledge.

Later years in Helmand

At the beginning of extensive foreign involvement in Helmand in 2006, the formal justice institutions in the province had no presence outside the urban centres of Lashkar Gah and Gereshk.[27] It took several years for the importance of the justice sector to be realised.

'The development of the judiciary and the rule of law is an increasing focus of ISAF', as Peter Watkins, director of operational policy,

Ministry of Defence, put it to a session of the House of Commons Defence Committee in 2010.[28] From an ancillary element of the 'counter-narcotics' effort in 2007, when I was justice advisor, justice and rule of law became a major priority of the overall effort. However, whether the international effort had demonstrated a continuity of approach, or even an internal consistency, was open to question. Whether the approach that was taken was concordant with Afghan priorities is also a matter of debate.

When asked whether it was realistic to try to build a justice system in a relatively short period, using an approach that appeared to prioritise a Western approach to rule of law, a senior official of the UK's Department for International Development operations in Helmand and an extremely experienced international aid official told me that 'The trouble is that PRT officials are often taken in by local officials ... who often see foreign officials not so much as occupiers as milch cows.'[29] He went on to say that:

> Quite a lot of the rule of law programme was a bit template based, so 'this is the establishment that a district should have'. There was indeed a lot of 'if we build it they will come'.[30]

The approach of international actors in counterinsurgency is to accept the fiction that the state is automatically to be aligned with counterinsurgent sentiment: 'The problem is that the conventional approach assumes that government authority and anti-insurgency sentiment go together ... This conclusion may be unwarranted; a local community could be both anti-insurgency and antigovernment.'[31] The relevance of this to lawfare in insurgency zones is that, paradoxically perhaps, a release from the obligation to identify incumbent government with counterinsurgent government will allow far greater flexibility of response in approach. There is no doubt that this was recognised in Helmand at least.

Professor Graham Woodman suggests that attempting to impose state law in place of customary law can in fact act to increase conflict.[32] Indeed, he suggests that reducing the application of state law will reduce conflict. Should efforts be made to harmonise the two kinds of law, the 'two goods', then this should be accomplished through community action (i.e. it should be bottom-up). Although Woodman is concerned primarily with African mechanisms, it is argued here that the same applies in other cultures where customary law, such as the Pashtunwali, applies.

Challenges for developing a counterinsurgent judicial strategy

1. Lack of planning for a judicial strategy

Particularly in the recent campaign in Afghanistan, there has been a lack of planning for the judicial element of counterinsurgency. This is an issue from the highest levels of military planning to the lowest. One former senior military legal officer, who has served with UK and US military rule of law missions and has dealt at the highest levels in such matters, has said:

> Rule of law is not part of the comprehensive military planning piece. It is planned, if at all, bit by bit. We need to develop a proper integrated planning process. During that process we need to have people who understand the pragmatic need for such an approach. Right now we don't have pragmatism in planning. We don't have planning at all. It is only at the last minute, or even after the last minute that military commanders get forced into this kind of planning. I don't think legal experts have been included at a high enough level.[33]

2. Lack of doctrinal coherence

In order for such planning to have positive effect, it needs to be integrated into a well-understood strategy, which must in turn be based on a practically oriented doctrine. As matters stand, counterinsurgency theory and practice is not situated within the extensive scholarship on pluralism, based on over a century of colonial experience and on more than fifty years of development work. Much of the colonial experience was founded on decades of thinking and practical strategic calculation. Much of it was geared to preventing, exploiting or ignoring what might (had current streams of counterinsurgent theory been established then) have been termed dangerous currents of 'insurgent' governance. It is not only in the counterinsurgency field that there has been a failure properly to engage with legal pluralism.

Underlying much of the West's recent efforts at justice within a counterinsurgency has been a strategic incoherence at several levels.

There has first been what might be described as 'vertical incoherence', in that efforts at the provincial level were rarely if ever fully coordinated with the Afghan national plans and priorities. In an interview with me, a British advisor to a senior Afghan minister put it like this: 'Look, the Afghan national plans are ramshackle and rickety. But they are there, and with effort could have begun to work. The countries, and I do mean here the British and Americans, carry on with their own work as if the central government did not exist.'[34]

3. Lack of coordination with other activities

There is also 'horizontal incoherence'—which is to say that within the mission in Helmand itself there has been a lack of a consistent or informed approach. At the military levels, there was never a single, continuous strategic approach. For example, in Helmand, the British military presence deployed in six-monthly increments of brigades, each of which had different perspectives, objectives and focuses.[35] Similarly, the various civilian advisors—on justice, as on other matters—were changed at intervals of six to eighteen months. The degree to which these advisors were briefed on their roles and the strategic objectives being pursued was very variable. There was no system of structured handover from one to the next; often it was done on a personally organised basis. One of the six justice advisors deployed to the province by the UK was given no briefings, save 'offer the people of Helmand a better deal'; others were given a half-page document.[36] Some justice advisors were instructed to assist the military effort in attempting to regularise detention policy; others had no involvement at all.[37] Even if the work had been coherent and consistent with an established strategy, there was little evidence of any link between proclaimed objectives of military counterinsurgency and civilian stabilisation efforts. Awareness of the legal environment into which these advisors were placed was patchy at best. The tensions and dilemmas of trying to develop a coherent judicial strategy within an already intensely complex environment were perhaps exacerbated by the needs of the military counterinsurgent effort.

4. Failure to engage with the 'facts on the ground'

Corruption

Looking at matters from a Western European perspective, we assume that judges exercise judicial function and that the police are concerned with enforcing law and order. As we saw in Chapter 2, Jonathan Foreman, a researcher and expert on aid policy, calls this 'the nomenclatural fallacy'.[38]

One UN justice advisor said that 'there was a real artificiality of office. A police chief may be called that, but he is not a police chief in the way that anyone in Europe would recognise in terms of his actual role.'[39]

A former stabilisation officer in southern Afghanistan is blunt about the reality of the West's efforts:

> The predations of the state here are so extreme that no-one could reasonably expect anything other than a negative response from ordinary people who really just want to be left alone in peace with the means to make a basic living, supported by some form of locally accountable justice and, fundamentally, order. We might have done better to have bothered to figure out what such people wanted, instead of trying to impose a 'best practice' governance solution for them in the way that we have.[40]

Consequent illegitimacy

The suggestion made in some quarters that informal justice undermines government legitimacy has been accepted implicitly.[41] Indeed, it can undermine government legitimacy, if thought is not given to how it is used and supported. It might equally well be argued that the imposition of a system that was regarded as corrupt, yet seen as the showcase of government, did more damage. A shrewder approach to lawfare might be to take the lessons of Lugard and the British systems on the North West Frontier and adapt them to today's strictures.

A UN justice advisor with seven years' experience in Central Afghanistan, and with many more years' work in the Balkans, the former Soviet Union and China, told me that:

> I realised I knew nothing pretty quickly. But then I had the distinct advantage of having worked, after ten years as a lawyer, in Albania. Even there

it took me six months to figure out what was going on. I came to Afghanistan with the full awareness that I knew absolutely nothing. Most military and many civilian officials have no experience of work in systems outside the Western legal world. Many never acquire real knowledge or even an awareness of their lack of knowledge.[42]

As may be recalled, this encapsulates Carothers' 'problem of knowledge' described earlier in this chapter. The UN officer went on:

Then there is the fact that most rule of law officers are lawyers. Many of these lawyers believe that you can abstract from all countries with 'rule of law' and pretend it's all a matter of engineering. There are also ideological reasons. For example, a shura's conclusions may be rejected because they are insufficiently 'human rights compliant'. One issue which is raised time and again is gender, which is a very hard sell indeed in the Pashtun world.[43]

5. Focus on Western priorities

Gender is one area where the clash between traditional Afghan and Western priorities is particularly evident. Clearly, Pashtun notions of gender relations—which might be summarised as defining women as possessions—do not sit well with Western priorities. This can have very positive effects. Fearon relates the case of one local judicial council set up by the British mission to resolve disputes. Here, two women were installed as members on the insistence of the British advisor. In at least one case, their presence was instrumental in avoiding appalling consequences for a very young woman. The girl concerned was being forced to marry an opium addict against her will. She stated—and this is not unusual—that if forced to do so, she would kill herself, the common method being self-immolation. The case was brought to the judicial council. The initial decision to confirm the marriage was overturned on the insistence of one of the female members of the committee and the girl went to school.[44]

Sadly, the priority attached to gender issues by key Afghan leaders is not the same as that attached to it by Western technical experts.

The UN official quoted above concluded his interview with me by saying:

A big strategic mistake the West made was to try to replicate our systems; apart from the obvious stupidity of that, a second mistake was not to match our legal reforms with the Sharia. An Afghan sees the reforms—

including the constitution—as a foreign imposition. Most people only know Sharia—so the Taliban come in and whatever we may think of its harshness, it is obviously Sharia. They know that. It is familiar; it is quick and you don't have to pay. We cannot compete with it. What we should have done is the really simple, but really vital stuff. We should have focused on one big, simple thing: fair dealing.[45]

6. The 'clash of two goods': centralism vs pluralism[46]

In his essay on legal pluralism, the scholar on jurisprudence Ronald Janse identifies seven reasons why ideas of legal pluralism have not caught on as they might have done in legal and 'rule of law development'.[47] An overriding problem, he suggests, is that legal and rule of law reform 'can briefly be summarised as "decades of stubborn refusal to learn"', an observation exactly replicated by the UN official 'I don't want to take these people's money away, but maybe someone should say "none of this works".'[48]

One serious problem identified to me by highly experienced development advisor and professor of law Cynthia Alkon in connection with that comment is that 'practitioners say "this doesn't work" all the time.'[49] She goes on to state that 'the problem is that they say it to each other and largely in private. There are no incentives for proclaiming failure in the development world, so it is very rare for failure to be admitted.' It seems that multi-million dollar projects must be seen to succeed, and reports written accordingly or the perception will be that the money has been wasted and that is simply not acceptable to governmental donors. Further, it is rare, with notable exceptions such as Carothers and Golub, for practitioners to enter the academic discourse with serious doubts to the effect that 'none of this works'.

Secondly, the fact that most of those dealing with rule of law reform are lawyers tends to predispose them to solutions that seem straightforward and to which they are professionally disposed, such as building courts. Third, and closely connected, is the fact that this kind of work has always been based on the 'empirical [for them] assertion that only the state is capable of providing social order ... or on the ideological claim that the state offers the best hope for the realisation of economic development, democracy and rule of law.'[50] There are echoes here of H. Patrick Glenn's observations on the invalidity of ideas of rule of law outside, or indeed he claims, inside the Western paradigm.

Fourth is the political pressure imposed by the fact that most such operations are founded on negotiations between the 'exogenous' (donor) interveners and their agents and governments, sometimes including judiciary and legislature. It is consequently understandable that high-level government officials seek assistance that helps them to strengthen the legal institutions of which they are in charge.

Fifth is the geopolitical factor of distrust of, for example, Islamic means of dispute resolution, which were seen as not sufficiently 'human rights compliant', or, even worse, may be perceived as presenting a threat cognate to terrorism.

The sixth (and closely linked to the fifth) is the normative under-standing that the so-called 'thick' definition of rule of law, which implies the inclusion of various civil, social and political rights, is the appropriate mechanism for the delivery of dispute resolution. Ganesh Sitaraman's *Counterinsurgent's Constitution* outlines the dilemma. On the one hand: 'The rule of law is one of those few but fortunate concepts that has universal support ... To stand against the rule of law is to stand with absolutism—against democracy, prosperity, peace, order, human rights, and liberty.'[51] On the other, however, it is 'enforced by central bureaucratic institutions like national police forces and court systems. The rule of law therefore looks much like a Western legal system.'[52] As was seen in the previous chapter, at the more extreme ends of the insurgent spectrum, ideas of human rights or international standards that cohere around the rule of law are seriously contested ideas.

Finally, the seventh factor that Janse identifies is the question of mandates—a matter closely linked with the fourth factor. All organisa-tions, such as the United Nations or the UK government, that are involved in this kind of activity have specific mandates that render it 'difficult to engage with non-state justice systems because these are regarded as falling short of international human rights law.'[53]

I would add an eighth and connected issue: that of the pervasiveness of Western cultural assumptions, or indeed 'political correctness': 'there is an element of "right thinking"' and if you don't think that way, you're out. In private everyone knows it won't work. They know what's going on.'[54]

The 'problem of knowledge' lies behind all of these features. There is an inadequate basic knowledge of the issues that play into the causes of insurgency and that pertain to the justice sector. This is particularly the case in places that do not in any way conform to the paradigms of Western political and legal theory.

Who is the insurgent?

Whether or not ungoverned space is a legitimate term, the reality of intervention in differently governed places requires a deep knowledge of the nuances and practices of the area into which outsiders stray with the ambition of quelling rebellion and assisting in setting up governance. Further, outsiders fail to appreciate the essential heart of the matter—that they are engaged in a competitive activity that means a great deal to their opponents. In my experience of legal reform in conflict, it rarely means anything truly visceral for the counterinsurgent.

In Afghanistan, 'legal experts from North America and Western Europe frequently come across as more interested in promoting the merit of the latest legal contrivances than in making a genuine effort to promote civilian welfare.'[55] The British effort in Helmand demonstrated this at the provincial level, with regular shifts in focus, matched by an equally incoherent Afghan national effort. The Taliban, however, were not encumbered by these contrivances and maintained an entirely consistent, indeed improving, approach. Recent examples of attempts to provide a rule of law element in counterinsurgency have demonstrated that, as Carothers says:

> there is a disturbingly thin basis of knowledge at every level—with respect to the core rationale of the work, the question of where the essence of the rule of law resides in different societies, how change in the rule of law occurs and what the real effects are of changes that are produced.[56]

His views are echoed by a recent UK advisor to the rule of law mission in Helmand: 'We needed to understand the pushes and pulls that run the place ... we dabbled with little or no understanding of the second or third-order consequences of our actions.'[57]

Thus, the rule of law practitioners have duplicated the efforts of military COIN practitioners. Whit Mason, editor of the leading study on rule of law efforts in Afghanistan, *Lost in Inaction*, told me that foreign rule of law experts were concerned with 'shaping the environment instead of shaping themselves around the environment.'[58] They were concerned with altering the status quo, whether or not they realised it. The role of 'rebel'—the agent of change—is usually that of the insurgent. Who, then, is the insurgent?

In an article in a 2013 edition of the US *Joint Force Quarterly*, Robert Egnell acknowledged that 'major counterinsurgency operations have historically achieved few successes. While it is indeed possible to learn from these few successes and numerous failures, counterinsurgency principles of the past are accepted outright a bit too easily in the 21st century.'[59] His further insight was that the nature of COIN operations, particularly in Afghanistan, was not in fact counterinsurgency; rather they were themselves rather more in the nature of insurgencies. There was a 'litany of assumptions' concerning the COIN campaign in Afghanistan.[60] He acknowledges that there was a serious problem concerning the legitimacy of the Afghan government and that Weberian democracy is not evident as an objective good for all populations of the world. The 'societal transformation' that seemed to be the purpose of the mission was, in fact, a revolutionary programme and therefore was more by way of an insurgency than a counterinsurgency.

This in itself is a sound insight. Egnell goes further, however, to prescribe the conceptual tactics of insurgents as an option for future operation of 'regime change', should such operations take place again. It is argued here that, howsoever reframed, Robert Pape's 'It's the occupation, stupid' will still apply.[61] In other words, we return to the problem of exogenous intervention. Astri Suhrke situates 'the history of state-formation in Europe' as typically 'forged in opposition to the other', rather than imposed by that 'other'.[62] She looks at several examples of endogenous state-building, such as the Meiji in Japan or the construction of the post-imperial Turkish state, and contrasts those with what she describes as the 'extreme case of international state-building' in Afghanistan.[63] This was characterised by a lack of ownership, failing Afghan leadership and an excess of possibly unfounded optimism and a deficiency of understanding of the practical need for sustainability.

Yet state-building in the West has taken centuries. Much of the foregoing has been concerned with the sliver of 'state-building' or at the local level, what was termed stabilisation, as it affects the construction of a justice sector. This has often been placed within the context of 'security sector reform' (SSR), a truly vast industry within the international development world. It is argued here that this is a category error of an archetypical kind. Justice in societies such as Afghanistan, Somalia or indeed any culture with a strong customary strain, is far more than an arm of the security forces, as indeed it is in Western societies. This category error has in turn bred an approach that has tended to relegate to the margins the far more important function of internal societal dispute resolution. Introducing elements foreign to the 'target' society—such as overlaying a formal justice sector along Western lines—has produced instabilities and internal conflicts, and has in fact made the security situation worse. It has built in, for example, further opportunities for theft, graft and corruption by state officials.[64] One former stabilisation officer, speaking about Afghanistan (where he works), expresses the views of some who have worked in such places: 'In short, public office is not regarded as a service to the people but as a means to extract resources from them. The state is a predatory, self-serving and hostile actor and not something that adds value to people's lives through the provision of public goods.'[65]

The combination of officials knowing that this is the case and yet continuing to add resources and opportunities for the same officials within that system may be considered to be an example of cognitive dissonance. This, in turn, has acted to reduce the legitimacy of the formal state, which was already at a very low ebb. 'To be legitimate and effective, legal reform has to relate to the normative basis of justice in Afghanistan.'[66] This was realised by legal reformers after the unfortunate experiences in the former Soviet Union in the late 1990s. The lessons of colonial authorities were never (or only rarely) examined. The 'breathtakingly mechanistic approach' based on the notion that 'a country achieves the rule of law by reshaping its key institutions to match those of countries that are considered to have the rule of law'[67] has resulted in the Taliban taking the lawfare initiative and using their considerable edge to great strategic effect, both in terms of the operational effect on the ground, where the formal sector has essentially been defeated in key areas, and in terms of the wider narrative of justice, which is dominated by their rhetoric and indeed to a very great extent backed up by reality.

The problems and questions arising from rule of law activities in places such as Afghanistan could and will arise in other areas of governance, such as education. Those areas, however—important and indeed vital though they are—are unlikely to affect the fight for legitimacy that lies at the heart of the recent Afghan war and that has been at the core of other military and stabilisation missions for much of the last decade.

CONCLUSION

'In large measure, our modern politics is legal politics. The terms of engagement are legal, and the players are legal institutions, their powers expanded and limited by law. To say that war is a legal institution is not only to say that war has also become an affair of rules or the military a legal bureaucracy; it is also to say something about the nature of the politics continued by military means.'[1]

Wars are horrific ways of making decisions, but they are ways of making decisions. For that reason, they can be thought of as a form of legal procedure. After all, law is nothing other than the science of making decisions.[2] At the outset of this book, the objective was to attempt to show that if war was once a form of legal process, then might the law not now be seen as at least a form of war? Perhaps even, as the father of the term lawfare, Charles Dunlap, has said, the 'decisive element'.[3]

Ultimately, insurgency and counterinsurgency are political acts; they constitute a form of warfare—indeed arguably the dominant form of warfare in the current international strategic environment. As such, if they are to succeed there should be a strategic appreciation made of the objectives, means and methods suited to the conflict. This has rarely been done in recent years. However, over the decades of the colonial period there developed a close appreciation of the need for such a strategy. There was a lengthy debate conducted by all levels of those involved, ranging from the practitioners on the frontiers themselves to the politicians deciding upon such strategies. Such awareness has not been evident over the last two decades.

Chapter 1 raised the question of whether there is a relationship between successful counterinsurgents and fair procedure. The case made in this book is not that this is a silver bullet or an undiscovered mine of counterinsurgency treasure; rather that there should be a legal policy that goes beyond the rhetorical and that moves into the practical. This is where an overall strategic perspective may help.

This comes against the background of an awareness of war as a multidimensional endeavour. The consequences of appreciating this are severe, if ruthlessly logical. If the courts of the occupying power lack legitimacy, then they must be attacked. Clearly, this can be done virtually, by setting up insurgent courts. The Irish Nationalists showed that it must also be done physically, by ensuring that the courts could not function—either by threatening or suborning staff or witnesses, or by destroying the buildings.

Not 'dealing fairly' leaves the way open for the insurgent to move in with what might now be called 'information operations', as we have seen at the grand strategic level with respect to Guantanamo and other detention issues in the 'Long War'. In a rather earlier generation in Northern Ireland, the Diplock Courts were presented (not without some justification) as being a derogation from basic notions of fairness, as understood in British law. Did the costs in legitimacy outweigh the gains from putting terrorists in jail? It may be so. This is a contingent circumstance and a clear-eyed stance needs to be taken at the outset to the legal approach to fighting insurgents. Taking an ad hoc approach to matters of detention and interrogation and the litigation procedures to which insurgents are subject lays the counterinsurgents open to the threat of legal action at home, lawfare in the way that it is traditionally understood.

As Porch has said in his *Counterinsurgency*, each war (and its results) is contingent upon circumstances. Each is, as it were, a law unto itself. Lessons to be drawn from Malaya are not necessarily to be applied to Afghanistan, save and insofar as it is necessary to have complete familiarity with the drivers and issues that the enemy relies upon.

The importance of procedural fairness lies in the sources of a conflict. For example, the land issues in Ireland, which for centuries drove many of the problems, were of a different nature from those in Afghanistan. However, mechanisms needed to be in place in order for those root causes to be dealt with. Failure to do so in Kenya and Ireland opened the way, especially in Ireland, for insurgent authority to begin to gain purchase on dispute resolution mechanisms, courts, which

CONCLUSION

eventually became a key strategic weapon, as seen in Chapter 3. A similar gap in legitimacy opened the way for the Taliban in Afghanistan,
both in the 1990s and more recently, to build their own 'brand' and to
start or continue the process of developing a message that they were to
be preferred to the government by those engaged of necessity in
forum-shopping. While from the Western perspective the Afghan War
is over, it certainly is not over for the Afghans. That theatre of justice
will continue to play itself out. The nostrums of formal justice on the
Western model have clearly failed, as they do not live sufficiently well
with Afghan culture and are considered to be part of the intensely
corrupt Afghan government.

What was and is the message of insurgent courts? It is simple: by
these instruments, insurgents demonstrate that they have the legitimacy to exercise one of the key functions of government. They demonstrate that they possess the authority to dispose of disputes, not only
among the members of their own groups but among the members of
the community they serve.

Once a belligerent group has got hold of the courts in a particular
disputed area, it is very difficult for the opposing party to dislodge it.
By 'courts', one means here the ability to decide disputes. The reason,
as Ireland and Afghanistan have shown, is that the ability to decide
disputes is an indicator of public trust not so much in propriety, as in
ability to enforce, and is therefore an indicator of legitimacy.
Commercial, farming and business interests understand the situation
better than COIN practitioners. In one sense, courts are an expression
of the 'wisdom of crowds', as to some extent the decision as to what
forum to use is a speculative one. For example, in the issue of land,
there is no interest in decisions that are only of temporary effectiveness. The party that aspires to 'win' in an insurgency needs to be able
to enforce its will, and one vital characteristic of that is the ability to
enforce the judgements of their courts.

Overall, however, counterinsurgents, whether conducting their campaigns as endogenous or exogenous interveners, need to be aware of the
requirement for a legal strategy—not just of how to use courts to counter insurgents, in other words as part of a security apparatus. They also
need to look at what may be needed to deal with the edge that insurgents
may have in the area of dispute resolution. The ideas presented in current

doctrinal documents are clearly inadequate, and have been shown to be so in Afghanistan. This gap in policy has been shown to be particularly obvious in relation to ungoverned space. In fighting wars of this nature, doctrinaire approaches based on Western notions of rule of law are ineffective, based as they are on premises that simply do not apply in ungoverned space. More thinking is required as to how the lessons of recent campaigns (and indeed older campaigns) can be developed. Much of that may draw on scholarship in legal anthropology.

It is also argued here that, seen through the lens of justice, the kind of thinking that is to be found in much military doctrine, written often by people with the haziest notion of how real societies work, is also profoundly conceptually flawed. This problem goes deeper than merely being an update of tired and anachronistic notions of 'hearts and minds' or 'winning the population' or, for that matter, 'governance'. Those templates are irrelevant in places where 'government' is not seen as a solution.

How should counterinsurgency theory cope with rupture strategy, forms of which range from the simple denial of authority or legitimacy, to using the courts to set a narrative tone for the conduct of counterinsurgency (as some may argue has happened pursuant to the cases in the UK dealing with detention)? One obvious tactic would be to ensure that this particular vulnerability, in this case concerning detention, is properly legally founded both at home and in the area of operations.

Such essential matters are not dealt with in current doctrine. The version of judicial strategy preferred by current counterinsurgency doctrine is the standard rule of law model, which is inappropriate in pluralist settings.

Yet there is a whole field of academic discourse that is inclined to show precisely the contrary—the field of legal pluralism: namely that 'the absence of a strong state will necessarily be followed by anarchic conditions.' [4] This is not necessarily so.

Implications for policy

Clearly there needs to be a full awareness of what it is that the counterinsurgent is trying to achieve, and a clear-eyed understanding that there may be internally conflicting objectives: for example, a national policy of gender promotion that is in direct opposition to the interest in ensuring that deeply held ideas are not challenged to the detriment of the overall mission.

The 'legal flank' may not always be open. US military lawyer Thomas Nachbar has this to say:

> To say counterinsurgents can use law to fight insurgents is not to say that they should … Both law and war have been around for as long as there have been governments, and the lessons we are learning in today's counterinsurgency and counterterrorism campaigns will likely play out for generations as, in each new conflict, law finds its place as both a constraint on war and a means of warfare.[5]

It is clear that there is far more awareness than there was of the importance of developing a soundly based judicial strategy. What is equally clear from recent practice is that, while this need has been identified by counterinsurgents, or many counterinsurgents, it has not been fulfilled in practice. Another scholar of counterinsurgency criticises Western counterinsurgency more generally, but his critique is just as valid for present purposes: 'When a state gets its strategy right in war, tactical problems tend to be subsumed and improved within it … But when a state fights a war under a botched strategy—as the United States is currently doing in Afghanistan—that fiction is exposed and laid bare with nothing for cover.'[6]

It may well be that, even after the setbacks of the last decades, there remains some validity in the dicta of counterinsurgency theory as applied to the provision of justice. However, as observed in Chapter 1, there remains very little coverage of the legal means available to insurgents, or indeed counterinsurgents, in prosecuting their operations. While there are the beginnings in stabilisation theory of an understanding of the importance of law and institutions of dispute resolution, this has not yet migrated across to the world of counterinsurgency beyond tired notions of rule of law development and security sector reform.

Equally, while there is most certainly a greatly increased global awareness of the potential for lawfare within the context of state-to-state conflict, the discussion of lawfare has largely been confined to questions surrounding detention and interrogation of terrorist suspects or the methods available to human rights activists in restraining the use, for example, of drones. These certainly have relevance to the prosecution of counterinsurgency, but they do not speak of the need to deal with insurgency at the operational legal level, let alone the strategic level. To adopt an aphorism: while we have been playing draughts, our adversaries have been playing chess.

At that level, the discourse remains at the default of building legal institutions ('rule of law field force', etc.). As was seen in Chapter 1, in the case of occupations, current international law allows a great deal of latitude, and therefore scope for initiative and original thought for the occupying power.

To get beyond that paradigm there will need to be a new approach to the planning of operations. A start could be made by including a legal element within 'intelligence preparation of the battlespace'. This idea lives well within advanced conceptions of intelligence. For example, in his 'Fixing Intel', General Michael Flynn, former ISAF chief of intelligence advocates taking intelligence away from the centrality of 'covert intelligence' and rendering it far more 'holistic' in nature, to include the legal battlespace.[7]

Finally, there must be an increased awareness of the multidimensional nature of war and along with it an increasing awareness of the multidimensional implications of law and war. Potential conventional opponents already have this awareness, and insurgent opponents have been, as this book has sought to demonstrate, aware of it for far longer.[8]

NOTES

INTRODUCTION

1. Whitman, James Q., *The Verdict of Battle*, Cambridge, MA: Harvard University Press, 2012, p. 94.
2. Ledwidge, Frank, 'Justice in Helmand: The Challenge of Law Reform in a Society at War', *Asian Affairs*, 40, 1 (2009), p. 40; Ledwidge, 'Justice and Counter-Insurgency in Afghanistan: A Missing Link', *RUSI Journal*, 154, 1 (2009), pp. 6–9.
3. Dunlap, Charles, 'Law and Military Interventions: Preserving Humanitarian Values in 21st-Century Conflicts', Harvard University Kennedy School of Government, Carr Center for Human Rights Working Paper, 29 November 2001, p. 8 available at http://people.duke.edu/~pfeaver/dunlap.pdf
4. Whitman, *The Verdict of Battle*, p. 3.
5. Whetham, David, *Just Wars and Moral Victories: Surprise, Deception and the Normative Framework of European War in the Later Middle Ages*, Leiden: Brill, 2009. See particularly Chapter III, 'The Role of Law as a Legal Instrument in the Middle Ages', p. 71.
6. Whitman, *The Verdict of Battle*, p. 3.
7. Kennedy, David, *Of War and Law*, Princeton, NJ: Princeton University Press, 2006, p. 13.
8. Cited in Townshend, Charles, *Britain's Civil Wars*, London: Faber, 1986, p. 20.
9. Bentham, Jeremy, 'Of Laws in General'.
10. Dunlap, 'Law and Military Interventions.'
11. Dunlap, Charles, 'Lawfare: A Decisive Element of 21st-Century Conflict', *Joint Forces Quarterly*, 59 (2009), p. 34, available at http://www.americanbar.org/content/dam/aba/migrated/2011_build/law_national_security/LawfareDunlapJun09.authcheckdam.pdf

12. Ibid., p. 34.
13. For example, Ledwidge, Frank, 'Soldiers Shouldn't Need to Go to Law for Justice', *The Times*, 20 June 2013, available (through paywall) at http://www.thetimes.co.uk/tto/opinion/columnists/article3795482. ece; see also Tugendhat, Tom and Croft, Laura, 'The Fog of Law: An Introduction to the Legal Erosion of British Fighting Power', Policy Exchange, 2013, available at http://www.policyexchange.org.uk/images/publications/the%20fog%20of%20law.pdf
14. Particularly the case of *Smith and Others* v. *Ministry of Defence*, judgement available at http://www.supremecourt.gov.uk/decided-cases/docs/UKSC_2012_0249_Judgment.pdf
15. For example, Heron, C.P., 'The Juridification of the British Armed Forces', Shrivenham Defence Research Paper, 2013, unpublished.
16. Kennedy, *Of War and Law*, p. 114.
17. See, for example, Cheng, Dean, 'Winning Without Fighting: Chinese Legal Warfare' (Heritage Foundation, 2012), available at http://www.heritage.org/research/reports/2012/05/winning-without-fighting-chinese-legal-warfare. See also Delex Systems, 'China's Three Warfares', 12 January 2012, available at http://www.delex.com/data/files/Three%20Warfares.pdf
18. Kittrie, Orde, *Lawfare: Law as a Weapon of War*, Oxford: Oxford University Press, 2015.
19. Kennedy, *Of War and Law*, p. 165.
20. Summarised at http://www.icty.org/x/cases/slobodan_milosevic/cis/en/cis_milosevic_slobodan.pdf
21. For one of many examples, see 'The Serbs Have Always Seen the ICTY as a Political and Not a Legal Body', at http://serbianna.com/analysis/archives/1708
22. Nachbar, Thomas B., 'Counterinsurgency, Legitimacy and the Rule of Law', Parameters, Spring 2012, Virginia Public Law and Legal Theory Research Paper No. 2013–19, p. 27.
23. Cheng, Dean, 'Winning without Fighting: The Chinese Psychological Warfare Challenge', Heritage Foundation Report, 12 July 2013, http://www.heritage.org/global-politics/report/winning-without-fighting-the-chinese-psychological-warfare-challenge
24. See also, for example, Lawfare, 'Lawfare Analysis on Defense Department Report on China', 21 August 2011, available at http://www.thelawfareproject.org/Blog/lawfare-analysis-in-defense-department-report-on-china.html
25. Keck, Zachary, 'With Air Defense Zone, China Is Waging Lawfare', The Diplomat, 30 November 2013, available at http://thediplomat.com/2013/11/with-air-defense-zone-china-is-waging-lawfare/

26. Whitman, *The Verdict of Battle*, p. 40.
27. Kennedy, *Of War and Law*, p. 25.
28. Betz, David, 'The Virtual Dimension of Contemporary Insurgency and Counterinsurgency', *Small Wars and Insurgencies*, 19, 4 (2008), p. 519.
29. Simpson, Emile, *War from the Ground Up: Twenty-First-Century Combat as Politics*, London: Hurst, 2013, p. 218.
30. FM 3–24, paragraph 1–13.
31. Strachan, Hew, *The Direction of War*, Cambridge: Cambridge University Press, 2013, p. 279.
32. Walzer, Michael, *Arguing about War*, New Haven, CT: Yale University Press, 2006, p. 9.
33. See, for example, Ucko, David H., 'Critics Gone Wild: Counterinsurgency as the Root of All Evil', *Small Wars & Insurgencies*, 25, 1 (2014), pp. 161–79 and the remarkable response of Douglas Porch at 'Reply to David Ucko', *Small Wars & Insurgencies*, 25, 1 (2014), pp. 180–5.
34. US Army Field Manual 3–24, *Counterinsurgency*, Washington, DC: Department of the Army, 2006 p 1–1, quoting a US special forces officer in Iraq.

1. LAW, LEGITIMACY AND INSURGENCY

1. Kennedy, *Of War and Law*, p. 45.
2. FM 3–24 (2006), paragraph 1–197.
3. Mary Kotsonouris, 'Lecture on Dail Courts', RTE, 27 February 2009, Dublin, available at http://www.rte.ie/radio1/thomasdavis/1251899.html
4. FM 3–24 (2014), paragraph 1–78.
5. FM 3–24 (2014), paragraph 1–2.
6. Kilcullen, *Out of the Mountains*, pp. 116ff.
7. Kilcullen, David, *Counterinsurgency*, London: Hurst, 2010, p. 155.
8. Nachbar, Thomas B, 'The Use of Law in Counterinsurgency', *Military Law Review*, 213 (2011), p. 142, available at https://www.jagcnet.army.mil/DOCLIBS/MILITARYLAWREVIEW.NSF/0/256fb1f93504c3478 5257b0c006b99d4/$FILE/By%20Thomas%20B.%20Nachbar.pdf
9. FM 3–24 (2006), paragraph 1–116; the 2014 edition does not set out indicators for legitimacy.
10. AFM 3–40, paragraph 12–26 and FM 3–24, paragraphs 6–101–106.
11. FM 3–24 (2014), paragraphs 13–65 and 13–67.
12. Anderson, E.G. and Black, L.J., 'Accumulations of Legitimacy: Exploring Insurgency and Counterinsurgency Dynamics', in the Proceedings of the International System Dynamics Conference, Boston, MA (2007),

p. 3. They go on to postulate that legitimacy grows and wanes over time as a result of several reinforcing loops, by representing legitimacy as a 'stock', or what might be described as a finite quantity. They also rather more conceptually discuss various 'causal loops' that feed into this essential competition, touching on various species of social capital that feed legitimacy. That approach is not adopted here.

13. Weber, *Politics as a Vocation*.

14. Mao Tse Tung, *Problems of War and Strategy*, Beijing: Foreign Languages Press, 1960, available at http://collections.mun.ca/PDFs/radical/ProblemsofWarandStrategy.pdf

15. Pirie, Fernanda, *The Anthropology of Law*, Oxford: Oxford University Press, 2013, p. 28.

16. Roberts, Simon, 'The Study of Dispute: Anthropological Perspectives', in J. Bossy (ed.), *Disputes and Settlements*, Cambridge: Cambridge University Press, 1985, p. 5.

17. Malinowski, Bronislaw, *Crime and Custom in Savage Society*, London: Kegan Paul, 1934.

18. See Pirie, *The Anthropology of Law* Chapter 2, passim.

19. Griffiths, John 'What Is Legal Pluralism', *Journal of Legal Pluralism*, 24, 2 (1986), p. 3.

20. Ibid., p. 4.

21. Isser, Deborah (ed.), *Customary Justice and the Rule of Law in War-Torn Societies*, Washington, DC: United States Institute of Peace, 2011, p. 4.

22. Anderson and Black, 'Accumulations of Legitimacy', p. 3.

23. Tyler, Tom R., *Why People Obey the Law*, Princeton, NJ: Princeton University Press, 2006.

24. Laird, Heather, *Subversive Law in Ireland, 1879–1920*, Dublin: Four Courts, 2005.

25. Thompson, E.P., *Whigs and Hunters: The Origins of the Black Act*, London: Penguin, 1975.

26. Laird, *Subversive Law in Ireland*, p. 24.

27. Ibid., p. 17.

28. Tyler, *Why People Obey the Law*, p. 21. See also Sunshine, J. and Tyler, T., 'The Role of Procedural Justice and Legitimacy in Shaping Public Support for Policing', *Law and Society Review*, 37, 3 (2003), p. 513. 'The procedural justice perspective argues that the legitimacy of the police is linked to public judgements about the fairness of the processes through which the police make decisions and exercise authority' (p. 514).

29. Tyler, *Why People Obey the Law*, p. 23.

30. Ibid., p. 26.

31. Fully reported in Tyler, *Why People Obey the Law*. See also Tyler, Tom R. and Rasinski, Kenneth, 'Procedural Justice, Institutional Legitimacy

and the Acceptance of Unpopular US Supreme Court Decisions: A Question of Causality', *Law and Society Review*, 25, 3 (1991), p. 469.

32. Tyler, *Why People Obey the Law*, p. 164.

33. Ibid., p. 178.

34. For an example of how Tyler's ideas translate in legal development work to systems with some form of established system of law, see Alkon, Cynthia, 'Plea-Bargaining as a Legal Transplant', *Transnational Law and Contemporary Problems*, 19 (2010), pp. 355–384

35. Roberts, *Order and Dispute*, p. 100. See also Lewis, Ioan and Samatar, Said, *A Pastoral Democracy*, London: James Currey, 1999, pp. 229–34.

36. Gentile, Gian, *Wrong Turn: America's Deadly Embrace of Counterinsurgency*, New York: New Press, 2013; Porch, Douglas, *Counterinsurgency: Exposing the Myths of the New Way of War*, Cambridge: Cambridge University Press, 2013.

37. See, for example, Abdo, Mohammed, 'Legal Pluralism, Sharia Courts and Constitutional Issues in Ethiopia', *Mizan Law Review*, 5, 1 (2011), http://www.ajol.info/index.php/mlr/article/view/68769.This outlines what might well be described as a 'hands-off' approach on the part of the state towards, in this case, sharia judgements. Much the same approach is taken with respect to decisions of *xeer* 'tribunals' in the Somali region.

38. Speech of Lord Chief Justice, 3 May 2008, at the London Muslim Centre: 'Lord Chief Justice Celebrates Equality before the Law', http://www.judiciary.gov.uk/media/media-releases/2008/1208

39. Rowan Williams stated that sharia law is 'unavoidable'; see 'Sharia Law Is "Unavoidable"', BBC News, 7 February 2008, http://news.bbc.co.uk/1/hi/uk/7232661.stm

40. See, for example, Weiss, Deborah, 'Britain's No Sharia Campaign', *American Thinker*, 18 November 2008, http://www.americanthinker.com/2008/12/britains_no_sharia_campaign.html

41. For example: 'If We Ignore Wrongs We Condone Them', *The Independent*, 20 June 2011, available at http://www.independent.co.uk/news/people/profiles/baroness-cox-if-we-ignore-wrongs-we-condone-them-2299937.html

42. Arbitration and Mediation Services (Equality) Bill, 2010–12, H.L. Bill [72] cl. 1 (England and Wales); text available at http://www.publications.parliament.uk/pa/bills/lbill/2013–2014/0020/14020.pdf. For further discussion of the issues raised, see Maret, Rebecca E., 'Mind the Gap: The Equality Bill and Sharia Arbitration in the United Kingdom', Boston College International and Comparative Law Review, 36, 1 (2013), http://lawdigitalcommons.bc.edu/iclr/vol36/iss1/7; for a full discussion of the legal issues raised, see Reiss, Maria, 'The

Materialization of Legal Pluralism in Britain: Why Sharia Council Decisions Should Be Non-binding', *Arizona Journal of International and Comparative Law*, 26 (2009).

43. Ibid., p. 26.

2. NEEDING A BETTER DEAL

1. Nachbar, Thomas B, 'The Use of Law in Counterinsurgency', Military Law Review, 213 (2011), p. 152, available at https://www.jagcnet. army.mil/DOCLIBS/MILITARYLAWREVIEW.NSF/0/256fb1f93504c 34785257b0c006b99d4/$FILE/By%20Thomas%20B.%20Nachbar.pdf, 'Use of Law in Counterinsurgency', p. 152.

2. See https://www.transparency.org/research/cpi/

3. Foreman, Jonathan; 'Aiding and Abetting', Civitas, 2012, p. 51

4. Chayes, Sarah, *Thieves of State: Why Corruption Threatens Global Security*, New York: W.W. Norton, 2015.

5. Chayes, Sarah, *Thieves of State: Why Corruption Threatens Global Security*, New York: W.W. Norton, 2015, p. 62.

6. Ibid.

7. See, for example, Tilly, Charles, 'War-Making and State-Making as Organised Crime', in Peter B. Evans, Dietrich Rueschemeyer, and Theda Skocpol (eds), *Bringing the State Back In*, Cambridge: Cambridge University Press, 1985, pp. 169–91.

8. See 'Corruption Perceptions Index', Ibid. Although Afghanistan appears on that index to be the third most corrupt place, the two countries below it are Somalia, where it is far too dangerous to obtain data, and North Korea where, likewise, it would be unwise to attempt an objective study of perceptions of corruption.

9. Kalyvas, Stathis, *The Logic of Violence in Civil War*, Cambridge: Cambridge University Press, 2006.

10. Whitman, James Q., *The Verdict of Battle*, Cambridge, MA: Harvard University Press, 2012, p. 94.

11. See Ledwige, Frank, 'Justice and Counter-Insurgency in Afghanistan: A Missing Link', *RUSI Journal*, 154, 1 (2009), pp. 6–9.

12. Galula, David, *Counterinsurgency Warfare: Theory and Practice*, Westport: Praeger, 2006, p. 63.

13. Clausewitz, *On War*, Chapter 1, Section 24.

14. McColl, Robert W., 'The Insurgent State: Territorial Bases of Revolution', *Annals of the Association of American Geographers*, 59, 4 (1969).

15. Kilcullen, David, *Out of the Mountains*: The Coming Age of the Urban Guerrilla, London: Hurst, 2014, p. 157.

16. Mahendrarajah, Shivan, 'Conceptual Failure, the Taliban's Parallel

Hierarchies, and America's Strategic Defeat in Afghanistan', *Small Wars and Insurgencies*, 25, 1 (2014), p. 93.

17. Sitaraman, Ganesh, *The Counterinsurgent's Constitution: Law in the Age of Small Wars,* Oxford: Oxford University Press, 2012, p. 10.
18. Guevara, Che, *Guerrilla Warfare*, n.p.: BN Publishing, 2007 [1960].
19. Ibid., p. 58.
20. For example, in Guevara, 'The Guerrilla as Social Reformer', p. 31; 'Civil Organisation', pp. 66–7; 'Epilogue', pp. 94–5.
21. Ibid., p. 67.
22. Talk at the Frontline Club discussing his book *Butcher and Bolt: Two Hundred Years of Foreign Engagement in Afghanistan*, London: Hutchinson, 2008, 9 October 2009, available at www.frontlineclub.com_videoevents
23. Clark, Kate and Carter, Stephen, 'No Shortcut to Stability: Justice, Politics and Insurgency in Afghanistan', Chatham House, December 2010, p. 4, http://www.chathamhouse.org/sites/default/files/public/Research/Asia/1210pr_afghanjustice.pdf
24. As examples of very many, see Quevedo, Archbishop Orlando B., 'Injustice: The Root of Conflict in Mindanao', address to 2005 Philippine bishops' conference, 'Injustice, Not Poverty, the Cause of Boko Haram Insurgency', Pointblank news, quoting former Nigerian President Gowon, http://pointblanknews.com/pbn/news/injustice-not-poverty-caused-boko-haram-insurgency-gowon/; a discussion paper by the Human Development Network of the Philippines finds that although poverty per se is not a cause, deprivation and injustice 'lie at the heart of armed conflict'. Deprivations include lack of water, healthcare, education and roadways. Injustices include rural families having no or too little land from which to make a living and being cheated or eased out of their fields. See Tria Kerkvliet, Ben, 'A Different View of Insurgencies', HDN Discussion Paper no 5 (2009), http://hdn.org.ph/wp-content/uploads/2010/07/A-Different-View-of-Insurgencies.pdf
25. *My Afghanistan*, Dir. Nagieb Khaja, Magic Hour Films 2012.
26. This ancient idea still subsists in some parts of the UK under the name 'common land'.
27. Tria Kerkvliet, 'A Different View of Insurgencies', p. 15.
28. Guevara, *Guerrilla Warfare*, p. 57.
29. Ibid., pp. 67, 93 and 94.
30. Giap, Vo Nguyen, *People's War, People's Army*, Honolulu: Hawaii University Press, 2001 [1961].
31. Ibid., p. 27.
32. Ibid.
33. Bergerud, Eric, *The Dynamics of Defeat: The Vietnam War in Han Nghia Province*, Boulder, CO: Westview Press, 1990, pp. 55–6.

34. Dodge, Toby, *Inventing Iraq: The Failure of Nation Building and a History Denied*, London: Hurst, 2003, p. 101; Dodge places great emphasis on the influence that the Indian experience of rule had on the British administrators in Iraq (see his Chapter 6).

35. Ibid., pp. 104, 106.

36. Mau Mau fighter interviewed by Caroline Elkins; see Elkins, *Britain's Gulag: The Brutal End of Empire in Kenya*, London: Pimlico, 2005, p. 74.

37. For an excellent full account of the importance of land to insurgency, see Kapstein, Ethan, 'Land and Rebellion: Lessons for Counter-Insurgency', *Survival*, 56, 2 (May 2014), pp. 109–28.

38. Huntington, Samuel P., *Political Order in Changing Societies*, New Haven, CT: Yale University Press, 1968, at p. 325.

39. 'A Bright Shining Narrative', Private distribution, 2012. The reference in the title is to an iconic book on the Vietnam War about the life of a former soldier who becomes disillusioned with ideas of 'pacification'.

40. Ibid.

41. Martin, Mike, *An Intimate War*, London: Hurst, 2014, pp. 43ff. This law 'outlined a programme of land redistribution, according to which all holdings over thirty *jereebs* were to be given out in packages of six *jereebs*. This was not enough to support a family of ten.'

42. Ibid., p. 43.

43. For a full account, see ibid.

44. For a full example, see the Juant Case outlined in Ledwidge, Frank, 'Justice in Helmand: The Challenge of Law Reform in a Society at War', *Asian Affairs*, 40, 1 (2009).

45. Cf. inter alia Martin, *An Intimate War*; Private distribution, 'A Bright Shining Narrative'; Ledwidge, 'Justice in Helmand'.

46. Conversation with head of education of the Helmandi provincial government. The area of the city concerned is called Mukhtar. From discussions with British military officials recently in the country, I have been unable to determine whether this issue has been addressed.

47. The best answer I received was 'the government', although there seemed to be no evidence that this was the case.

48. Jones, Ann, 'In Bed with the US Army', Tom Dispatch, 11 August 2014, http://www.tomdispatch.com/blog/175879/best_of_tomdispatch %3A_ann_jones%2C_in_bed_with_the_u.s._army

49. Mahendrarajah, 'Conceptual Failure', p. 111.

50. Ibid., pp. 111–12.

51. Ibid., p. 104.

52. Griffith, Arthur, 'The Resurrection of Hungary' (1904), p. 163, https://ia600204.us.archive.org/2/items/resurrectionofhu00grifiala/resurrectionofhu00grifiala.pdf

53. Ibid., p. 93.

3. OFFERING A BETTER DEAL: INSURGENT COURTS IN THE TWENTIETH CENTURY

1. It is interesting that courts did not seem to feature heavily among the funded roles. Kosovars constituted a separate ethnic and linguistic group and it is highly unlikely that the judgement of a Kosovar rebel court would carry any weight among the Serbian population. Further, among the majority of Kosovars, who constituted about 90 per cent of Kosovo's population, there was little doubt about the legitimacy of their shadow state. What was at issue was whether they could gain an ascendancy militarily over the incumbent Serbian one.

2. Baylouny, Anne Marie, 'Authority Outside the State: Non-state Actors and New Institutions in the Middle East', in Anne Clunan and Harold Trinkunas (eds), *Ungoverned Spaces: Alternatives to State Authority in an Era of Softened Sovereignty*, Stanford: Stanford University Press, 2010.

3. For fuller discussion of this matter see below, Chapter 7.

4. William Kraus in Spencer Tucker (ed.), *The Encyclopaedia of Insurgency and Counterinsurgency: A New Era of Modern Warfare*, ABC-CLIO 2013, p. 276.

5. Beckett, Ian F.W., *Modern Insurgencies and Counter-Insurgencies*, London: Routledge, 2001, p. 16.

6. Ibid., p. 17

7. Heffer, Simon, 'Why Does Ken Loach Loathe His Country So Much?', *Daily Mail*, 30 May 2006.

8. Technically, there were two concurrent jurisdictions. One was founded on regulations made under the Defence of the Realm (Consolidation) Act 1915, the other power was a residual power accorded to the military in common law. It was the former that was brought into operation. The first test case concerning the detention and trials of Gerald Doyle and Cornelius O'Donovan was lost (see Foxton, David, *Sinn Féin and Crown Courts*, Dublin: Four Courts Press, 2008, pp. 117ff.)

9. Although ninety-three were sentenced to death by court martial, the other sentences were commuted.

10. The National Arbitration Courts Committee, see Townshend, Charles, *The Republic*, London: Allen Lane, 2013, p. 125.

11. Ibid., p. 126.

12. Brayden, John, 'Sinn Féin Courts in Operation', *American Bar Association Journal*, 4 (September 1920), p. 10.

13. Foxton, *Sinn Féin and Crown Courts*, p. 195.

14. Ibid., p. 189; Townshend, *Republic*, p. 127.

15. Ibid., p. 127.

16. Brayden, 'Sinn Féin Courts in Operation', pp. 8–11.

17. One of his two sons had been killed in the British army during the First World War; the other was serving on operations in India at the time the article was written.

18. Brayden, 'Sinn Féin Courts in Operation', p. 10.

19. Ibid., p. 8.

20. Foxton, *Sinn Féin and Crown Courts*, p. 194.

21. Brayden, 'Sinn Féin Courts in Operation', p. 9.

22. Ibid., p. 10.

23. Foxton, *Sinn Féin and Crown Courts*, p. 188.

24. 'Letter from A.M. Sullivan', *The Times*, 10 July 1920.

25. Townshend, *The Republic*, p. 129.

26. Foxton, *Sinn Féin and Crown Courts*, p. 192.

27. RTE (Irish Radio) interview of Conor Maguire (19 January 1969), http://www.rte.ie/archives/exhibitions/920-first-dail-eireann-1919/289506-the-first-dail-sinn-fein-courts/

28. Tyler, Tom R., *Why People Obey the Law*, Princeton, NJ: Princeton University Press, 2006, p. 19.

29. Proclamation quoted in Foxton, *Sinn Féin and Crown Courts*, p. 181, from PRO/TS27/85.

30. Townshend, *The Republic*, p. 338.

31. Foxton, *Sinn Féin and Crown Courts*, p. 185.

32. 'Letter from A.M. Sullivan', *The Times*, 10 July 1920. The Irish Bar Council declared that barristers appearing before the Sinn Féin Courts were committing professional misconduct.

33. Letter to *The Times* quoted in Brayden, 'Sinn Féin Courts in Operation', p. 10.

34. Quoted in Townshend, *The Republic*, p. 130 (no attribution).

35. Kotsonouris, Mary, *The Dail Courts, 1920–24*, Dublin: Irish Academic Press, 1994, p. 5.

36. Mampilly, Zachariah, *Rebel Rulers: Insurgent Governance and Civilian Life during War*, Ithaca, NY: Cornell University Press, 2011, p. 72.

37. Monaghan, Rachel, 'The Return of Captain Moonlight', *Studies in Conflict and Terrorism*, 25 (2002), p. 48.

38. Porch, Douglas, *Counterinsurgency: Exposing the Myths of the New Way of War*, Cambridge: Cambridge University Press, 2013. p. xii.

39. Anderson, Jon Lee, *Guerrillas*, London: Abacus, 1992, p. 172.

40. See also Sivakumaran, Sandesh, *Law of Non-international Armed Conflict*, Oxford: Oxford University Press, 2012, p. 555.

41. Ibid., p. 555, n. 322. See also the classic film *Battle of Algiers* featuring a marriage between two insurgents, presided over by an official who seems to be a judge. Apparently a brief and unremarkable scene, its implications are great, because what is happening is that the new

state, represented by the insurgent officials, is deciding and validating the institution of marriage.

42. Ibid., p. 554.

43. Ibid. It was the author's observation as a 'ceasefire verifier' during the Kosovo War before the NATO intervention that there were insurgent courts in Kosovo, but they were run by, and drew their legitimacy from, the shadow government run by the Lidhja Demokratike e Kosovës (LDK) political party and its allies. The Kosovo Liberation Army—drawn from a different political tradition—did not run courts or any other civil infrastructure. There is little or no literature on this.

44. The SPLM judicial system was clearly impressive, consisting of a full panoply of first instance, appeal and supreme courts founded on an extensive legislative basis. See http://www.nyulawglobal.org/globalex/South_Sudan.htm

45. Anderson, *Guerrillas*, p. 187.

46. FMLN, *Legitimacy of Our Methods of Struggle*, Berkeley: Inkworks Press, 1988.

47. 'Inter-American Commission on Human Rights Periodic Report for 1990–1991', Chapter VI, 'El Salvador', http://www.cidh.org/annualrep/90.91eng/chap. 4a.htm

48. For a discussion of this, see Sivakumaran, *Law of Non-international Armed Conflict*, pp. 552–3.

49. Kalyvas, Stathis, *The Logic of Violence in Civil War*, Cambridge: Cambridge University Press, 2006, pp. 89–90.

50. The mission is known by its acronym MINURSO.

51. 'Periodic Report of the Sahrawi Arab Democratic Republic to the African Commission for Human and People's Rights', October 2001, paragraphs 56–60, http://www.achpr.org/files/sessions/55th/state-reports/2nd-2002–2012/periodic_report_sahrawi_eng.pdf

52. 'Nang Lydia's House: Arbitration at the Barrio Level', Philippine Revolution Web Central, posted March 2013, http://www.philippinerevolution.net/publications/ang_bayan/20130421/arbitration-at-the-barrio-level

53. See, for example, http://www.philippinerevolution.net/statements/20061228_garci-case-being-considered-for-proceedings-in-people-s-court-cpp, where a state governor acquitted in the state courts is referred to the People's Courts.

54. NFDP Guide (October 1972) Part II, Chapter III, Article 2.

55. UN General Assembly, 'Report of the United Nations Special Rapporteur on Extrajudicial, Summary or Arbitrary Executions Phillip Alston from the Mission to the Philippines', 16 April 2008, http://www.refworld.org/cgi-bin/texis/vtx/rwmain?page=search&docid=4

84d2b2f2&skip=0&advsearch=y&process=y&allwords=&exactphrase
=&atleastone=&without=&title=special rapporteur extrajudicial exe
cutions&monthfrom=&yearfrom=&monthto=&yearto=&coa=&langu
age=&citation=

56. The CPN—M is now called the 'Unified' Communist Party of Nepal—Maoist (UCPN—M).
57. 'Parallel Justice Maoist Style', BBC News, 14 October 2006, http://news.bbc.co.uk/1/hi/world/south_asia/6048272.stm
58. 'Judged by the People: The Maoists Grow Stronger', The Economist, 5 October 2006, http://www.economist.com/node/8001629
59. Ibid.
60. See comment by Kunda Dixit, chief editor of the Nepal Times, 'Parallel Justice, Maoist Style', BBC News.
61. Ibid.
62. Ibid.
63. For a fine account of the sophistication of the courts system of the Tamil Tigers' state, see Sivakumaran, 'Courts of Armed Opposition Groups', pp. 493ff. For a detailed account of this court system from a senior Tamil official, see Kamalendran, C., 'The Inside Story of "Eelam Courts"', Sunday Times (Sri Lanka), 14 November 2004, http://sundaytimes.lk/021208/news/courts.html
64. Sivakumaran, Law of Non-international Armed Conflict, p. 562.
65. Ibid., p. 490; also pp. 17–20.
66. The Geneva Conventions 12 August 1949 (International Committee of the Red Cross 2009 edition).
67. Common Article 3.1.
68. Ibid.
69. Common Article 3.1(a).
70. See, for example, Sivakumaran, 'Courts of Armed Opposition Groups'; Somer, Jonathan, 'Jungle Justice: Passing Sentence on the Equality of Belligerents in Non-international Armed Conflict', International Review of the Red Cross, 89, 867 (September 2007), http://www.icrc.org/eng/assets/files/other/irrc-867-somer.pdf; Gejji, Parth S., 'Can Insurgent Courts Be Legitimate within International Humanitarian Law?', Texas Law Review, 91 (2012–13), p. 1525, http://www.texaslrev.com/wp-content/uploads/Gejji.pdf
71. Gejji, 'Can Insurgent Courts Be Legitimate?', p. 1554.
72. Sivakumaran, Law of Non-international Armed Conflict, p. 558.
73. Ibid., p. 562.

4. CALIPHATES OF LAW: INSURGENT COURTS TODAY

1. 'Haidara' in Vice News, 'Inside the Islamic State', August 2014, https://news.vice.com/video/the-islamic-state-full-length
2. Anderson, Jon Lee, *Guerrillas*, London: Abacus, 1992, p. 173.
3. Ibid.
4. Ibid., p. 181.
5. For a full and informed discussion of the degree to which there is distinct 'Taliban' in Helmand, see Martin, Mike, *An Intimate War*, London: Hurst, 2014.
6. Zaeef, Abdul Salam, *My Life with the Taliban*, London: Hurst, 2010, p. 65. See also Rashid, Ahmed, *Taliban*, London: I.B. Tauris, 2010, p. 25.
7. Mahendrarajah, Shivan, 'Conceptual Failure, the Taliban's Parallel Hierarchies, and America's Strategic Defeat in Afghanistan', *Small Wars and Insurgencies*, 25, 1 (2014), p. 100.
8. Interview by author with Helmandi member of provincial council, September 2007.
9. Clark, Kate and Carter, Stephen, 'No Shortcut to Stability: Justice, Politics and Insurgency in Afghanistan', Chatham House, December 2010, p. 4, http://www.chathamhouse.org/sites/default/files/public/Research/Asia/1210pr_afghanjustice.pdf p. 21.
10. For other cases like this, see Ledwidge, Frank, 'Justice in Helmand: The Challenge of Law Reform in a Society at War', *Asian Affairs*, 40, 1 (2009), and Ledwidge, Frank, 'Justice in Helmand: The Challenge of Law Reform in a Society at War', *Asian Affairs*, 40, 1 (2009).
11. Interview with Ahmed Tassal, Helmandi journalist. Tassal had himself interviewed several Taliban judges.
12. This account is taken from my report of the case made at the time, in August 2007. It has been reported elsewhere, in Ledwidge, 'Justice in Helmand'. For other similar cases, see the body of the report and appendices in Antonio Giustozzi, Adam Baczko, and Claudio Franco, 'Shadow Justice: How the Taliban Run Their Judiciary', Integrity Watch, 2012, http://www.iwaweb.org/_docs/reports/research/shadow_justice-how_the_taliban_run_their_judiciary.pdf
13. This account is taken from my report of the case to the UK Provincial Reconstruction Team made in August 2007. It has been reported elsewhere, in Ledwidge, 'Justice in Helmand'.
14. Clark and Carter, 'No Shortcut to Stability', p. 21.
15. Giustozzi, Baczko and Franco, 'Shadow Justice'.
16. Ibid.
17. Ibid., p. 22.

18. There have been allegations of corruption by Taliban courts. However, the Taliban are acutely conscious of this and take steps to redress the problem (see ibid., pp. 27 ff.). See also Giustozzi, Antonio, 'The Taliban's "Military Courts"', *Small Wars and Insurgencies*, 25, 2 (2014), pp. 284–96.
19. Giustozzi, Baczko and Franco, 'Shadow Justice', p. 21.
20. Ledwidge, 'Justice and Counter-Insurgency in Afghanistan'.
21. See 'On the Frontlines with the Taliban', *Fault Lines*, Al-Jazeera America, 4 April 2014 (presented and produced by Nagieb Khaja), http://america.aljazeera.com/watch/shows/fault-lines.html
22. Ibid., p. 27.
23. Ibid., p. 28.
24. See also Mahendrarajah, 'Conceptual Failure', pp. 107–9; Giustozzi, 'Taliban's "Military Courts"', pp. 284–96.
25. Giustozzi, Baczko and Franco, 'Shadow Justice', p. 32.
26. International Crisis Group, 'Reforming Afghanistan's Broken Judiciary', report no. 195 (Brussels 2010), p. 24, http://www.crisisgroup.org/en/regions/asia/south-asia/afghanistan/195-reforming-afghanistans-broken-judiciary.aspx
27. 'Gunmen Kill Afghan Government Prosecutor', *The Hindu*, 21 August 2011, http://www.thehindu.com/news/international/article2379032.ece. See also Patel, Naina, 'The Long Road to Justice', *Guardian*, 15 September 2011, http://www.theguardian.com/world/2011/sep/15/long-road-justice-afghanistan
28. Steele, Jonathan, *Ghosts of Afghanistan: The Haunted Battleground*, London: Portobello, 2012, p. 28.
29. Although the author's interviews would suggest they have had success at the very least in the southern cities of Lashkar Gah and Kandahar.
30. Giustozzi, Baczko and Franco, 'Shadow Justice', p. 40. See many media reports, for example: 'Why Many Afghans Opt for Taliban Justice', BBC News, 2 December 2013, http://www.bbc.co.uk/news/world-asia-24628136
31. 'Somalia's Islamic Courts', *Unreported World* (Reporter Aidan Hartley), Channel 4, Series 12, http://www.sidereel.com/Unreported_World/season-12/episode-10
32. Barnes, Cedric and Hassan, Harun, 'The Rise and Fall of Mogadishu's Islamic Courts', *Journal of Eastern African Studies*, 1, 2 (2007), pp. 151–60.
33. Mwangi, Oscar Gakuo, 'The Union of Islamic Courts and Security Governance in Somalia', *African Security Review*, 19, 1 (2010), p. 92.
34. Ibid., passim.
35. Ibid., p. 91.

36. Channel 4, 'Somalia's Islamic Courts'.
37. Verhoeven, Harry, 'The Self-Fulfilling Prophecy of Failed States: Somalia, State Collapse and the Global War on Terror', *Journal of Eastern African Studies*, 3, 3 (2009), p. 417.
38. Mwangi, 'Union of Islamic Courts', p. 91.
39. Hansen, Stig Jarle, *Al Shabaab in Somalia: The History and Ideology of a Militant Islamist Group 2005–2012*, London: Hurst, 2013, for a detailed account of Al-Shabaab.
40. MacFarquhar, Neil, 'A Battle for Syria, One Court at a Time', *New York Times*, 13 March 2013, http://www.nytimes.com/2013/03/14/world/middleeast/a-battle-for-syria-one-court-at-a-time.html?pagewanted=all&_r=0
41. CNN, 'Rebel Court Fills Void amid Syrian Civil War', 26 January 2013, http://edition.cnn.com/2013/01/25/world/meast/syria-rebel-court/index.html
42. Ibid.
43. Baczko, Adam, Dorronsoro, Gilles and Quesney, Charles, 'The Civilian Administration of the Insurgency in Aleppo, Syria', Global Observatory, 19 November 2013, http://www.theglobalobservatory.org/analysis/624-the-civilian-administration-of-the-insurgency-in-aleppo.html
44. Channel 7 France, 'Syrian Rebels Establish Brutal Sharia Courts in Captured Areas', Clarion Project, 8 September 2013, http://www.clarionproject.org/videos/syrian-rebels-establish-brutal-sharia-courts-captured-areas
45. Agence France Presse, 'Syrian Rebels Set Up Courts in Aleppo', Huffington Post, 12 April 2013, http://www.huffingtonpost.com/2013/04/12/syrian-rebels-courts-aleppo_n_3066264.html
46. Channel 7 France, 'Syrian Rebels Establish Brutal Sharia Courts in Captured Areas'.
47. Baczko, Dorronsoro and Quesney, 'The Civilian Administration of the Insurgency in Aleppo, Syria'.
48. For a full account, see Warrick, Joby, *Black Flags: The Rise of ISIS*, New York: Corgi 2016, especially pp. 345–7.
49. March, Andrew F. and Revkin, Mara, 'Caliphate of Law', *Foreign Affairs*, April 2015 https://mararevkin.wordpress.com/2015/04/15/caliphate-of-law/
50. Revkin, Mara, 'ISIS' Social Contract', *Foreign Affairs*, 12 January 2016 https://mararevkin.wordpress.com/
51. See Revkin, Mara, 'The Legal Foundations of the Islamic State', Brookings paper, 16 July 2016, p. 11, https://www.brookings.edu/research/the-legal-foundations-of-the-islamic-state/
52. Napoleoni, Loretta, *The Islamist Phoenix: The Islamic State (ISIS) and the Redrawing of the Middle East*, New York: Seven Stories, 2014, pp. 48–9.

53. Napoleoni, *The Islamist Phoenix*, p. 55.

54. Ibid.

55. For an extended discussion of ISIS and its social contract, see Revkin, 'ISIS' Social Contract'.

56. Zelin, Aaron, 'The Islamic State of Iraq and Syria Has a Consumer Protection Office', *The Atlantic*, 13 June 2014, http://www.theatlantic.com/international/archive/2014/06/the-isis-guide-to-building-an-islamic-state/372769/

57. Karouny, Mariam, 'In Raqqa, ISIS Governs with Fear and Efficiency', *The National* (Pakistan), 5 September 2014, http://www.thenational.ae/world/middle-east/in-raqqa-isil-governs-with-fear-and-efficiency#ixzz3CS8248zo

58. Ibid.

59. Lister, 'Profiling the Islamic State', p. 26.

60. March and Revkin, 'Caliphate of Law'.

61. Vice News, 'Inside the Islamic State'.

62. Ibid., minute 27.

63. Ibid., minute 28:50.

64. Cockburn, Patrick, *The Jihadis Return: ISIS and the New Sunni Uprising*, New York: OR Books, 2014, p. 119.

65. See Revkin, 'Legal Foundations of the Islamic State', pp. 22ff.

66. Ibid., p. 26.

67. The case is also referred to in 'Legal Foundations of the Islamic State', p. 30.

68. Ibid.

69. See Revkin, Mara; 'Is ISIS Good at Governing?', The Experts Weigh In (Part One), Brookings Online, 20 November 2015, https://mararevkin.wordpress.com/2015/11/20/brookings-experts-weigh-in-is-isis-good-at-governing/; https://mararevkin.wordpress.com/2015/11/20/brookings-experts-weigh-in-is-isis-good-at-governing/

70. Discussion with UN official June 2016. It may well be that the seeds of this project are to be found here; 'The Importance of Planning Syria's Reconstruction', World Bank, http://www.worldbank.org/en/news/feature/2016/05/24/the-importance-of-planning-syria-s-eventual-reconstruction

71. Kadri, Sadakat, *'Heaven on Earth': A Journey through Shari'a Law*, London: Vintage, 2013, p. 263.

72. Ibid.

5. DISRUPTIVE LITIGATION

1. Quoted from Robertson, Geoffrey, *The Tyrannicide Brief*: The Story of the Man who sent Charles I to the Scaffold, London: Vintage, 2010, p. 156.

2. Vergès, Jacques, *Terror's Advocate*, Dir. Barbet Shroeder, 2010 at minute 20
3. Vergès, Jacques, *De la stratégie judiciaire*, Paris: Editions de minuit, 1968.
4. Ibid., introduction.
5. Ibid., p. 94.
6. Foxton, David, *Sinn Féin and Crown Courts, Dublin*: Four Courts Press, 2008, p. 174.
7. Cobain, Ian, *Cruel Britannia: A Secret History of Torture*, London: Portobello, 2012, p. 189. McGonigal was one of the 'originals' of the SAS regiment and a Catholic.
8. Quoted in Easton, Richard, 'A Case in Point: A Once Powerful Weapon', *Solicitors Journal*, 20 September 2013, http://www.solicitorsjournal.com/blog/case-point-once-powerful-weapon
9. Ibid.
10. Vergès, *De la stratégie judiciaire*, p. 97.
11. See Saint-Pierre, François, 'Non, Jacques Vergès n'a pas inventé la défense de rupture', *Le Monde*, 20 August 2013, http://www.lemonde.fr/idees/article/2013/08/20/non-jacques-verges-n-a-pas-invente-la-defense-de-rupture_3463953_3232.html; Easton, 'Case in Point'.
12. Saint-Pierre, 'Non, Jacques Vergès'.
13. Morgan, Ted, *My Battle for Algiers*, New York: Smithsonian Books, 2007, p. 213.
14. Ibid.
15. Vergès, *De la stratégie judiciaire*, p. 22.
16. Quoted in Foxton, *Sinn Féin and Crown Courts*, p. 228.
17. Ibid., p. 266.
18. Ibid., p. 200.
19. Ibid., p. 204.
20. Dáil debates, 11 March 1921,
21. Townshend, Charles, *The Republic*, London: Allen Lane, 2013, pp. 129–31.
22. Bravin, Jess, *The Terror Courts: Rough Justice at Guantanamo Bay*, New Haven, CT: Yale University Press, 2014, p. 368.
23. *Sandar et al. v. State of Chattisgargh*, 5 July 2011, Supreme Court of India, quoted in Bhandar, Brenna, 'Strategies of Legal Rupture: The Politics of Judgement', *Windsor Yearbook of Access to Justice*, 30, 2 (2012), p. 59.
24. Ibid., p. 75.
25. Ibid., p. 77.
26. Ibid., p. 78.

27. Foxton, *Sinn Féin and Crown Courts*, p. 193.
28. Healy, Tim (KC), 'Letters and Leaders', quoted in ibid., p. 262.
29. Morgan, *My Battle for Algiers*, p. 213.
30. 'History Will Absolve Me', Castro's speech in his own defence at the Moncada Barracks Trial 1953, available in English translation at http://www.marxists.org/history/cuba/archive/castro/1953/10/16.htm— The speech as it now exists is Castro's recollection of what was said, as no contemporaneous record exists.
31. Dunlap, Charles, 'Law and Military Interventions: Preserving Humanitarian Values in 21st-Century Conflicts', Harvard University Kennedy School of Government, Carr Center for Human Rights Working Paper, 29 November 2001, p. 8 available at http://people.duke.edu/~pfeaver/dunlap.pdf
32. The terms are my terms.
33. Kittrie, Orde, *Lawfare: Law as a Weapon of War*, Oxford: Oxford University Press, 2015. pp. 284–5.
34. Cheng, Dean, 'Winning without Fighting: The Chinese Psychological Warfare Challenge', Heritage Foundation Report, 12 July 2013, http://www.heritage.org/global-politics/report/winning-without-fighting-the-chinese-psychological-warfare-challenge
35. Conversation with Dr Cheng, December 2013.
36. See also Kittrie, *Lawfare*, pp. 161–97 for an extensive account of how the People's Republic of China has applied lawfare at the grand strategic level.
37. Padilla, Juan Manuel, 'Lawfare: The Colombian Case', paper presented to Fort Leavenworth School of Advanced Military Studies, 2010, available at http://www.restauracionacional.org/lawfare-the-colombian-case/
38. See, for example, 'State Department Cable Says Colombian Army Was Responsible for Palace of Justice Deaths, Disappearances', National Security Archive, 28 October 2009, http://www2.gwu.edu/~nsarchiv/NSAEBB/NSAEBB289/index.htm
39. The events of 30 January 1972 resulted in the deaths from British army fire of fourteen men. Two extensive inquiries followed. The first by Lord Widgery is often criticised as a 'whitewash' (see, for example, Cohen, Nick, 'Schooled in Scandal', *The Guardian*, 1 February 2004, http://www.theguardian.com/politics/2004/feb/01/davidkelly.politicalcolumnists); the second, under Lord Saville, was the most expensive inquiry in British legal history and ended in 2010.
40. Coughlin, Con, 'Hamas Helping British Lawyers Target Israel', *The Telegraph*, 21 December 2009, http://www.telegraph.co.uk/news/worldnews/middleeast/israel/6850900/Hamas-helping-British-lawyers-target-Israel.html

41. *Ireland* v. *United Kingdom* application no. 5321/71 (judgment dated 18 January 1978), http://www.cvce.eu/en/obj/judgement_of_the_european_court_of_human_rights_ireland_v_the_united_kingdom_18_january_1978-en-e07eaf5f-6d09–4207–8822–0add3176f8e6. html

42. Although there have been successful efforts in the civil courts to sue alleged members of a 'real IRA' team who were found to have caused the Omagh bombings in 1998, killing twenty-eight. See 'Omagh Bomb Families Win Multi-million Pound Legal Case', *Belfast Telegraph*, 8 June 2009, http://www.belfasttelegraph.co.uk/news/local-national/omagh-bomb-families-win-multimillion-pound-legal-case-28482210.html; one solicitor, Jason McCue, who brought the case, is also engaged in actions against the Libyan government for support of the IRA during the 'Troubles'.

43. Kaufman, Alan G., 'Review of *Justice in Blue and Gray*' (by Stephen Neff, 2010), 7 March 2012, http://www.lawfareblog.com/2012/03/justice-in-blue-and-grey-a-legal-history-of-the-civil-war/#UvonBkDivIV

44. Gates, Robert M., 'A Balanced Strategy: Reprogramming the Pentagon for a New Age', *Foreign Affairs*, 88, January–February 2009 http://www.jmhinternational.com/news/news/selectednews/files/2009/01/20090201_20090101_ForeignAffairs_ABalancedStrategy.pdf

45. Holzer, Mark, 'Offensive Lawfare and the Current Conflict', *Harvard National Security Journal*, 20 April 2013 http://harvardnsj.org/2012/04/offensive-lawfare-and-the-current-conflict/

46. Ibid., paragraph 3.

47. See 'Italy Indicts 31 in Alleged CIA Kidnapping', Associated Press, 16 February 2007, http://www.msnbc.msn.com/id/17184663/

48. *Almog* v. *Arab Bank, PLC, 471 F. Supp. 2d 257 (E.D.N.Y. 2007) (No. 04–CV-5564)*, http://www.motleyrice.com/files/9-11-to-bankrupt-documents/almog-et-al-v-arab-bank-complaint-12-21-04.pdf

49. General V. Giap, quoted in Langer, Howard, *The Vietnam War: An Encyclopedia of Quotations*, Westport, CT: Greenwood Press, 2005), p. 318.

50. Dannat, General Sir Richard, *Leading from the Front: An Autobiography*, New York: Corgi, 2011, p. 382.

51. Bravin, *Terror Courts*, pp. 322–3 describes the Qahtani case in some detail; the case was dropped, as were many others due to evidence being determined as inadmissible because it had been obtained under torture by CIA operatives.

52. Quoted in Sands, Philippe, *Torture Team: Deception, Cruelty and the Compromise of Law*, London: Penguin, 2009, p. xiv.

53. See, for example, the stream of cases referred to in the United States

Federal and Supreme Court's judgment of *Hamdan* v. *Rumsfeld* (US SC), http://www.supremecourt.gov/opinions/05pdf/05-184.pdf; See also Bravin, *Terror Courts*, p. 204.

54. Ahmed, Dawood, 'America's Army of Lawyers Is Almost as Deadly as Its Drones', *The Guardian*, 20 November 2013, http://www.theguardian.com/commentisfree/2013/nov/20/us-drone-strikes-pakistan-legal-debate

55. For example Dunlap, Charles, 'Lawfare: A Decisive Element of 21st-Century Conflict', Joint Forces Quarterly, 59 (2009), p. 34, available at http://www.americanbar.org/content/dam/aba/migrated/2011_build/law_national_security/LawfareDunlapJun09.authcheckdam.pdf; and Kennedy, David, *Of War and Law*, Princeton, NJ: Princeton University Press, 2006, p. 119.

56. For full details of this case and its aftermath, see TSO, 'Report of the Baha Mousa Inquiry', TSO, 2011, http://webarchive.nationalarchives.gov.uk/+/http://www.bahamousainquiry.org/; See also TSO, 'The Report of the Detainee Inquiry', TSO, 2013, available at http://www.detaineeinquiry.org.uk/, and Al-Sweady Public Inquiry Team, 'The Al-Sweady Public Inquiry', available at http://www.alsweadyinquiry.org/ (the inquiry is ongoing at the time of writing).

57. *Al Skeini and others* v. *United Kingdom*, application no. 55721/07 at European Court of Human Rights. *Al Jeddah* v. *United Kingdom* application no. 27021/08 at European Court of Human Rights. For a sound summary of these rather complex issues, see http://www.interights.org/al-skeini/index.html

58. Al-Sweady Public Inquiry Team, 'The Al-Sweady Public Inquiry', http://www.alsweadyinquiry.org/

59. *R (on the application of Maya Evans)* v. *Secretary of State for Defence* (2010 EWHC 1445 Admin), http://www.judiciary.gov.uk/Resources/JCO/Documents/Judgments/r-evans-v-ssd-judgment.pdf and *R (on the application of Maya Evans)* v. *Secretary of State for Defence* (2013 EWHC 3068), http://www.bailii.org/ew/cases/EWHC/Admin/2013/3068.html

60. *R (on the application of Serdar Mohammed)* v. *Secretary of State for Defence* detailed 'Grounds of Claim', http://www.reprieve.org.uk/static/downloads/2012_03_23_PUB_Serdar_Mohammed_Grounds_of_Claim.pdf

61. *R (on the application of Serdar Mohammed)* v. *Secretary of State for Defence* (2012 EWHC 3454 Admin), http://www.bailii.org/cgi-bin/markup.cgi?doc=/ew/cases/EWHC/Admin/2012/3454.html&query=Serdar+and+Mohammed&method=boolean. The case continues; see http://www.leighday.co.uk/International-and-group-claims/Afghanistan for updates.

62. Lord Justice Richards in *R (on the application of Maya Evans)* v. *Secretary of State for Defence* (2010 EWHC 1445 Admin), paragraph 1.
63. For a fuller discussion, see Maya Evans (2010) case at paragraphs 58–75.
64. Discussions with several legal and military intelligence officers.
65. Strachan, Hew, *The Direction of War*, Cambridge: Cambridge University Press, 2013, p. 279.
66. Discussion with solicitor closely involved in the Maya Evans cases.
67. Kennedy, *Of War and Law*, p. 119.
68. Discussion with NATO military intelligence officer, March 2014. A similar account was rendered (by a different officer) of another targeting meeting in the same campaign where the legal constraint was not slander but the possibility that capture might result in ill-treatment. In such circumstances, authority was given in that case to kill. These accounts have something of the nature of anecdote, but they certainly reflect at the very least a perceived excessive punctiliousness on the part of military lawyers as a result of pressure from domestic litigation.
69. See *Al Skeini and others* v. *United Kingdom*, application no. 55721/07 at European Court of Human Rights, judgment *Al Jeddah* v. *United Kingdom*, application no. 27021/08 at European Court of Human Rights. For a discussion of these cases, see Milanovic, Marko 'Al Skeini and Al Jedda in Strasbourg', *European Journal of International Law*, 23 (2012), pp. 121–39.
70. See, for example, the many cases litigated concerning detention and interrogation in US facilities such as Guantanamo Bay.
71. Interview with civilian justice advisor to the UK Provincial Reconstruction Team, Lashkar Gah, 2011. Interview dated 29 April 2014.
72. For an excellent review of this toxic practice, see 'Libel Tourism: A Growing Threat to Free Speech', Article 19/Freedom House (27 May 2008), https://www.article19.org/data/files/pdfs/publications/uk-libel-tourism.pdf. Matters became so bad that the New York State Legislature passed the 'Libel Tourism Act', which effectively prevented judgments in foreign libel courts from being enforced in New York State. This statute was essentially aimed at 'forum shoppers' and 'libel tourists' using UK courts.
73. Kittrie, *Lawfare*.
74. Ibid., pp. 295–305.
75. In the UK, the government has outlined some of the crimes subject to universal jurisdiction; they include torture, kidnapping, hostage-taking. However, a warrant may only be issued with the consent of the politically nominated attorney-general. See, for example, UK Govern-

ment Press Release, 'Universal Jurisdiction', 11 September 2011, https://www.gov.uk/government/news/universal-jurisdiction

76. See *Regina* v. *Bartle and the Commissioner of Police for the Metropolis and others ex parte Pinochet* (1999 House of Lords). There was along legal saga surrounding this case, which eventually resulted in Pinochet being returned to Chile.

77. These efforts take place in various countries fairly regularly. On the day this section was being written, for example, the BBC reported that Israeli politician Tzipi Livni was being 'summonsed by UK police' during a visit to the UK. See 'Israeli Politician Tzipi Livni "Summonsed by UK Police"', BBC News, 4 July 2016, http://www.bbc.co.uk/news/world-middle-east-36697324

78. Padilla, 'Lawfare'.

6. COUNTERINSURGENT DILEMMAS: HINTS FROM HISTORY

1. Callwell, Charles, *Small Wars, Their Principles and Practice*, Tales End Press edn, 2012, Chapter XIII

2. Clunan, Anne and Trinkunas, Harold, 'Alternative Governance and Security', in Anne Clunan and Harold Trinkunas (eds), *Ungoverned Spaces*, Stanford, CA: Stanford University Press, 2010, p. 277.

3. Clunan, Anne and Trinkunas, Harold, 'Conceptualising Ungoverned Spaces', in Clunan and Trinkunas (eds), *Ungoverned Spaces*, p. 27.

4. Straw, J., 'Failed and Failing States', European Research Institute Speech, September 2002.

5. Rabasa, Angel et al., *Ungoverned Territories*, Santa Monica: RAND, 2007, p. iii, http://www.rand.org/content/dam/rand/pubs/monographs/2007/RAND_MG561.pdf; see also Lamb, R.D., 'Ungoverned Areas and Threats from Safe Havens', Final Report of the Ungoverned Areas Project, Prepared for the Office of the Under Secretary of Defense for Policy, http://www.cissm.umd.edu/papers/files/ugash_report_final.pdf

6. Lengthy chapters in the book cover the Pakistani–Afghan border region, the Arabian peninsula, the 'Sulawesi-Mindanao Arc', the East Africa corridor, West Africa, the North Caucasus, the Colombia–Venezuela border, the Guatemala–Chiapas border.

7. See, for example, Wheelan, Theresa, 'African Security and US Interest: The Problem of Ungoverned Space', Presentation by Theresa Wheelan, US deputy assistant secretary of defense for African affairs on establishment of 'Africa Command' (2007), http://www.youtube.com/watch?v=0zd2uE5l33E

8. For example, Call, Charles T., 'The Fallacy of the "Failed State"', *Third*

World Quarterly, 29, 8 (2008), pp. 1391–407; Hehir, Aidan, 'The Myth of the Failed State and the War on Terror: A Challenge to the Conventional Wisdom', Journal of Intervention and Statebuilding, 1, 3 (2007), pp. 307–32; Boas, Morten, 'The Rhetoric of the Failed State', European Journal of Development Research, 17, 3 (2005), pp. 385–95.

9. Hehir, 'The Myth of the Failed State', p. 328.
10. Ibid., p. 329.
11. Johnson, T.H. and Mason, C., 'No Sign until the Burst of Fire', International Security, 32, 4 (Spring 2008), p. 55.
12. Clunan and Trinkunas, 'Conceptualising Ungoverned Spaces', p. 27.
13. Mampilly, Zachariah, Rebel Rulers: Insurgent Governance and Civilian Life During War, Ithaca, NY: Cornell University Press, 2011, p. 46.
14. Clapham, C., 'The Global–Local Politics of State Decay', in Robert Rotberg (ed.), When States Fail: Causes and Consequences, Princeton: Princeton University Press, 2003, pp. 78–9.
15. From 2011 to 2013, Afghanistan was assessed by Transparency International as the most corrupt country in the world. See Transparency International, 'Corruption Perceptions Index' (annual), http://www.transparency.org/cpi2013/results
16. Griffiths, John 'What Is Legal Pluralism', Journal of Legal Pluralism, 24, 2 (1986), p. 1.
17. Ibid., p. 4.
18. Ordinance of the East Indian Company 1772, quoted in ibid., p. 6.
19. Pirie, Fernanda, The Anthropology of Law, Oxford: Oxford University Press, 2013, p. 46.
20. Lugard, Frederick, The Dual Mandate in British Tropical West Africa, Forgotten Books, 2012.
21. Lugard also served as an administrator in Hong Kong from 1905 to 1912
22. Lugard, Dual Mandate, pp. 199–200, where the system that was applied to Northern Nigeria is described. Today, this is the heartland of Boko Haram.
23. Ibid., p. 194
24. Roberts, Simon, Order and Dispute, New Orleans: Quid Pro Quo Books, 2013, p. 163.
25. Ibid., p. 164.
26. Porter, Doug in Brian Tamanaha, Caroline Sage, and Michael Woolcock (eds), Legal Pluralism and Development: Scholars and Practitioners in Dialogue, Cambridge: Cambridge University Press, 2012, p. 166.
27. Santos, Boaventura de Sousa, Toward a New Common Sense: Law, Globalisation and Emancipation, London: Butterworth, 2002, p. 114–15, quoted in Griffiths, 'What Is Legal Pluralism?', p. 7.

28. French colonial administration did not devolve power to local poten-
tates; they tended to be subordinate to the local political officer; see
Crowder, Michael, 'Indirect Rule: French and British Style', *Journal of
the International African Institute*, 34, 3 (July 1964), p. 197.

29. Hasluck, Margaret, 'The Albanian Blood Feud', in Paul Bohannan (ed.),
Law and Warfare: Studies in the Anthropology of Conflict, Garden City, NY:
Natural History Press, 1967, p. 381.

30. Gawrych, George, *The Crescent and the Eagle (1871–1913): Ottoman
Rule, Islam and the Albanians*, London: I.B. Tauris, 2006.

31. Ibid., p. 30.

32. Oakley-Hill, David, *An Englishman in Albania: Memoirs of a British Officer
1929–1955*, London: I.B. Tauris/Centre for Albanian Studies, 2002.

33. Kuehn, Thomas, *Empire, Islam and the Politics of Difference: Yemen 1849–
1918*, Leiden: Brill, 2011, pp. 144–5; Kuehn takes the view that,
unlike the British and French, it was not the policy, or at least the
intention, of the Ottomans to institutionalise the differences between
the rulers and the ruled and create a permanent or long-lasting hier-
archical order. It was the intention of the Ottoman central government to develop modes of governance that on the contrary would
bring the conquered peoples into the Ottoman polity. In places such
as Northern Albania and Yemen, this was not possible.

34. Abdo, Mohammed, 'Legal Pluralism, Sharia Courts and Constitutional
Issues in Ethiopia', *Mizan Law Review*, 5, 1 (2011), available at http://
www.ajol.info/index.php/mlr/article/view/68769; Hagmann, Tobias,
'The Return of Garrison Rule to Ethiopia', Paper presented at
G.M. Carter conference, 'The Politics of Permanent Flux: State–
Society Relations in the Horn of Africa', 15–16 March 2013,
University of Florida, Gainesville. This paper describes an Ethiopian
'Forward Approach' to its intractable Somali Region with military,
special police and other security bodies garrisoned in an area where
legal and political authority is essentially devolved to clan interests
ostensibly favourable to Ethiopian government interests. For an account
of Somali society and law, see Lewis, Ioan and Samatar, Said, *A Pastoral
Democracy*, London: James Currey, 1999; and for a somewhat libertar-
ian description of Somali Law (known as *xeer*) see van Notten, Michael,
The Law of the Somalis, Trenton, NJ: Red Sea Press, 2005.

35. Interview with Sarah Vaughan, September 2014.

36. Sitaraman, Ganesh, *The Counterinsurgent's Constitution: Law in the Age of
Small Wars*, Oxford: Oxford University Press, 2012, p. 178.

37. See, for example, Crowder, 'Indirect Rule', p. 197.

38. See ibid., and Tripodi, Christian, *Edge of Empire: The British Political
Officer and Tribal Administration on the North West Frontier 1877–1947*,
Aldershot: Ashgate, 2011.

39. Stewart, Rory and Knaus, Gerald, *Can Intervention Work?*, New York: Norton Global Ethics Series, 2011, p. 22.

40. Ibid., p. 20.

41. Porch, Douglas, *Counterinsurgency: Exposing the Myths of the New Way of War*, Cambridge: Cambridge University Press, 2013, p. 32.

42. Tripodi, Christian, 'Peacemaking through Bribes or Cultural Empathy: The Political Officer and Britain's Strategy towards the North West Frontier 1901–1945', *Journal of Strategic Studies*, 31, 1 (February 2008), pp. 123ff.

43. Centred on the *bureaux arabes*.

44. Porch, *Counterinsurgency*, p. 33.

45. Ibid., p. 36.

46. For a full account of Sandeman's life, see Tucker, A.L.F., 'Sandeman: Peaceful Conqueror of Baluchistan' (1921), http://archive.org/stream/sirrobertgsandem00tuckrich/sirrobertgsandem00tuckrich_djvu.txt

47. Gilmour, David, *The Ruling Caste: Imperial Lives in the Victorian Raj*, London: Pimlico, 2007, p. 171.

48. Imperial War Museum interview with Olaf Caroe.

49. Porch, *Counterinsurgency*, p. 36.

50. For an extended discussion of the importance of 'holistic intelligence', see Ledwidge, Frank, *Losing Small Wars: British Military Failure in Iraq and Afghanistan*, New Haven, CT: Yale University Press, 2011, pp. 223–30.

51. Under article 247(3) of the Constitution of 1973, no act of parliament is applicable to the FATA or any part thereof unless the president of Pakistan so directs. He rules directly and elected representatives have no say in the governance of the FATA.

52. FATA comprises seven agencies and six frontier regions, including Waziristan.

53. A former chief justice of the Supreme Court of Pakistan, Alvin Robert Cornelius, declared the FCR to be 'obnoxious to all recognised modern principles governing the dispensation of justice'; *Sumunder* v. *State* (PLD 1954 FC 228).

54. That said, significant amendments were made in 2011, including a restriction on collective punishment of tribes, a measure that remarkably was still available to authorities until 2011.

55. Carothers, Thomas, 'Promoting the Rule of Law Abroad: The Problem of Knowledge', in Carothers, Thomas, *Critical Mission: Essays on Democracy Promotion*, Washington, DC: Carnegie Endowment for International Peace, 2004, pp. 15ff.

56. Simpson, A. W. B. 'Round up the Usual Suspects: The Legacy of British

Colonialism and the European Convention on Human Rights, *Loyola Law Review*, 629 (1995–96), p. 648; the Criminal Tribes Act of Burma allowed the authorities to categorise a tribe, gang or class 'addicted to the systematic commission of non-bailable offences' as a 'criminal tribe'. Various consequences followed: for example, the entire tribe could be fingerprinted and each person's residence controlled. In parts of upper Burma, the entire tribe could be detained; see 1 Burma Code 401; India Act VI (1924).

57. Gilmour, *Ruling Caste*, p. 171.

58. Chiefs Courts Ordinance 1931 was itself a modification of the Civil Courts Ordinance of 1929. For a full discussion, see Jok, Aleu et al., 'A Study of Customary Law in Southern Sudan', World Vision and South Sudan Secretariat on Legal and Constitutional Affairs, 2004. For a complete discussion of the impact of this and other similar enactments in Southern Sudan and their legacy, see Fadlalla, Mohammed, *The Customary Laws of Southern Sudan, Customary Law of Dinka and Nuer*, iUniverse, 2009.

59. Section 7 Chiefs Courts Ordinance 1931; see Jok et al., *Study of Customary Law*, p. 14.

60. Fadlalla, *Customary Laws*, p. 21.

61. South Sudan Local Government Act 2009, section 98(1).

62. Roberts, *Order and Dispute*, p. xiii.

63. Deng, Francis M., 'Customary Law in the Cross Fire of Sudan's War of Identities', in Isser, Deborah (ed.), *Customary Justice and the Rule of Law in War-Torn Societies*, Washington, DC: United States Institute of Peace, 2011, pp. 285–323.

64. Ibid., p. 307.

65. A case can be made that the current Ethiopian 'ethnic federalist' state is adopting a similar approach to the government of its regions. This is an intensely contested and controversial arrangement.

66. Dodge, Toby, *Inventing Iraq: The Failure of Nation Building and a History Denied*, London: Hurst, 2003.

67. Ibid., p. 120.

7. TWENTIETH-CENTURY COUNTERINSURGENCY JUDICIAL STRATEGY: THE BRITISH EXPERIENCE

1. Kennedy, David, *Of War and Law*, Princeton, NJ: Princeton University Press, 2006, pp. 13ff.

2. Ibid., p. 21.

3. Most notably *Small Wars Journal* (http://smallwarsjournal.com/). Many others along those lines have been set up to promote discussion amongst COIN 'practitioners'.

4. For example, there is no mention in FM 3–24 of the US Civil War. There is a mention of an 1847 proto-Fenian document advising rebels to 'break up' the 'force of England'; see FM 3–24 (2006 edition), paragraphs 3–102.

5. Suhrke, Astri, 'Exogenous State-Building: The Contradictions of International State-Building in Afghanistan', in Whit Mason (ed.), *The Rule of Law in Afghanistan: Missing in Inaction*, Oxford: Oxford University Press, 2011.

6. Few, Michael, 'This Isn't the COIN You're Looking For', *Foreign Policy* (December 2011).

7. The third stanza reads: 'Take up the White Man's burden/The savage wars of peace/Fill full the mouth of Famine/And bid the sickness cease;/And when your goal is nearest/(The end for others sought)/ Watch sloth and heathen folly/Bring all your hope to nought.'

8. Kilcullen, David, *Out of the Mountains: The Coming Age of the Urban Guerrilla*, 2013, p. 23.

9. Crawshaw, Michael, 'The Evolution of British COIN', attachment to MOD JDP 3–40 (undated UK government publication), https://www. gov.uk/government/uploads/system/uploads/attachment_data/ file/43334/jdp340theevolutionofbritishcoinbymichaelcrawshaw.pdf

10. Colonel David Benest in 'British Atrocities in Counterinsurgency', http://www.militaryethics.org/British-Atrocities-in-Counter-Insurgency/10/

11. For example, Porch, Douglas, *Counterinsurgency: Exposing the Myths of the New Way of War*, Cambridge: Cambridge University Press, 2013; Nagl, John, *Learning to Eat Soup with a Knife*, Chicago: University of Chicago Press, 2002; Ledwidge, Frank, *Losing Small Wars: British Military Failure in Iraq and Afghanistan*, New Haven, CT: Yale University Press, 2011, pp. 223–30.

12. Mockaitis, Thomas, *British Counterinsurgency in the Post-imperial Era*, Manchester: Manchester University Press, 1995, p. 12. Examples of scholars extolling the 'British approach' were plentiful—before 2005.

13. Farwell, Byron, *Queen Victoria's Little Wars*, London: Wordsworth, 1999, p. 364.

14. See 'Human Security Report 2005', www.hsrgroup.org/human-security-reports/2005/text.aspx. This reports states that Britain was involved in twenty-one 'international conflicts' between 1946 and 2003, ahead of France (nineteen), the United States (sixteen) and the Soviet Union (nine).

15. Army Staff College, *Handbook on Counter-Revolutionary Warfare*, Camberley: Army Staff College, 1995. In chronological order: Greece (1945–6); Palestine (1945–8); Egypt (1946–56); Malaya (1948–60);

Eritrea (1949); Kenya (1952–6); Cyprus (1954–8); Aden (1955, 1956–8); Togoland (1957); Brunei (1962); Borneo (1963–6); Radfan (1964); Aden (1965–7); Dhofar (1970–6); Northern Ireland (1969–2007); Afghanistan (2001 to date); and Iraq (2003 to date). I am grateful to Martin Bayly for allowing me to read his thesis for his Oxford MPhil—'COINing a New Doctrine', unpublished MPhil thesis, Oxford University, 2009—containing this information, and for the insights gained from extensive conversations with this emerging scholar.

16. General Charles James Napier, cited in Farwell, *Queen Victoria's Little Wars*, p. 20.

17. 'Duties in Aid of the Civil Power', London: HMSO, 1923, p. 3, cited in Mockaitis, Thomas, *British Counterinsurgency 1919–1960*, London: Macmillan, 1990, p. 18.

18. Only four years before, in 1919, there had been a departure from the concept of minimum force at Amritsar, when General Reginald Dyer had given the order for soldiers to open fire on a demonstrating crowd, killing 379 and wounding over 1,000 others. For a discussion of the reality behind the rhetoric, see most recently Mockaitis, Thomas, 'The Minimum Force Debate: Contemporary Sensibilities Meet Imperial Practice', *Small Wars and Insurgencies*, 23, 4–5 (2012), pp. 762–80.

19. Gwynn, Major General Sir Charles, *Imperial Policing*, London: Macmillan, 1936; Simson, H.J., *Rule and Rebellion in the British Empire*, Edinburgh: Blackwood, 1937.

20. Alderson, Colonel Alex, 'The Validity of British Counterinsurgency Doctrine after the War in Iraq 2003–2009', PhD thesis, Cranfield University, 2010, https://dspace.lib.cranfield.ac.uk/bitstream/1826/4264/1/100126-Alderson-PhD%20Thesis.pdf

21. Ibid., p. 80.

22. 'Duties in Aid of the Civil Power'. This 1923 publication was followed in 1934 by *Imperial Policing* by Major General Sir Charles Gwynn (not a formal doctrinal publication) and 'Notes on Imperial Policing', which certainly was published by the War Office (but, says Alderson, possibly also authored by Gwynn), also in 1934. In 1949, 'Imperial Policing and Duties in Aid of the Civil Power' was published as a single document.

23. Counter Insurgency Operations, Army Field Manual Volume 1, Part 10 (2001 edn), http://www.scribd.com/doc/53578088/Counter-Insurgency-Operations-UK-Army; Alderson, 'Validity of British Counterinsurgency Doctrine', p. 80.

24. Cf. Kiszely, General Sir John, 'Learning about Counterinsurgency', *RUSI Journal*, 151, 6 (2006), pp. 16–21; Moreman, T.R., 'Small Wars and Imperial Policing: The British Army and the Theory and Practice

of Colonial Warfare in the British Empire 1919–1939', *Journal of Strategic Studies*, 19, 4 (1996), p. 105; Rigden, Col. I.A. 'The British Approach to Counter-Insurgency: Myths, Realities, and Strategic Challenges', USAWC Strategy Research Project, 15 March 2008; Strachan, Hew, 'British Counterinsurgency from Malaya to Iraq', *RUSI Journal*, 152, 6 (2007), pp. 8–11; Wither, James K., 'Basra's Not Belfast: The British Army, Small Wars and Iraq', *Small Wars and Insurgencies*, 20, 3–4 (2009), pp. 611–35. See also (more generally) *Small Wars and Insurgencies*, 23, 4–5 (2012), for a recent set of articles on this topic. All the above articles question the degree to which UK doctrine was incorporated into practice.

25. Strachan, Hew, 'Conclusion', in Jonathan Bailey, Richard Iron, and Hew Strachan (eds), *British Generals in Blair's Wars*, Aldershot: Ashgate, 2013, p. 336.

26. Alderson, 'Validity of British Counterinsurgency Doctrine'.

27. Ibid., p. 130.

28. AFM vol. 1–10, paragraphs 12.2 and 12.4.

29. Ibid., paragraph 12.13.

30. Ibid., paragraph 12.19.

31. Ibid., paragraph 12.10.

32. Ibid., paragraph 12.22.

33. Ibid., paragraph 12.23.

34. Ibid., paragraph 12.29.

35. Ibid., paragraph 12.26.

36. A statement based on extensive conversations with UK army legal advisors in Afghanistan and elsewhere.

37. UK Ministry of Defence, 'Security and Stabilisation: The Military Contribution', Joint Doctrine Publication 3–40, https://www.gov.uk/government/uploads/system/uploads/attachment_data/file/49948/jdp3_40a4.pdf

38. JDP 3–40, paragraph 615, p. 172.

39. JDP 3–40, paragraph 617, p. 173.

40. Crawshaw, 'Evolution of British COIN'.

41. Brigadier Andrew Mackay's command guidance to 52 Brigade, Helmand, October 2007.

42. Kilcullen, *Out of the Mountains*, p. 160.

43. Nachbar, Thomas B, 'The Use of Law in Counterinsurgency', Military Law Review, 213 (2011), p. 155, available at https://www.jagcnet.army.mil/DOCLIBS/MILITARYLAWREVIEW.NSF/0/256fb1f93504c34785257b0c006b99d4/$FILE/By%20Thomas%20B.%20Nachbar.pdf

44. Cobain, Ian, *Cruel Britannia: A Secret History of Torture*, London: Portobello, 2012, p. 171. Kitson was a contemporary of Bill Clinton

at University College Oxford; Kitson, Frank, *Low Intensity Operations*, London: Faber and Faber, 1971, p. 69.

45. French, David, *The British Way in Counterinsurgency 1945–1967*, Oxford: Oxford University Press, 2012, p. 82.

46. Ibid., pp. 81–2.

47. *Liversidge* v. *Anderson*, 3 All E.R. 338, 361 (1941) (Atkins, L.J., minority opinion).

48. Israeli Supreme Court judgment H.C. 320/80, *Kwasama* v. *Minister of Def.*, 5(3) P.D. 113, 132.

49. French, *The British Way in Counterinsurgency*, p. 76.

50. Ibid., p. 74.

51. Defined as 'Government by the Military Authorities when the normal machinery of government has broken down as a result of invasion, civil war or large scale insurrection …' See *Oxford Dictionary of Law*, 7th edn, Oxford: Oxford University Press, 2009. Martial law was proclaimed on 29 September 1936 in Palestine, but not put into force.

52. Emergency Powers Act 1945; 8&9 Geo. 6, Chapter 31 (1945). For example: Government of Palestine Ordinances, Regulations, Rules, Orders and Notices 259 Suppl. no. 2 to Palestine Gazette Extraordinary no. 584 (19 April 1936) (Government Printing Press, 1936); Government of Palestine Ordinances, Regulations, Rules, Orders and Notices no. 723 (30 September 1937). For a wider view of the British approach in Palestine, see Hughes, Matthew, 'The Practice and Theory of British Counterinsurgency: The Histories of the Atrocities at the Palestinian Villages of al-Bassa and Halhul, 1938–1939', Small Wars & Insurgencies, 20, 3 (2009).

53. Dispatch to Colonial Office of 5 May 1949, quoted in Coates, John, *Suppressing Insurgency: An Analysis of the Malayan Emergency 1948–54*, Boulder, CO: Westfield Press, 1992, p. 46.

54. Orders in Council are enacted as 'subordinate legislation' by the Privy Council, and therefore do not require parliamentary scrutiny.

55. Emergency Powers Order in Council 1939 (9 March 1939); 2& 3 Geo 6 Chapter 62 (1939) (UK).

56. Regulation 6(2)e; Regulation 6(2)b.1; Regulation 6(2)d; Regulation 6(2)g.

57. Regulation 7.

58. French, *The British Way in Counterinsurgency*, p. 78.

50. This was a decision taken by Neville Chamberlain on the basis that such a bill might not be passed in parliament (see ibid., p. 71). As was seen above, it was only in 1945 that emergency powers were placed on a statutory basis.

60. Jones, A. Creech, 'Note on Powers for Dealing with Subversive

Activities', 18 February 1950 (TNA CAB 134.535/ODC (50) 14) (per French, *British Way in Counterinsurgency*, p. 78).

61. Thompson, Robert, *Defeating Communist Insurgency*, London: Hailer, 1966.
62. Ibid., p. 52.
63. Ibid., p. 50.
64. Ibid., p. 55.
65. 'It helps to make all officers and civilian officials responsible and accountable for their actions.' Ibid., p. 54.
66. Minute by Sir G. Templer to Mr Churchill PREM 11/639. From *British Documents on the End of Empire*, vol. 2, London: HMSO, 1995, p. 361.
67. The reply outlined the policy of the government for the development of a Malay nation, with full citizenship, 'partnership' and democracy for all its races. This required the defeat of communist 'terrorism' and a 'worthy and continuing British involvement in the life of the country'. This constitutes what would now be called a 'desired end-state': Directive issued by Mr Lyttleton on behalf of HMG PREM 11/639. From *British Documents on the End of Empire*, p. 372.
68. Interview with Robert Thompson; Imperial War Museum Sound Archive (IMSA 10192).
69. Ibid., p. 82.
70. Strachan, 'British Counterinsurgency from Malaya to Iraq', pp. 8–11.
71. Ibid.
72. Russia in Chechnya being a signal example.
73. See *Mutua v. Foreign and Commonwealth Office*, http://www.judiciary.gov.uk/Resources/JCO/Documents/Judgments/mutua-fco-judgment-05102012.pdf
74. 'Malaysians Lose Fight for 1948 "Massacre" Enquiry', BBC News, 4 September 2012, http://www.bbc.co.uk/news/world-19473258. See also Ward, Ian and Miraflor, Norma, *Slaughter and Deception at Batang Kali*, Singapore: Media Masters Singapore, 2009.
75. See *Keyu and Others v. Secretary of State for Foreign and Commonwealth Affairs* (UK Court of Appeal judgment dated 17 March 2014), http://www.judiciary.gov.uk/media/judgments/2014/keyu-and-others-v-foreign-secretary
76. Harding, Andrew, *Law, Government and the Constitution in Malaysia*, The Hague: Kluwer Law International, 1996, p. 1.
77. In 1948, very shortly after independence, the Israeli parliament (the Knesset) allowed for a state of emergency to be promulgated. In due course, an emergency was declared on 21 May. These provisions have essentially survived in terms of their effect virtually untouched until

1979 with the passage of the Emergency Powers (Detention) Law. The idea of 'emergency' very much remains current.

78. 'Report of the Commission to Consider Legal Procedures to Deal with Terrorist Activities in Northern Ireland', 1972, Cmnd 5185; better known as the 'Diplock Commission'. See http://cain.ulster.ac.uk/hmso/diplock.htm for summary of conclusions

79. Diplock Commission report paragraph 7 7(a).

80. The courts were, in due course, established by the Northern Ireland (Emergency Provisions) Act 1973. This was supported and continued by the Prevention of Terrorism (Temporary Provisions) Act 1974. The ancestor of this act was a 1939 statute, the Prevention of Violence (Temporary Provisions) Act, similar in effect to the Emergency Powers Order in Council 1939 (see above). Diplock Commission report paragraph 1(e).

81. Ibid., paragraph 1(g).

82. See *Hansard*, 20 December 1972, http://hansard.millbanksystems.com/commons/1972/dec/20/diplock-commission-report

83. See, for example, Korff, Douwe, 'Diplock Courts in Northern Ireland: A Fair Trial?', Amnesty International, 1984, http://amnesty.org/en/library/asset/EUR45/004/1983/en/070b71c5–47c3–4ffd-add8–6108adb415b7/eur450041983en.pdf

84. Provisional IRA 'Green Book', p. 8, http://tensmiths.files.wordpress.com/2012/08/15914572-ira-green-book-volumes-1-and-2.pdf

85. Justice and Security (Northern Ireland) Act 2007.

86. See Jackson, John and Doran, Sean, 'Conventional Trials in Unconventional Times: The Diplock Court Experience', *Criminal Law Forum*, 4, 3 (1993), p. 503.

8. COUNTERINSURGENT JUDICIAL STRATEGY TODAY

1. Caroe, Olaf, *The Pathans*, Oxford: Oxford University Press, 1958, p. 347. This is the 'must read' on Pashtun history and culture. It is available in reprint. Caroe can be heard talking about his work at length at the Imperial War Museum tape number IWM 4909/07.

2. For a full and accessible account of this, see AlkonCynthia, 'The Cookie Cutter Syndrome: Legal Reform Assistance under Post-Communist Democratization Programs', *Journal of Dispute Resolution*, 2002, http://scholarship.law.missouri.edu/jdr/vol2002/iss2/2; Carothers, Thomas, 'Promoting the Rule of Law Abroad: The Problem of Knowledge', in Carothers, Thomas, *Critical Mission: Essays on Democracy Promotion*, Washington, DC: Carnegie Endowment for International Peace, 2004, pp. 15ff. at p. 21.

3. Clunan, Anne and Trinkunas, Harold, 'Alternative Governance and Security', in Anne Clunan, Anne and Harold Trinkunas (eds), *Ungoverned Spaces*, Stanford, CA: Stanford University Press, 2010, p. 288.

4. Carothers, 'Promoting the Rule of Law Abroad', p. 20.

5. Carothers, Thomas, 'The Rule of Law Revival', *Foreign Affairs*, 77 (April 1998), p. 95, http://www.foreignaffairs.com/articles/53809/thomas-carothers/the-rule-of-law-revival

6. De Soto, Hernando, 'Preface', in Buscaglia, Edgardo et al. (eds), *The Law and Economics of Development*, Greenwich, JAI Press, 1997, p. xiv. Cited in Stromseth, Jane, Wippman, David and Brooks, Rosa, *Can Might Make Right? Building the Rule of Law after Military Interventions*, Cambridge: Cambridge University Press, 2006, p. 58.

7. Carothers, 'Promoting the Rule of Law Abroad', p. 17.

8. Stromseth et al., *Can Might Make Right?*, p. 77.

9. Carothers, 'Promoting the Rule of Law Abroad', pp. 15ff.

10. Ibid., p. 26.

11. Golub, Stephen, 'Beyond the Rule of Law Orthodoxy: The Legal Empowerment Alternative', Carnegie Endowment for International Peace, 2003, http://carnegieendowment.org/files/wp41.pdf. For an extended conceptual deconstruction of recent rule of law failures, see also Brooks, Rosa, 'The New Imperialism: Violence, Norms and the "Rule of Law"', *Michigan Law Review*, 101, 7 (2003), pp. 2275–340. Brooks discusses what she calls a 'string of expensive disappointments' in rule of law promotion.

12. US Center for Law and Military Operations, 'Rule of Law Handbook: A Practitioner's Guide for Judge Advocates', 2011, http://www.loc.gov/rr/frd/Military_Law/pdf/rule-of-law_2011.pdf

13. 'Commander Says Rule of Law Needed to Combat Taliban', http://www.army.mil/article/51708/; see also Chesney, Robert, 'General Martins on Rule of Law Green Zones, Afghan Criminal Prosecution, and Other Updates from the ROLFF in Afghanistan', Lawfare, 10 February 2011, http://www.lawfareblog.com/2011/02/general-martins-on-rule-of-lawgreen-zones-afghan-criminal-prosecution-and-other-updates-from-the-rolff-in-afghanistan/; US Embassy, Kabul, Afghanistan, 'Coordinating Director of Rule of Law and Law Enforcement', available at http://kabul.usembassy.gov/klemm.html

14. 'Bridging the Potomac: How a Rule of Law Field Force Strikes Balance between Security and Development Operations', *Small Wars Journal* (25 March 2013), http://smallwarsjournal.com/jrnl/art/bridging-the-potomac-how-a-rule-of-law-field-force-strikes-balance-between-security-and-dev

15. US Center for Law and Military Operations, 'Rule of Law Handbook'.

16. Although see Ledwidge, Frank, 'Justice a Center of Gravity Analysis', in ibid., p. 251; FM 3–24.
17. See, for example, International Crisis Group, 'Reforming Afghanistan's Broken Judiciary',report no. 195 (Brussels 2010), p. 24, http://www. crisisgroup.org/en/regions/asia/south-asia/afghanistan/195-reformin-gafghanistans-broken-judiciary.aspx Afghanistan's justice system is described as being in a 'catastrophic state of disrepair'.
18. Interview with senior UNAMA official, April 2014.
19. This account is summarised from Major Mullin's essay in US Center for Law and Military Operations, 'Rule of Law Handbook' (2009 edn), p. 265, http://loc.gov/rr/frd/Military_Law/pdf/rule-of-law_2009. pdf
20. Ibid., p. 269.
21. Fearon, Kate, 'Pragmatism, Proximity and Pashtunwali: Informal Justice at the District Level in Helmand Province', in P. Albrecht, P. et al. (eds), *Perspectives on Involving Non-state and Customary Actors in Justice and Security Reform*, Rome: International Development Law Organization, 2011, p. 11.
22. Conversation with the education secretary to the Helmand provincial government.
23. The 'Provincial Reconstruction Team' based in a fort in the outskirts of Lashkar Gah.
24. Account taken from a contemporary report made by me, August 2007. For further such examples, see Ledwidge, Frank, 'Justice in Helmand: The Challenge of Law Reform in a Society at War', *Asian Affairs*, 40, 1 (2009).
25. Conversation with UK police advisor, August 2007.
26. Kilcullen, David, *Counterinsurgency*, London: Hurst, 2010, p. 155.
27. The provincial justice institutions that report to the Supreme Court, Attorney General's Office and Ministry of Justice in Kabul, which notionally provide oversight and links to national-level justice programmes. These comprise the formal courts, the Office of the Chief Prosecutor for the province and the various Ministry of Justice components, including the Huquq (Civil Rights) Department, the Kazai Dowlat (Land Registry Court), the Juvenile Justice Administration Department and the Prison Service
28. Evidence of Peter Watkins to Parliamentary Defence Committee report on operations in Helmand, http://www.publications.parliament.uk/ pa/cm201012/cmselect/cmdfence/554/554.pdf, Q 314
29. Interview by telephone with senior cultural advisor to UK armed forces, 26 November 2011.
30. Interview with senior DFID official deployed to Helmand.

31. Sitaraman, Ganesh, *The Counterinsurgent's Constitution: Law in the Age of Small Wars*, Oxford: Oxford University Press, 2012, p. 180.

32. Woodman, Graham R., 'A Survey of Customary Laws in Africa, in Search of Lessons for the Future', abstract available at Proceedings of Conference on Customary Law in Africa, October 2008, Gabarone, http://www.customarylawrevisited.com/abstracts.lc

33. Interview with senior UK military legal officer, April 2014.

34. Interview with advisor to an Afghan minister, May 2014.

35. Units of between 5,000 and 10,000 soldiers; Ledwidge, Losing Small Wars, pp. 133–4.

36. Such as the author on his deployment in 2007; UK justice advisor interviewed, April 2014.

37. Interviews with four of the six justice advisors deployed.

38. Foreman, Jonathan; 'Aiding and Abetting', Civitas, 2013,; see p51ff.

39. Interview with senior UN justice advisor April 2014.

40. Private distribution, 'Bright Shining Narrative'.

41. Nachbar, Thomas B, 'The Use of Law in Counterinsurgency', Military Law Review, 213 (2011), p. 153, available at https://www.jagcnet. army.mil/DOCLIBS/MILITARYLAWREVIEW.NSF/0/256fb1f93504c 34785257b0c006b99d4/$FILE/By%20Thomas%20B.%20Nachbar.pdf

42. Interview with senior UN justice advisor, April 2014.

43. Interview with senior UN justice advisor, Jeffrey Rustand, April 2014.

44. Fearon, 'Pragmatism, Proximity and Pashtunwali', p. 32.

45. Interview with senior UNAMA justice advisor, April 2014.

46. Barfield, Thomas, Nojumi, Neamat, and Thier, J. Alexander, 'The Clash of Two Goods: State and Non-State Dispute Resolution in Afghanistan', United States Institute of Peace, http://www.usip.org/sites/default/ files/file/clash_two_goods.pdf

47. Janse, Ronald, 'A Turn to Legal Pluralism in Rule of Law Promotion', *Erasmus Law Review*, 3 (December 2013), p. 6, http://www.erasmus-lawreview.nl/files/ELR_2013_03_005.pdf

48. Interview with senior UN justice advisor, Jeffrey Rustand, April 2014.

49. Interview with Cynthia Alkon December 2014.

50. Janse, 'Turn to Legal Pluralism', p. 8.

51. Sitaraman, *Counterinsurgent's Constitution*, p. 183.

52. Ibid., p. 15; for a legal critique of the rule of law concept, see Fallon, Richard H., 'The Rule of Law as a Contested Concept', *Columbia Law Review*, 97, 1 (1998).

53. Janse, 'Turn to Legal Pluralism', p. 10.

54. Interview with Jeffrey Rustand, April 2014.

55. Mampilly, Zachariah, *Rebel Rulers: Insurgent Governance and Civilian Life During War*, Ithaca, NY: Cornell University Press, 2011, p. 243.

56. Carothers, 'Promoting the Rule of Law Abroad', p. 27.
57. UK police advisor in Helmand, interviewed April 2014.
58. Interview with Whit Mason, March 2014.
59. Egnell, Robert, 'Western Insurgency in Afghanistan', *Joint Force Quarterly* (October 2013), p. 10, http://www.dtic.mil/doctrine/jfq/jfq-70.pdfp
60. Ibid., p. 14.
61. Pape, Robert 'It's the occupation, stupid' *Foreign Policy*, October 2010, http://foreignpolicy.com/2010/10/18/its-the-occupation-stupid/
62. Suhrke, Astri, 'Exogenous State-Building: The Contradictions of International State-Building in Afghanistan', in Whit Mason (ed.), *The Rule of Law in Afghanistan: Missing in Inaction*, Oxford: Oxford University Press, 2011. p. 227.
63. Ibid., p. 237.
64. See, for example, the 'Juant Case', reported in detail in Ledwidge, 'Justice in Helmand'.
65. Private distribution, 'Bright Shining Narrative'.
66. Suhrke, 'Exogenous State-Building', p. 244.
67. Carothers, 'Promoting the Rule of Law Abroad', p. 21.

CONCLUSION

1. Kennedy, David, *Of War and Law*, Princeton, NJ: Princeton University Press, 2006, p. 13.
2. Whitman, James Q., *The Verdict of Battle*, Cambridge, MA: Harvard University Press, 2012, p. 23.
3. Dunlap, Charles, 'Lawfare: A Decisive Element of 21st-Century Conflict', Joint Forces Quarterly, 59 (2009), p. 34, available at http://www.americanbar.org/content/dam/aba/migrated/2011_build/law_national_security/LawfareDunlapJun09.authcheckdam.pdf
4. See, for example, *Journal of Legal Pluralism*, http://www.jlp.bham.ac.uk/volumes/index.htm; Mampilly, Zachariah, *Rebel Rulers: Insurgent Governance and Civilian Life During War*, Ithaca, NY: Cornell University Press, 2011, p. 7.
5. Nachbar, Thomas B, 'The Use of Law in Counterinsurgency', Military Law Review, 213 (2011), p. 164, available at https://www.jagcnet.army.mil/DOCLIBS/MILITARYLAWREVIEW.NSF/0/256fb1f93504c34785257b0c006b99d4/$FILE/By%20Thomas%20B.%20Nachbar.pdf
6. Gentile, Gian, *Wrong Turn: America's Deadly Embrace of Counterinsurgency*, New York: New Press, 2013, p. 117.
7. Flynn, Michael T., Pottinger, Matt and Batchelor, Paul, 'Fixing Intel: A Blueprint for Making Intelligence Relevant in Afghanistan', Center for

a New American Security, 2010; see also General Flynn's lecture at the Brookings Institution, 13 November 2013, podcast http://www.lawfareblog.com/2013/11/lawfare-podcast-episode-50-dia-chief-lt-general-michael-t-flynn-speaks-at-brookings/

8. See Qiao Liang and Wang Xiangsui, *Unrestricted Warfare*, Beijing: PLA Literature and Arts Publishing House, 1999, http://www.cryptome.org/cuw.htm

INDEX

INDEX

INDEX

INDEX

INDEX